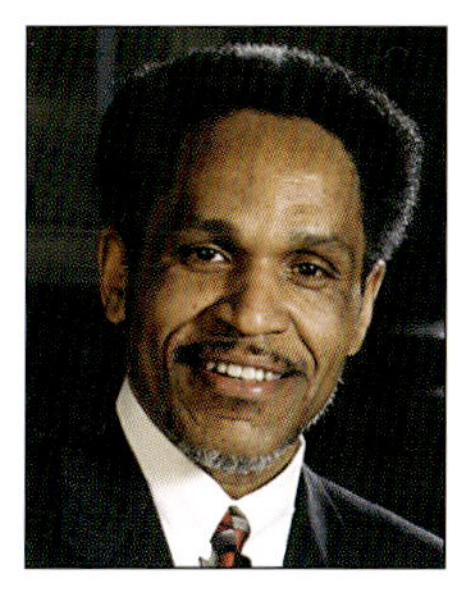

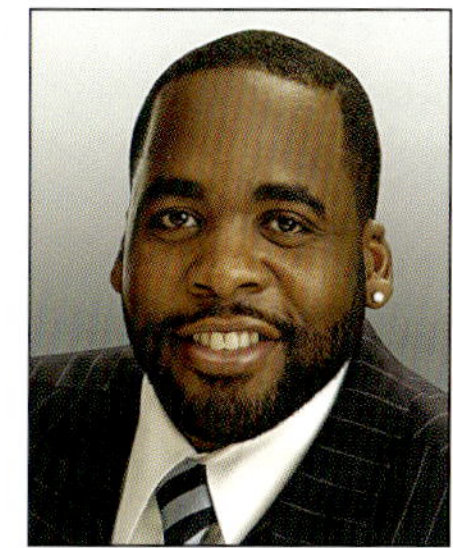

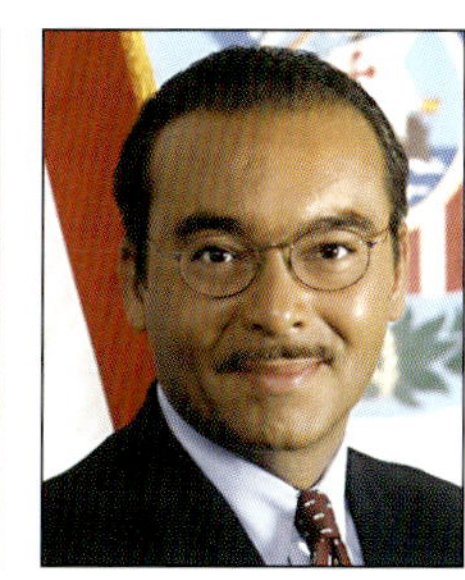

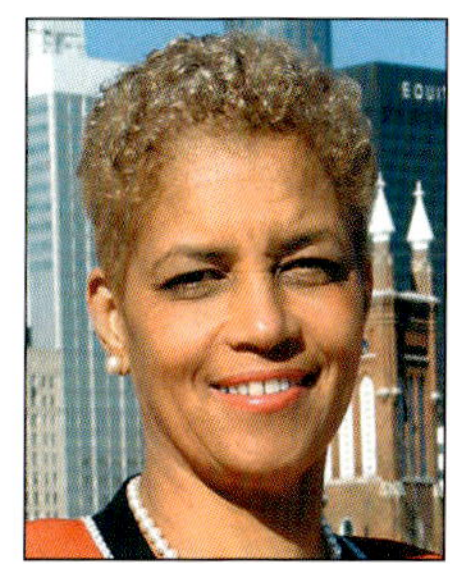

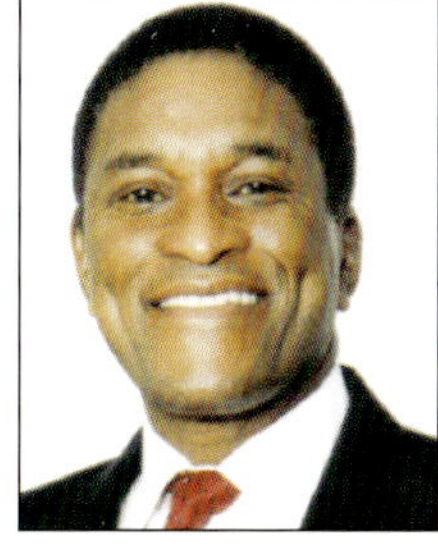

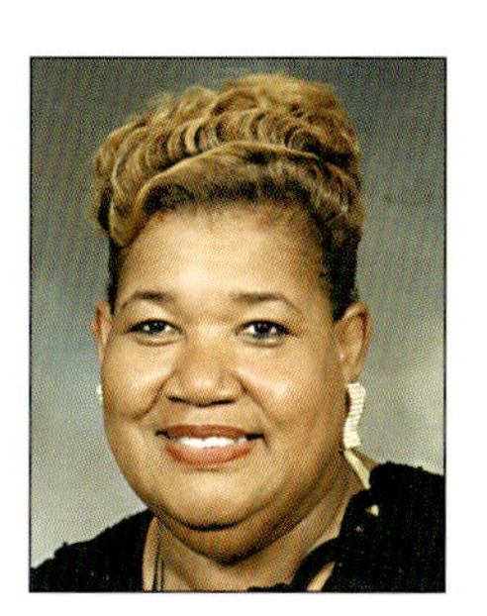

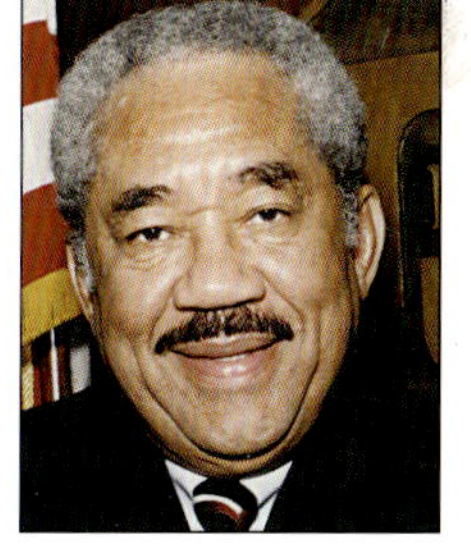

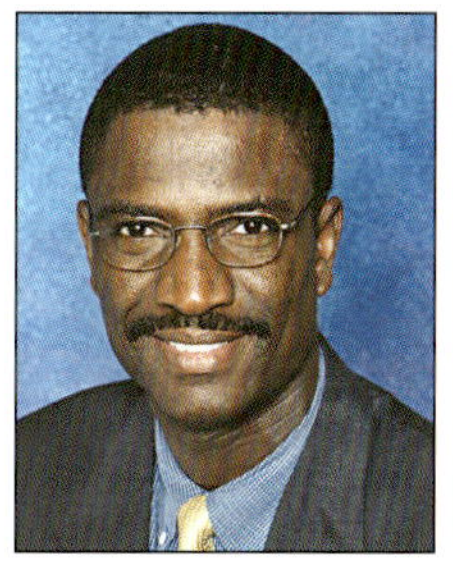

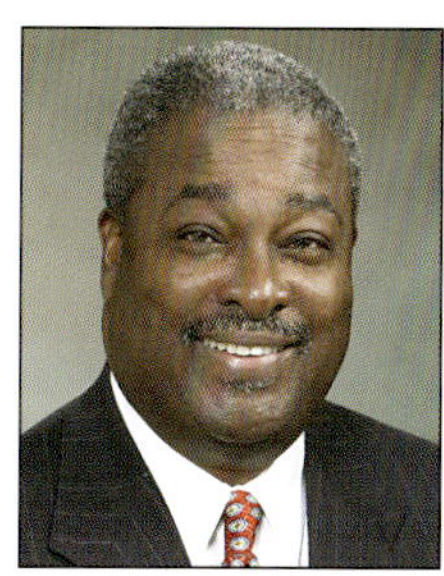

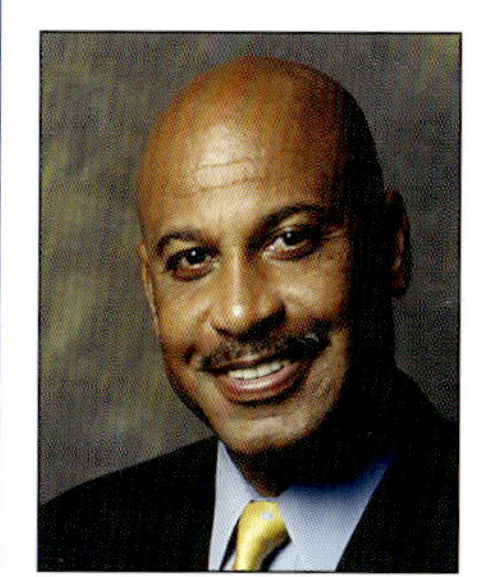

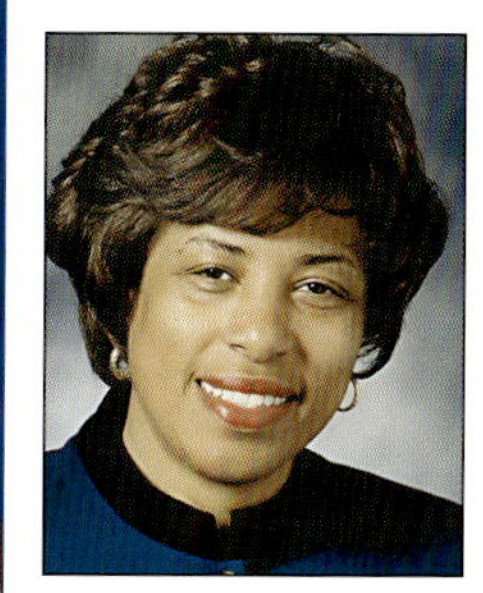

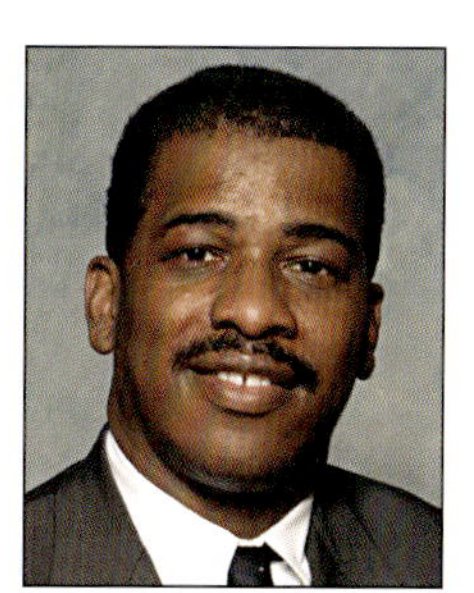

Black Mayors in America™

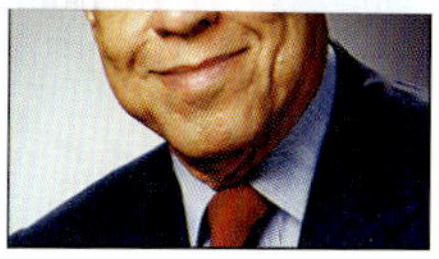

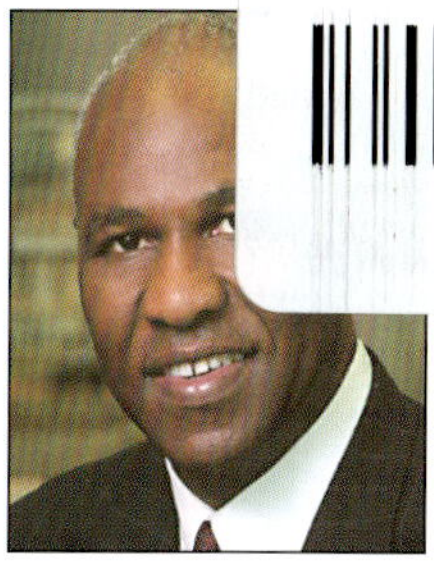

—THE 2005 EDITION—

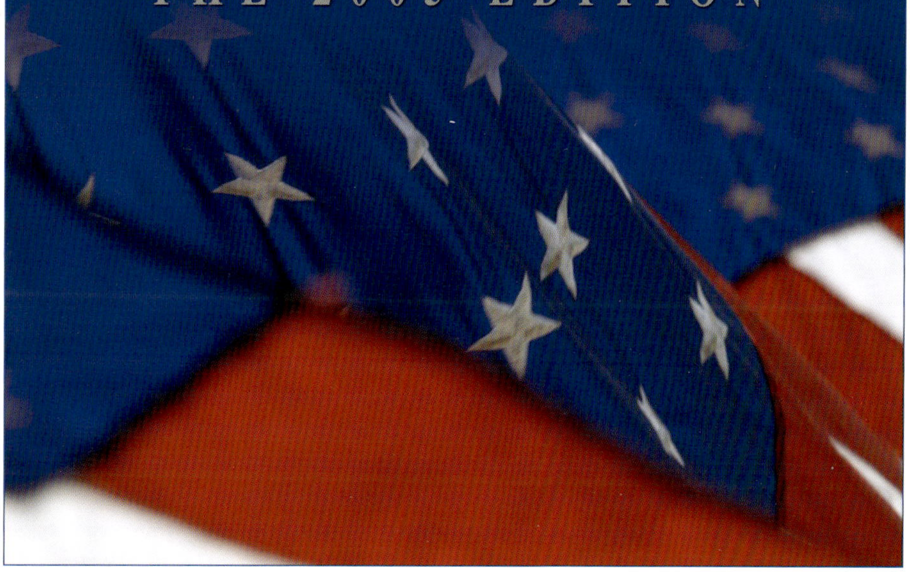

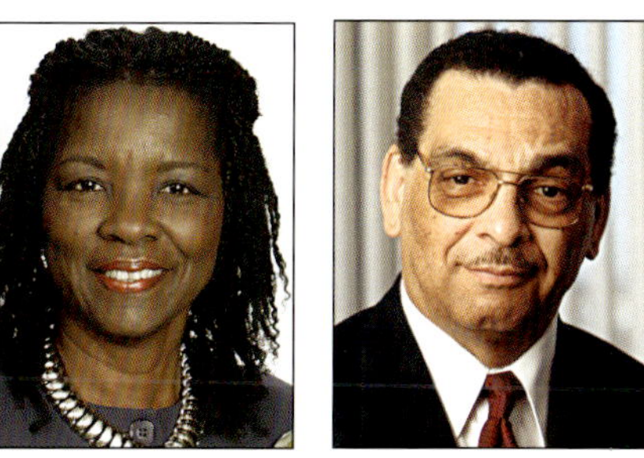

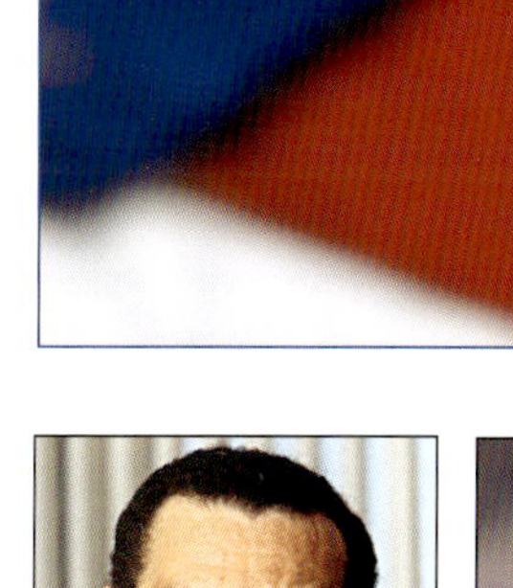

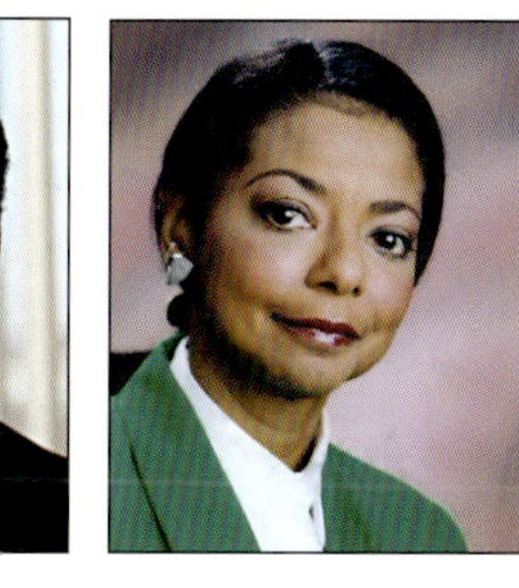

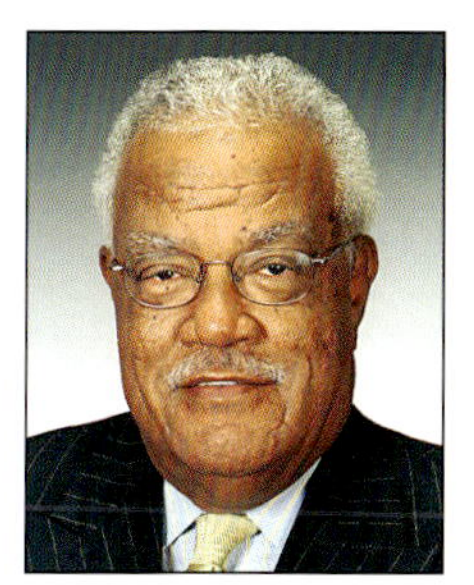

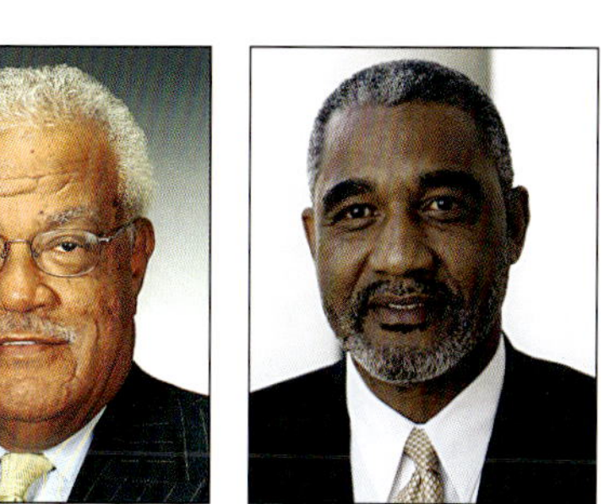

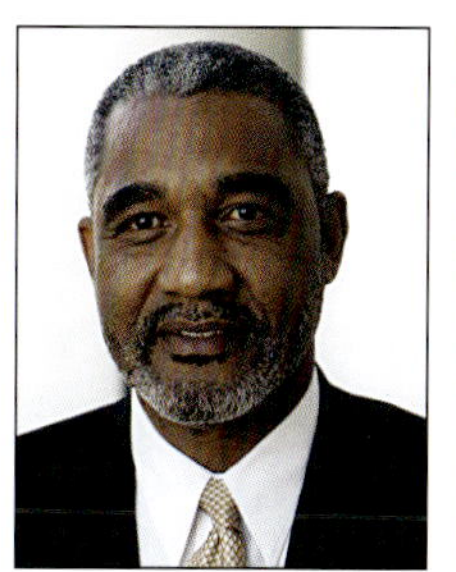

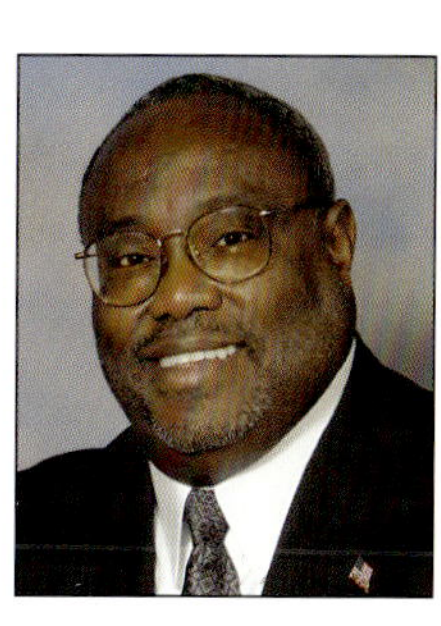

Black Mayors in America

— THE 2005 EDITION —

Purchase additional copies online @

www.whoswhopublishing.com

Our Corporate Headquarters
Who's Who Publishing Co., LLC
1650 Lake Shore Drive, Ste. 250
Columbus, Ohio 43204

All Credit Cards Accepted

Inquiries for bulk purchases for youth
groups, schools, churches, civic or
professional organizations please call
our office for volume discounts.

(614) 481-7300

Copyright © 2005 by C. Sunny Martin,
Briscoe Media Group, LLC

Who's Who Publishing Co., LLC Personnel:

C. Sunny Martin – CEO & Founder
Ernie L. Sullivan – Senior Partner
Paula M. Gray – Assistant to Publisher

Melanie Diggs – Senior Editor
Nathan Wylder and Philip Hickman – Copy Editors

Christy Smith – Production Manager
Ivory D. Payne – Senior Art & Layout Director

ISBN # 0-9763069-4-8
$29.95 each-USA

CONTENTS

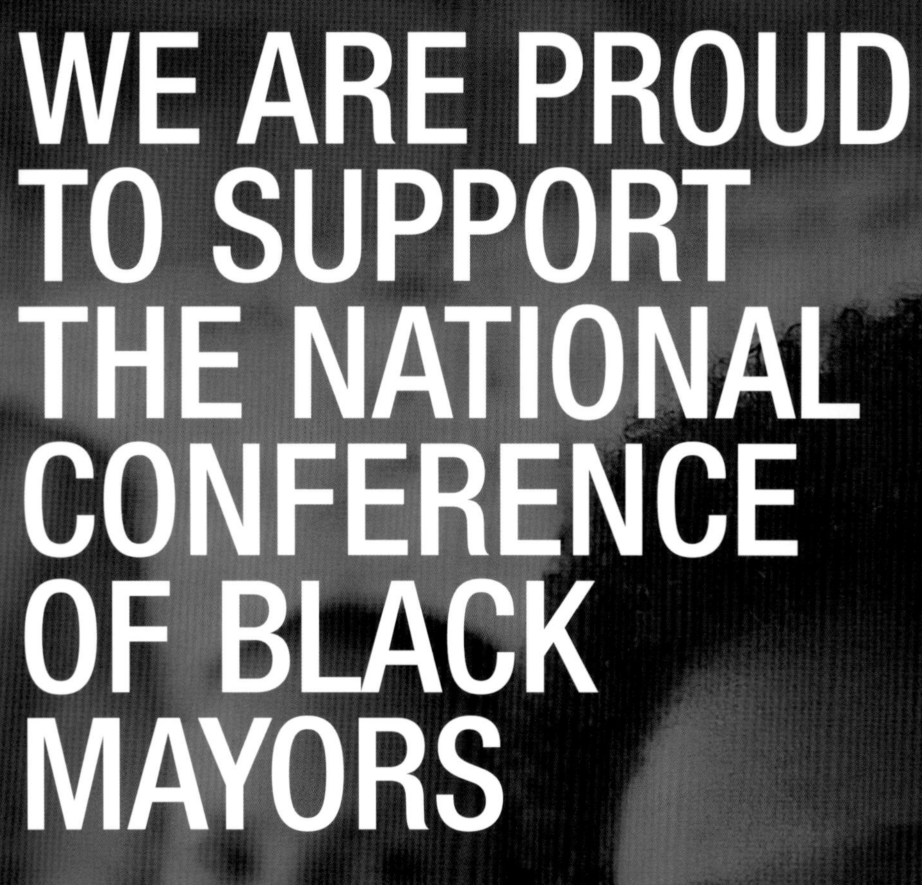

WE ARE PROUD
TO SUPPORT
THE NATIONAL
CONFERENCE
OF BLACK
MAYORS

Limitedbrands

BATH & BODY WORKS / C.O. BIGELOW / EXPRESS / HENRI BENDEL
THE LIMITED / VICTORIA'S SECRET / THE WHITE BARN CANDLE COMPANY

Office of the Mayor
Harvey Johnson, Jr., Mayor

Greetings!

It brings me great pleasure to welcome each of you to the National Conference of Black Mayors 31st Annual Convention! I am certain that this year's convention will be very successful.

I also commend the Who's Who Publishing Company for producing *Black Mayors In America.* This publication highlights African-American mayors who are performing vital work in our communities across the country. These individuals are truly forging positive change in their cities and I applaud them!

Who's Who Publishing Company's willingness to create a publication that profiles black public servants is very significant, and I thank them for their commitment. I am certain that each of you will enjoy browsing the profiles.

Again, I welcome you to the convention!

Sincerely,

Harvey Johnson, Jr.
HJJ/cdm

National Conference of Black Mayors, Inc.

March 23, 2005

Greetings:

As the new Executive Director of the National Conference of Black Mayors, Inc., I would like to graciously extend my congratulations to the publishers, sponsors and honorees of the commemorative edition of *Black Mayors In America*, 2005.

This publication is historic in highlighting the exemplary contributions that are made by African American mayors across the United States. This publication is both powerful and refreshing as we celebrate the leadership and integrity of some of the nation's finest leaders, who continue to make invaluable contributions not only to their individual communities, but as examples to communities across this nation.

As we commemorate the importance and significance of yet another form of African American leadership, On behalf of the National Conference of Black Mayors, Inc, (NCBM) we are enthusiastic about our 31st Annual Convention being held April 27- May 1, 2005 in Columbus, Ohio at the Hyatt Regency Columbus. The convention theme is, *"The 21st Century: Meeting The New Challenges for Economic Growth"*, hosted by the Honorable Mayor Michael Coleman. We have planned a strong convention program coupled with some exciting evening events. The National Conference of Black Mayors, Inc. currently represents over 535 African American Mayors nationwide and count among it's membership some of America's largest, as well as moderate, and small urban and rural communities, collectively representing in excess of 20 million people!

As the National Conference of Black Mayors, Inc. enthusiastically move into another decade, we are looking forward to the new vision of a creative and innovative means to continue to strengthen not only the individual cities of our mayoral membership, but to eventually strengthen all cities throughout the United States, in leading by example and blazing new trails in municipal growth and development.

I earnestly believe that this publication is monumental in ensuring that the entire nation is aware of this type of leadership helping to ensure that there will be a place set for the next generation of exceptional leaders because of the wisdom and foresight of the leaders honored in this publication.

Thank you for your continued dedication and commitment to acknowledging the nations most brilliant leaders!

Sincerely,

Vanessa R. Williams
Executive Director

Building America's 21st Century Cities

Keeping Neighborhoods Safe and Securing Our Economic Future

Launching South Side Neighborhood Pride

Selling the first homes on Taylor Ave.

Welcome to the inaugural edition of Black Mayors in America, a publication dedicated to capturing history, sharing lessons and telling success stories that may have once seemed impossible.

As America's African American mayors gather together in Columbus, Ohio, for the 2005 National Conference of Black Mayors, this special publication is being made available by Who's Who Publishing and C. Sunny Martin. This special publication and great NCBM Conference also would not have been possible without the hard work, diligence, foresight, creativity and passion of my wife Frankie, host team leaders Danni Palmore and Gary Cavin, and all of our local host committee.

There are only a select group of individuals in every generation who move forward to change the course of history, change the hearts and minds of their communities and step out of the every day and into their duty as great public servants. Mayors are vigilant every day, leading, inspiring, doing what is right for all people in our cities and improving the world for future generations. It is a blessing and an honor representing the heart and soul of a city, charged with the health and safety of neighborhoods and empowered to forge new paths for an ever more diverse nation.

I am proud to see so many friends within these pages, mayors who have stood up in their hometowns to build a better tomorrow.

Honoring the Tuskegee Airmen

*Mayor Coleman with
the Capital Kids*

As we do our jobs every day, providing housing, creating jobs, managing budgets, delivering basic city services like police and fire protection, building neighborhoods, we are also living out dreams once thought impossible. The election of hundreds of African Americans as city mayors comes only after generations of struggle, and it is a credit to the great ideas that founded America that our nation has continued to march towards its destiny as the greatest, most diverse, most inclusive and most dynamic society in history.

When I was 9 years old, growing up during much tougher times in Toledo, Ohio, my mother took me to Scott High School Gymnasium to hear the Reverend Dr. Martin Luther King, Jr. speak. While the words of this great leader were inspiring, it was Dr. King's ability to bring people together and stir their passion for equality, for fairness and for justice that remains with me even to this day. The room vibrated with his words and energy, and in response the congregation rose up in one voice to call for change. When the bucket was passed that afternoon, I reached into my pocket and gave all I had - a nickel. To a civil rights leader on a persistent march for freedom, that nickel may not have bought much more than a soda pop, but for me it represented that I was now a soldier for my community, my first memory of giving back selflessly.

Giving back to the community through public service is the most powerful action we can take. I believe that there is no stopping a community that is willing to give of itself without consideration of what its members will get in return. In all paths, business, science, medicine, academics, law, media, politics, we must encourage our citizens to make the most of these opportunities to help others succeed and prosper through our service.

Dr. King's words are an inspiration to me every day, and he captured the essence of giving when he spoke of our interdependence. As he said, "Everybody can be great. Because anybody can serve. You don't have to have a college degree to serve. You don't have to make your subject and your verb agree to serve. You don't have to know about Plato or Aristotle to serve. You don't have to know Einstein's Theory of Relativity to serve. You don't have to know the second theory of thermo-dynamics in physics to serve. You only need a heart full of grace. A soul generated by love."

When we step forward today, we do so on the shoulders of great leaders and greater ideas. This book, Black Mayors in America, is a testament to this moment in history, built upon our shared heritage, our hard work and our commitment to remember the lessons of great leaders like Dr. King. These stories of real lives and real leaders serve as a new benchmark in our ongoing American story of interdependence, and I am proud to congratulate all who share in the honor today.

Together we can do more than even our forefathers dreamed, and we must blaze the path for the next generation.

Sincerely,

Michael B. Coleman
Mayor
Columbus, Ohio

A Message From The Publisher

C. Sunny Martin

"To lead suggests that you must have followers. For others to follow you, you must be superior to them in the things that they must follow you for. People only respect leaders and follow them when there is something superior in them."

—*Marcus Garvey (1887-1940)*

Welcome to the first edition of ***Black Mayors In America!***

I am extremely honored and proud that we have this opportunity to present to you this historical and comprehensive publication that chronicles the rich history of African-American mayoral leadership in cities across this great nation.

Our company's mission is deeply rooted in documenting the positive achievements of African-Americans from all walks of life, and we are most happy to include ***Black Mayors In America*** to our long list of publishing titles.

I want to extend our thanks to Columbus, Ohio Mayor Michael B. Coleman and his wife, Columbus' first lady, Frankie Coleman, for their combined creative vision for seeing that this publication became a reality.

Additionally, much credit is given to Vanessa Williams, executive director of the National Conference of Black Mayors, Inc. I must also credit Bunny Jackson-Ransom of FirstClass Inc., Dannette Palmore of PolicyWorks, and Gary Cavin and other members of the Columbus 2005 host committee for their assistance in this project.

This publication could not be possible without your combined effort and input. I sincerely thank all of you for your dedication to this effort.

Finally, I am most indebted to my staff. It is perhaps one of the great diversity testimonies of team commitment and accomplishment that this publication has become a reality. Carter, Christy, Ernie, Ivory, Melanie, Nathan, Paula, Philip, Randy, and Rochelle, you have made a considerable contribution to documenting a part of our nation's history!

Be blessed in all you do!

C. Sunny Martin
Founder/CEO
Who's Who Publishing Co., LLC
sunny@whoswhopublishing.com

Visit Us Online @ www.whoswhopublishing.com

Houghton Mifflin Company

congratulates the

Black Mayors In America

as you convene for your

31st Annual Conference.

Black Mayors In America

Solutions for Classrooms, Grades PreK–12

HOUGHTON MIFFLIN

Riverside Publishing
A HOUGHTON MIFFLIN COMPANY

Edusoft

Great Source
EDUCATION GROUP

earobics

McDougal Littell

For more information, visit www.hmco.com
© Houghton Mifflin Company. All rights reserved. 03/05 SS04065

Granville Woods' (the "Black Thomas Edison") inventions are known around the world for providing safer travel on trains.

Granville Woods
1856-1910

When it came to railway communication, Granville Woods put us on the right track.

Granville Woods formed Woods Railway Telegraph Company in 1884. His early inventions included the "telegraphony" allowing telegraph stations to send voice and telegraph messages over a single wire. The "Synchronous Multiplex Railway Telegraph" made communication possible between train stations and moving trains. This invention continues to provide for greater railway safety even today. Woods' concept of "third rail" is also currently used in the U.S. as a source of subway power allowing trains to receive more electricity and less friction. Despite other inventors' attempts to make claim to his devices, Granville Woods fought them and won. Over time, he obtained more than fifty patents, including improvements to existing inventions such as safety circuits, the telegraph, phonograph and telephone. Sprint proudly salutes this great innovator of communications.

Diversity recruiting is more and more important as the world becomes more global. Initially, legal compliance was the primary driver behind most Diversity strategies. However, today high performing organizations understand that Diversity makes good business sense for customers and employees. In short, having a diverse workforce is no longer an option. It has become an absolute requirement for business success.

Ensuring that your organization has the human resources necessary to meet business goals and market competition is a key challenge. Welcome to the world of Sullivan Staffing Strategies. We are an executive recruiting and Diversity consulting organization whose mission is to help our client companies meet their Diversity staffing needs in the most efficient and cost effective way possible. We have already had the opportunity to research best practices in some of the country's largest staffing organizations. In addition, our network of strategic partners provides us extensive support for specialized staffing products and services.

Services

Executive Recruiting
- Specialized target searches

Professional Recruiting
- Accounting/Finance
- Health care
- Information technology

College Recruiting Programs
- Specialized partnerships
- Key schools approach

Diversity Strategies
- Internal recruiting strategies
- External partnership development
- Executive search

Community Based Recruiting
- Identifying community partners
- Community partners orientation development

For more information contact Ernest L. Sullivan at 614-258-7815 or 614-537-7506

www.sullivanss.com   elsulllivan1@msn.com

INCLUDE YOUR CITY!

If you would like to include your city as part of the Who's Who family of publications, please call our corporate office at (614) 481-7300.

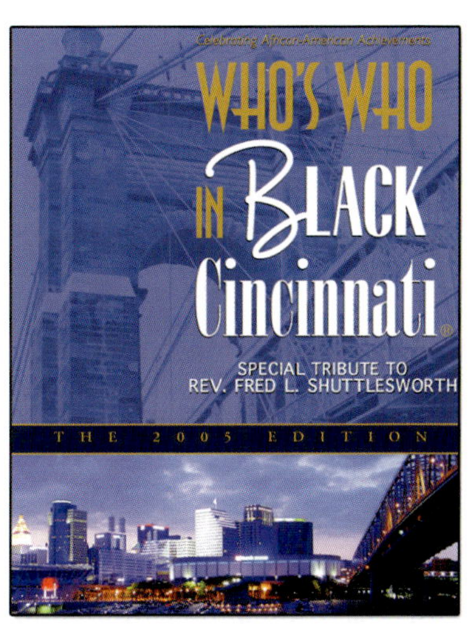

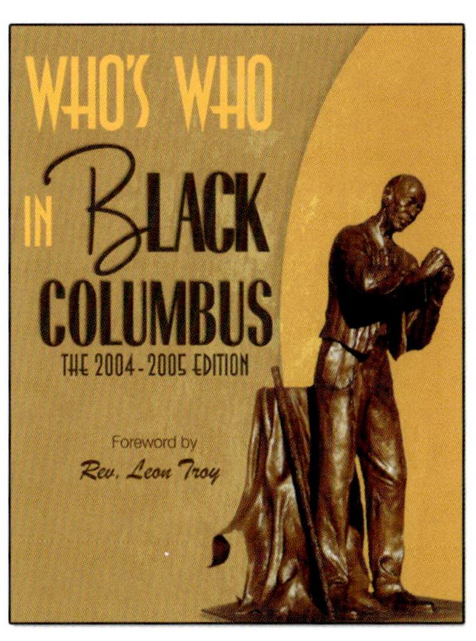

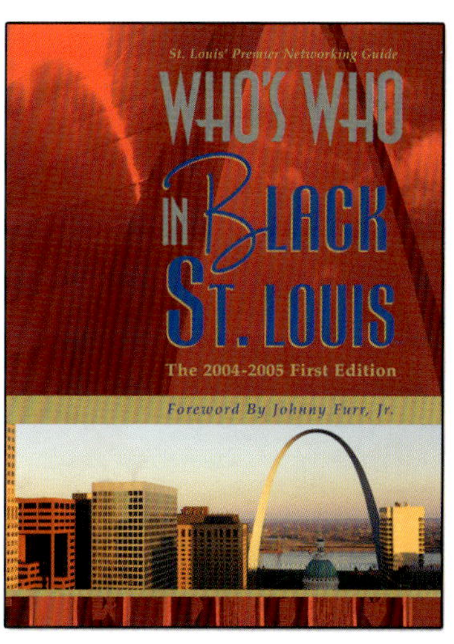

WWW.WHOSWHOPUBLISHING.COM

Commemorate your appearance in Black Mayors In America with a beautiful, handcrafted plaque.

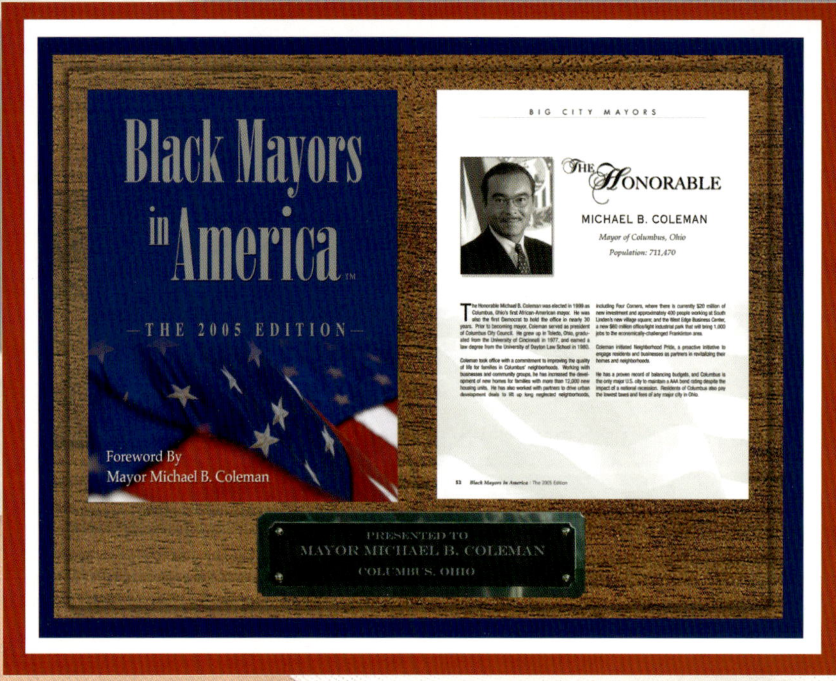

Your picture and biographical data will be mounted on a 16" x 20" rich, hand staine 3/4" birchwood plaque and sealed with a non-glare finish.

Perfect for your office or lobby!

Only $169.95 + S&H

Order Your Commemorative Plaque Today!

Order online or call (614) 481-7300

www.whoswhopublishing.com

SQUIRE SANDERS
LEGAL
COUNSEL
WORLDWIDE

Merrill Lynch

proudly supports the

2005 NATIONAL CONFERENCE OF BLACK MAYORS

*C*ongratulations to all the African-American mayors converging in Columbus, and to all those mayors who have come before. We celebrate your achievements. You, truly, have a great place in our nation's history.

EXCEPTIONAL
SOLUTIONS
FOR EXCEPTIONAL CLIENTS

ml.com

Central State University

College of Business and Industry

**Charles H. Showell, Jr., Ph.D.,
Dean**

www.centralstate.edu

- *Water Resources Management*
- *Manufacturing Engineering*
- *Business Administration*
- *Accounting and Economics*

Preparing business leaders for the 21st Century

AMERICA'S BLACK MAYORAL LEGACY

By Melanie L. Diggs

Despite the odds, cultural barriers, city demographics and opposition by traditional power structures, black mayoral leadership continues to be an emerging factor in cities and villages, both large and small, across the United States. With each election, from the 1800s through the present, the foundation of local politics with national implications is laid as a testimony to African-American leadership that will not accept boundaries of any sort. Men and women, both highly educated and barely educated, those from poverty and privilege, and those from places renowned and unknown have stepped into history to ensure that people without a voice receive representation. Thanks to their courage and the constituencies that support them, the face of rural, urban, and suburban politics is forever changed.

There are so many African-American mayoral "firsts" that space will not allow us to individually cite each. Within this context, we journeyed and explored a few of our past and contemporary mayoral trailblazers and their effect on the cities, communities, and people they touched. We discovered that those who govern do so during times of economic hardship, seasons of unrest and political upheaval, and periods of peace and prosperity. They are judged by what they promise and what they deliver, and by what they inherit and what they leave as an inheritance. The impact they leave may be small ripples of revival and restoration or tidal waves of transition that force local, state, national, and international change. For some mayors, history has told their story. For others the day of examination has yet to dawn.

MAYOR NED SHERMAN

(1807-1907) • ELECTED 1878

Believed by historians to lay in an unmarked grave in the village cemetery of Oneida Lake in Cleveland, New York, Edward "Ned" Sherman rests. Serving one term, it was in 1878 that he was elected president (mayor) of the village, which was incorporated in 1857.[1] Village of Cleveland historian Charlene Weed is in the process of verifying that Ned Sherman may be the first black mayor in the state of New York, and perhaps in the United States.

In speaking with Ms. Weed and Barbara Dix, Oswego County historian, Who's Who Publishing discovered that centenarian Ned Sherman was born June 9, 1807 in Saratoga, New York and died August 5, 1907. Before relocating to the Village of Cleveland he worked as a mule team driver on an Erie Canal packet boat; in the off-season he was a barber. In 1851 he worked for William

Foster who would later become a New York state senator (1872-1873). On July 10, 1875 Sherman became a widower when his wife, Elizabeth, died at age 39; they had five children. Oswego County records also reveal that Sherman owned property and that he married a second wife, Harriet.

Ned Sherman's rise to mayor came about in an unusual way. When the president of the Cleveland village board quit during a heated meeting, a replacement was needed. Within a climate of controversy and a lack of consensus, they voted right there and then. Sherman, the village barber who could neither read nor write, was elected. Says Weed, "It seemed he was viewed as a peacemaker, one who was impartial and who understood the villager's needs." And although he was illiterate, it was recorded that he governed "in a right, smart manner."

MAYOR CARL BURTON STOKES

(1927-1996) • ELECTED 1967

Ambassador Carl Burton Stokes was America's first black mayor of a major American city and he became the first African American ever to be elected to all three branches of government - the legislative, the executive, and the judicial.

The second son of Charles and Louise Stokes, Carl Stokes was born on June 21, 1927 in Cleveland, Ohio. A laundry worker, Charles died in 1929 leaving Louise Stokes to support her two sons by working as a domestic. In his autobiography *Promises of Power,* Stokes recalls, "We lived in a rickety ol' two family house. We covered rat holes with the tops of tin cans."[2] A step up, Louise Stokes found an apartment in Outhwaite Estates, the nation's first federally funded housing project. Carl and his older brother, Louis, who served for more than 30 years as Ohio's first black U.S. congressman, contributed to the household income by working in neighborhood stores and as carriers for the *Cleveland News.*

A high school dropout, Stokes worked in a foundry and then joined the Army. After receiving an honorable discharge as a corporal he obtained his high school diploma and supported himself as a dining car waiter. He later earned a bachelor of science degree in law at the University of Minnesota, a law degree from Cleveland Marshall Law School, and was presented with honorary doctorate degrees from 14 colleges and universities across the U.S. He was a visiting lecturer at universities and business institutions throughout the United States, Europe, and the Caribbean.

In November of 1962, Stokes became the first black Democrat in the history of the state of Ohio elected to the General Assembly. He was reelected in 1964 and 1966. At that time, members of the assembly were elected countywide, and Cuyahoga County's population was only 14 percent black. Stokes remains the only black Democrat ever elected countywide to the Ohio Legislature.

AMERICA'S BLACK MAYORAL LEGACY

Carl Burton Stokes is sworn in as Cleveland's 48th mayor. Holding the Bible is his brother, Louis, and looking on is his wife, Shirley. (Photo courtesy of Western Reserve Historical Society)

On November 13, 1967, Stokes attracted international attention when he was sworn in as mayor of the City of Cleveland, the first black mayor of a major American city, which had a population of 810,000. The black population in Cleveland was only 37 percent at that time, and it therefore, signified the first time an African American was elected mayor of a predominantly white major U.S. city. Cleveland selected Stokes, the grandson of a slave, over Seth Taft, the grandson of a U.S. president. Because he was a former resident of public housing, Stokes' win over the wealthy Taft was symbolic to poor blacks in Cleveland. Ninth grader Norris Bunch was inspired by Stokes' achievement, "I know he was a high school dropout...but he finished and went on to college. If he can make good, why can't I?"[3]

Subsequently, Mayor Stokes was asked by the White House to represent the United States on goodwill trips to Europe. He was also sent to the Caribbean on missions to Puerto Rico, the Bahamas, Barbados, and Trinidad. This was not the end of his achievements as mayor, however. In 1970, the 15,000-member National League of Cities composed of mayors and city and county officials nationwide, unanimously voted Stokes as president of their organization - the first black official ever to hold that office.

Stokes' administration was navigated through the rough waters of race and economic challenges. It was his desire to improve the lives of Cleveland's black poor and to give them a voice in municipal government.

AMERICA'S BLACK MAYORAL LEGACY

Despite some successes, he fell short of achieving his goals in the manner he envisioned. This was largely due to a declining tax base, a conservative state and federal government, and a constant migration of the poor into the city.[4] After two terms as mayor, Stokes decided to end his political career and begin a new one in broadcast journalism.

In April 1972, Carl Stokes became the first black anchorman to appear daily on a television news program in New York City. At WNBC-TV, NBC's flagship station, Stokes also served as an urban affairs editor and a correspondent. He traveled throughout Africa and was frequently assigned to the United Nations, where he interviewed heads of state and other foreign dignitaries.

After eight years as an award-winning broadcast journalist, Stokes returned to Cleveland and the practice of law in 1980. He became the first black lawyer to serve as general counsel to a major American labor union, the United Auto Workers-Region 2 and 2A. He likewise represented Laborers' Local 1099, Cleveland's largest city labor union.

On November 8, 1983, Stokes was elected judge of Cleveland Municipal Court, Ohio's largest court. Two months later on December 22, his colleagues elected him administrative judge of the court. Immediately thereafter, on January 9, 1984, his fellow judges elected him as their presiding judge. This was the first time a freshman judge was elected administrative and presiding judge of the 13-judge Municipal Court. Stokes served two terms

in this position. His election was another standard of political measurement in American history since few Americans - and no other African American - had ever been elected to the legislative, executive, and judicial branches of government in our nation.

On November 2, 1993, Stokes was elected to a third six-year term as judge of Cleveland Municipal Court. On August 26, 1994, President Bill Clinton appointed then Judge Stokes as his Ambassador Extraordinary and Plenipotentiary of the United States to the Republic of the Seychelles. Seychelles is a small cluster of islands in the Indian Ocean off the coast of Africa. Stokes served as ambassador until the time of his death at age 68 from cancer of the esophagus.

Before his death Stokes remarried his second wife, Raija, a former model from Finland. They were first married in 1981 and adopted a daughter, Cynthia Sofia, in 1988. The couple divorced in 1993.

In addition to his wife, brother Rep. Louis Stokes, and adopted daughter, three adult children survive him from his first marriage to Shirley Edwards - Carl Stokes, Jr., Cordell Stokes, and Cordi McBee-Awad. Stepson Sasha Kostadinov, and three grandchildren, Cordell Stokes, Jr., Jevonna Laraija Stokes, and Cybil Quinn McBee, also survive him.

MAYOR RICHARD GORDON HATCHER

(1933-) • ELECTED 1967

Sharing a place in black history, Richard Gordon Hatcher was elected mayor of Gary, Indiana on the same day that Carl Stokes was elected mayor of Cleveland, November 7, 1967. He became the first black mayor in the state of Indiana, the first black mayor of a large industrial Midwest city, and held that office for an unprecedented five terms.

Twenty-five miles east of Gary, Hatcher was born in Michigan City, Indiana July 10, 1933. He was the youngest of 13 children; six of his siblings died before reaching maturity. His parents Carlton and Katherine Hatcher worked as laborers. Carlton, a Baptist deacon, worked at Pullman Standard, a rail and passenger

car manufacturer. Katherine worked in a factory plucking hairs from pigs' tails for cushion stuffing.

Like other mayors, Hatcher overcame the handicap of poverty and growing up in a post-Depression era. His athleticism in track and football helped him excel, despite his introverted nature and a stuttering problem. Track and football also enabled him to obtain an athletic scholarship to Indiana University in 1951. With the assistance of two black churches and his two older sisters, Hatcher graduated with a bachelor's degree in business and government in 1956. He continued his studies earning a law degree at Valparaiso University School of Law in 1959. While in law school, he worked as a psychiatric aide.[5]

AMERICA'S BLACK MAYORAL LEGACY

Newly elected, Mayor Richard Hatcher at a press conference November 7, 1967.
Top and bottom photos courtesy of Calumet Regional Archives, Indiana University Northwest Library.

Hatcher moved to Gary, Indiana and practiced law in East Chicago. In 1961 he became a deputy prosecutor for Lake County, Indiana and served in that capacity until 1963 when he was elected to the Gary City Council. During the early years of his political career Hatcher became involved in the same civil rights issues facing many urban centers: discrimination in employment, housing, education, law enforcement and medical care. His reputation in Gary was built on his activism in police brutality cases and his participation in a school desegregation case. He is credited with founding Migwithania, (Swahili for "unity," or "we are together") a group of young, black professional activists. It was this group that helped to promote Hatcher's mayoral campaign.

Hatcher was the first and only freshman elected president of the City Council in Gary's history, and in 1967 he became Gary's first popularly elected African-American mayor. "When he became mayor, there was not an open housing ordinance in the city of Gary.

I couldn't live where I live now," shared Gary Councilmember Chuck Hughes in a 2003 interview with the *Clarion-Ledger.* [6]

Hatcher's leadership was marked with white flight by residents and businesses, most particularly to the suburb of Merrillville, Indiana. A northwest Indiana steel town, Gary began its corresponding decline with the steel industry. In Merrillville residents took advantage of lower property taxes, less crime, and residential and commercial development that included retail shopping. Conversely, Gary became known for its high crime rates, decreasing downtown businesses, and poorer population. With an eroding tax base, the racially polarized city's fiscal problems continued despite redevelopment efforts.

Hatcher is, however, credited with completing an airport transportation terminal, a city-run sports and fitness center, the Genesis Center, and transforming a hotel into a senior citizen high rise. Unfortunately, Hatcher was never able to transform Gary into an example of strong African-American economic and political power. Although he was blamed for much of Gary's economic demise, neighboring cities Hammond and East Chicago, which had white mayors, experienced the same dilemma.

After his 1987 defeat in a bid for a sixth term, Hatcher started his own consulting firm, R. Gordon Hatcher & Associates. He worked as an Institute of Politics fellow at Harvard University's Kennedy School from 1988-1989. In 1989 he began teaching political science at Roosevelt University and likewise at Valparaiso University in 1991, where he was a senior research professor. He is an adjunct professor of African-American studies at Indiana University Northwest. Hatcher ran unsuccessfully for mayor of Gary in 1991 and was defeated in the primary. He served as Jesse Jackson's campaign chairman in the 1984 presidential race and as an advisor in the 1988 race. [7]

Hatcher is known for continuing to speak out on civil rights issues, and he has written several articles on this subject as well as politics and law.

MAYOR SOPHIA M. MITCHELL

(1888-1978) • APPOINTED 1969

Sophia Mitchell was the first black woman appointed mayor in the United States. She served as mayor of Rendville, Ohio from 1969-1975. Rendville is a small town 72 miles southeast of Columbus, Ohio. Born February 27, 1888, she died March 19, 1978 at the age of 90. **(Photo unavailable)**

MAYOR ELLEN WALKER CRAIG-JONES

(1906-2000) • ELECTED 1971

According to the Ohio Historical Society and the Joint Center for Political Studies in Washington, D.C., in 1971, Ellen Walker Craig became the first African-American woman to be popularly elected to the office of mayor in the United States. She served from 1971-1975 as mayor of the Village of Urbancrest, ten miles south of Columbus, Ohio.

Known as "Aunt Dolly," Ellen Walker was born June 5, 1906 in Truro Township, within Franklin County. At the age of four months, her parents moved to Urbancrest. At age 10 her mother died. One year later tragedy struck again when their home burned to the ground. "We had nothing," she shared with *Today's Columbus Woman* in 1994. The fire did more than damage a home; it deeply affected her. For years she kept money hidden in "God's drawer" for those people in genuine need.

With no more than a high school education, Craig-Jones began her political career in the early 1950s on the Urbancrest Village Council. At the time, both her brother and her first husband, James Craig, were members. They challenged her to run for a seat on the six-member council. She won a seat in 1952 and served from 1952-1964. Encouraged by friends, she ran for mayor in 1971 and won, becoming the nation's first popularly elected African-American female mayor.

Under her administration, she is credited for annexing about 60 acres of additional land, the purchase and remodeling of a new city administration building, and the installation of mercury vapor street lights, to name a few. Moreover, she strengthened cooperative ties with officials of Grove City, Columbus, Franklin County, and the State of Ohio. To achieve these results, Craig-Jones had to work full-time at what was technically a part-time job with part-time pay. She declined to run for a second term due to her husband's health.

The Craigs were married for 60 years before James' death in 1983. At the age of 86 she was remarried to William Jones, a retired college professor. She continued to be active in Urbancrest, and even after she retired as mayor was known to call the White House and receive the action she needed. In spite of her accomplishments and contacts, she considered her family and her church, Union Baptist Church, to mean more to her than anything else.

Craig-Jones died of leukemia January 23, 2000. One son, James P. Craig, and one daughter, Estherleen Moore, grandchildren, great grandchildren, and great great-grandchildren survive her.

Mayor Walker Craig-Jones next to one of the wheels from the wagon that carried her family to Urbancrest, Ohio in 1906.
Photos courtesy of The Walker-Craig family archives

Mayor Tom Bradley in his City Hall office
Photo courtesy of the Los Angeles City Archives

AMERICA'S BLACK MAYORAL LEGACY

MAYOR TOM BRADLEY

(1917-1998) • ELECTED 1973

Mayor Tom Bradley, circa 1973
Photo courtesy of the Los Angeles City Archives

The grandson of a slave and the son of a sharecropper and a maid, Tom Bradley overcame the obstacles of color, childhood and career to be "first." He became the first African-American lieutenant on the Los Angeles Police Department (LAPD), the first African American elected to the Los Angeles City Council, and the city's first black mayor.

His parents, Lee and Crenner Bradley, lived in a log cabin outside of Calvert, Texas. They moved from Texas to Arizona to pick cotton, and in 1924, they settled in Los Angeles. There, his father worked as a porter on the Santa Fe railroad and as a crewmember on an ocean liner; his mother found work as a maid. Eventually his parents divorced, and with five children, his mother continued her domestic work.

AMERICA'S BLACK MAYORAL LEGACY

Through his academics, track, and football, Bradley earned a full scholarship to UCLA in 1936. He accomplished this by going against the advice of his high school guidance counselor, who told him to focus on vocational classes. In his junior year at UCLA he took an exam for the LAPD, scoring near the top. To say discrimination existed within the department and the city was an understatement. In 1940 there were 100 African-American police officers among the ranks of 4,000. Despite the discrimination, Bradley's 21-year career was highlighted with his promotion to lieutenant, the highest rank achieved by an African American at the time.[8]

While working with the LAPD, Bradley attended law school in the evening. Upon retiring in 1961, he practiced law and became active with the Democratic Party. In 1963, he was elected to the Los Angeles City Council, serving a district comprised of a majority of white voters. While on City Council, he spoke out against the LAPD's internal racist practices, its handling of the Watts Riots in 1965, and the excessive use of force in the shooting of a black man.

Bradley ran for mayor in 1969 against incumbent Sam Yorty. However, his stance of the above issues opened the door for Yorty to label him a militant. Although Bradley placed first in the primary, he lost the general election as a result of Yorty's racist tactics.

For his second mayoral bid, Bradley's support came from friendships developed during his previous years of public service. "Old friends, loyal and supportive, responding to the friendships which we had established over the years, became the essence of that multiethnic community that became my campaign supporters," he shared.[9] In Cleveland, Atlanta, and Newark, where Carl Stokes, Maynard Jackson, and Kenneth Gibson respectively were elected, African Americans made up a large percentage of the population. However, in 1973, blacks comprised less than 18 percent of the Los Angeles population. Bradley's challenge was to engage both the majority and black voters without alienating either, and to simultaneously disallow race to become an issue. Grassroots support came from black ministers, their congregations and Jewish activists. Advertising and campaign financing came from wealthy investors, many of whom were liberal Jews. He also received support from the Latino and Asian communities.[10] Bradley was reelected an unprecedented four times before he retired in 1993.

During Bradley's administration, Los Angeles surpassed San Francisco as the West Coast's economic power in Pacific Rim trading. The downtown skyline changed and the city gained international recognition. Further, he is credited with increasing mass transit with new rail lines and buses, and helping the Los Angeles International Airport to become a success. Bradley's personal and one of his most significant triumphs was bringing the 1984 Olympic Games to Los Angeles. Calling it "the highlight of his entire political career," the Olympics garnered $250 million in revenues for the city of Los Angeles.[11]

Bradley's promise of impartiality and his determination not to allow race to become a core component of his administration worked for and against him. His programs were designed to benefit all of Los Angeles, not just the disenfranchised, who were predominately African American. In the mid 70s, he created programs that rehabilitated abandoned houses, thus increasing African-American home ownership. He likewise initiated summer recreation programs for disadvantaged youth. He changed the demographics of the city's commissioners as well as the Civil Service Commission, which determined the city's hiring policies. Moreover, Los Angeles' black middle-class benefited from his affirmative policies, and he tapped prominent members of minority groups for influential city government positions.

Although his quiet, yet effective impartial practices benefited African Americans and other ethnic groups, many within the black community viewed him as weak and not willing to defy his white support base. Heather Parker summarizes Bradley's style, "What they failed to recognize was that Bradley's leadership reflected his political values and his belief that his approach was the most effective way to bring black Angelenos [sic] into the political and economic mainstream. In his own worldview he could not be an outspoken advocate for African Americans and, at the same time, impartially service the multivariate interests of Los Angeles' diverse electorate. Bradley's strength was his courage to remain true to his ideals even when, in doing so, he alienated many of his own people who had so strongly supported him and provided the political foundation for his election."[12]

In 1981 Bradley ran for governor of California as a Democrat. He lost to Republican George Deukmejian by less than one percentage point. He subsequently lost a second governor's race in 1986.

While Bradley tried to unify Los Angeles' diverse ethnic and racial groups through economic and social policies, the riots that followed the verdicts of four white LAPD officers who were acquitted in the Rodney King beating marked the end of his administration.

AMERICA'S BLACK MAYORAL LEGACY

His soft-spoken, coalition-building leadership style that served him for five administrations came to an end. He retired at age 75 and joined a downtown law firm.

In March 1996, Bradley suffered a heart attack. The following April he suffered a paralyzing stroke a day after triple bypass surgery, which left him unable to speak. Bradley died on September 29, 1998 at the age of 80 after a heart attack. His wife, Ethel, and two daughters survive him.

One of his staffers, now Councilmember Wendy Greuel, recalls Mayor Bradley imparting his wisdom to young people about reaching their potential and not giving up hope. "He was an inspiration to kids who didn't believe they had any hope of succeeding in life," she shared.[13]

Former Vice President Al Gore eulogized Tom Bradley by quoting Dr. Martin Luther King Jr., "'The arc of the universe is long, but it bends toward justice.' And so it did for Tom Bradley, whose life was a testament to justice, hope, and an audacious faith in the future."

MAYOR MAYNARD HOLBROOK JACKSON, JR.

(1938-2003) • ELECTED 1973

In 1973 at age 35, Maynard Holbrook Jackson, Jr. became the first African American elected mayor of a major southern city, capturing 95 percent of the black vote and 17.5 percent of the white vote. At the time he was the city's youngest mayor and his blueprint for black and white business ventures made Atlanta the Black Mecca of the South.

"Let me tell you how [Atlanta's Black Mecca reputation] started," Mack Wilbourn, owner of thriving Popeye's Chicken and Edy's Ice Cream airport concessions, revealed to Who's Who Publishing. "All of a sudden, you had a black mayor who was very elegant and engaging, who made black people all over the country very happy and very pleased. He was so good looking, so well spoken, so charismatic-he was someone your mother could be proud of. Then he brought bright black people into his administration who traveled all over the United States, and the word was out: 'You could get a better shot in Atlanta because somebody black was in charge.' With other black mayors at the time, you didn't feel it was a welcome sign out like it was in Atlanta with Maynard. Maynard always promoted Atlanta. Wherever he went to speak, it made people feel good and they wanted to come here. I know people who came to Atlanta and enjoyed it so much that they'd send back for their clothes and never leave."

Jackson was born in Dallas, Texas March 23, 1938. When he was 14, his family moved to Atlanta when his father became pastor of the influential Friendship Baptist Church. His grandfather, John Wesley Dobbs was a prominent minister and civil rights leader. Dobbs served as co-chairman of the Atlanta Negro Voters

AMERICA'S BLACK MAYORAL LEGACY

League, and his father, the Rev. Maynard H. Jackson, Sr. founded the Georgia Voters League. Acknowledged as a child prodigy, Jackson completed high school at age 14. At age 18 he graduated from Morehouse College with a bachelor's degree in political science and history, even younger than his idol, Dr. Martin Luther King, Jr. He went on to North Carolina Central University School of Law to earn a juris doctor degree, cum laude. He later received eight honorary degrees and was a Visitor of the Kennedy School of Government at Harvard University and a Chubb fellow at Yale University. A Phi Beta Kappa, Jackson worked his way through school as a waiter, tobacco picker, librarian, and an encyclopedia national sales trainer and salesman.

Jackson's political career began in 1969 when he campaigned and won the office of vice mayor, the first black to do so. After a run-off election in 1973, he assumed the mayoral office from Sam Massell, Atlanta's first Jewish mayor in 1974. He served three terms - from 1974 to 1982 and again from 1990-1994.

Jackson was described by many as a big man with a big heart who spearheaded radical change in Atlanta and throughout the nation. He was the embodiment of the shift from the civil rights movement in the streets to the quest for clout and influence in government and corporate America. Jackson is widely viewed as the architect of affirmative action-a controversial concept he introduced in 1975 during the expansion of Hartsfield International Airport, now ranked as one of the nation's busiest. He vowed to halt the $400 million project unless 25 percent of the construction contracts were awarded to minority-owned businesses. This landmark program, which required that minority-owned enterprises get a larger share of government contracts by partnering with white-owned firms, became a national model.

"He saw how much good affirmative action did for well-connected white folks and he thought it ought to be tried for other people as well," remarked former President Bill Clinton to a rousing ovation at Jackson's funeral service. "Sure enough, it worked." The mid-field terminal opened its doors in 1978 on time and under budget-a phenomenal feat that shocked critics. More significantly, it also represented the first time that African Americans, minority, and female vendors shared in a huge slice of the economic pie from a major capital project. When Jackson took office in 1973, black business owners had received less than one percent of city contracts. By 1978 they were receiving almost 39 percent, helping to establish a viable African-American middle-class in Atlanta and several millionaires.

Jackson's other accomplishments as mayor were equally amazing. During his three terms he lowered Atlanta's crime rate, helped to initiate the Metropolitan Atlanta Rapid Transit Authority (MARTA), Atlanta's rapid rail system, and streamlined the city's administration structure. He used the city's bank accounts to pressure local banks to open their boards of directors to blacks and women,[14] and pressured major law firms to hire black lawyers. Similar to his Los Angeles counterpart, Mayor Tom Bradley, he was essential in bringing the 1996 Olympics to Atlanta. Former Atlanta Mayor Bill Campbell told CNN, "Jackson was to affirmative action what Martin Luther King was to civil rights. His affirmative action program became a model for governments around the country."[15]

Despite being viewed as the nation's quintessential big-city mayor, when Maynard Jackson completed his second stint as Atlanta's first African-American mayor, he could not find a job. And despite his superstar status as a vote getter and political powerbroker, there was no higher political office available or on the horizon. Jackson had battled and bruised Atlanta's business community with his forceful demands for inclusion and his eloquent, albeit assertive style, so much so that the Phi Beta Kappa Morehouse graduate was forced to open an Atlanta office for a Chicago law firm. He managed Chapman & Cutler's lucrative municipal bond practice. "Those were tough, humbling times," admits Jackson's ex-wife Bunnie Jackson-Ransom.

In 1987, Jackson bought a small investment-banking firm that he renamed Jackson Securities. The prospering enterprise has now become his business legacy. It is one of only two black-owned securities firms in Atlanta with eleven offices across the country. "We go all over the country trying to convince people to give us a chance to show what we can do and to get the business," Jackson told the venerable Hungry Club Forum in one of his last public speeches to the city in February of 2003. "We're still struggling, still fighting for crumbs from America's economic table."

In 1996, Jackson Securities was named one of the nation's top five black investment firms. Critics charged that Jackson parlayed his contacts, friendships, and clout to win city bond deals in Atlanta and throughout the country. "Maynard was a rainmaker, a fierce competitor, a top notch investment banker, and probably as good, if not better, a businessman than he was a politician," opines Bruce Dobbs, co-owner of the Malachi Group, Atlanta's other black-owned brokerage firm. To his entrepreneurial credit, Jackson also owned Jackmont Hospitality, an airport operations outfit.

Jackson suffered from diabetes and had major heart surgery in 1992. On June 23, 2003, after disembarking his flight, he collapsed at Reagan National Airport in Washington, D.C. He was revived but suffered a heart attack while in route to the Virginia Medical Center in Arlington, Virginia and died. Ironically, he died on the same day his principles were upheld by the U.S. Supreme Court. He is survived by his wife of 25 years, Valerie Jackson, her two children with Jackson, three children from his marriage to Bunnie Jackson-Ransom, three grandchildren, and one brother and two sisters.

MAYOR COLEMAN ALEXANDER YOUNG

(1918-1997) • ELECTED 1973

Detroit's first black and longest serving mayor was also one of its most controversial. Elected in 1973, Coleman A. Young served until 1993. His early encounters with racism stimulated a life of social activism and change in the labor movement, the military, and politics. Succinctly and summarily stated, The *Detroit Free Press* described him as "...revered and reviled, eloquent and profane, a leader and a loner. He dominated Detroit for 20 years, serving longer than any other mayor."[16]

Named in honor of his father and grandfather, Alex Young, Coleman Alexander Young was born May 24, 1918 in Tuscaloosa, Alabama to William Coleman and Ida Reese Young. Like thousands of blacks in the 1920s and 1930s, his father, frustrated with the Jim Crow laws of the South and looking for better economic opportunities, moved his family north. As destiny would have it, they moved to Black Bottom, an eastside Detroit neighborhood located a mere two miles from the mayor's office Young would eventually maintain for two decades.

The oldest of five children, his adversarial yet protective leadership abilities evolved from parental upbringing and experiencing discrimination first-hand in school. Young was denied scholarships to three area high schools despite his straight "A" average at St. Mary's Catholic School. In 1935 he graduated second in his class at Eastern High School, and once again was denied academic scholarships, this time to Wayne State University and the University of Michigan.

Young's activism began with organized labor, which he saw as a vehicle to fight discrimination and simultaneously earn good wages. As an automotive worker, his efforts as a union organizer for the Congress of Industrial Organizations (CIO) kept him unemployed and blacklisted. He was likewise fired from the U.S. Post Office for recruiting employees to form a union, and for his protests against racial segregation at Sojourner Truth, a public housing project in Detroit.[17]

His military career was equally controversial. At age 24, he enlisted in the U.S. Army during World War II. There, he received commission as a second lieutenant in the infantry, and subsequently transferred to the air corps. It was in the air corps that he became the nation's first black bombardier. He and his fellow black servicemen became known as the Tuskegee Airmen. Unfortunately, racism impeded them from their purpose. Instead of fighting Hitler and his forces, they fought the U.S. Army. With his organizational abilities, he and 100 black officers protested through a sit-in at an all-white Officers' Club in Freedom Field, Indiana.[18] Jailed, they avoided an attempt to be court-martialed and shot because of Young's ability to get their case in the headlines of black newspapers and his letters to the Adjutant General's office. As a result of failed efforts by the Army's investigative team and the negative publicity, they were released. Segregation at the Club ended, but according to Wilbur C. Rich in *Coleman Young and Detroit Politics*, the incident marked the beginning of "Young's first purely civil rights activity."[19]

Young picked up his union organization activities after the War, becoming director of the Wayne County AFL-CIO and a leader of the National Negro Labor Council. These roles landed him on the House Un-American Activities Committee's list of individuals thought to be communists. His defiance to their interrogation of him kept him blacklisted and invited the FBI to monitor him from the 1940s through the 1980s.

Mayor Coleman Alexander Young
Photo courtesy of The Coleman A. Young Foundation

AMERICA'S BLACK MAYORAL LEGACY

Young's subsequent political career was marked by a successful run for the Michigan Constitutional Convention in 1961; winning a Senate seat in 1964; becoming the Democratic floor leader in 1966; and in 1968 he became the first black member of the Democratic National Committee.

With racial tensions, rioting, and a steadily deteriorating relationship between the black community and Detroit's police department, Senator Young ran for mayor. Toughened by his past, the lack of finances did not hinder his bid. In 1974 at age 55 he became Detroit's first black mayor. His tenure was marked by the city's economic hardships and white flight to the suburbs. It was also highlighted by his creation of jobs for women and blacks in the police department, thus improving community relations. Under Young's leadership, the Detroit Police Department eventually became known worldwide for its crime prevention programs. Moreover, Young kept Detroit from bankruptcy, making alliances with leadership in the labor, business, political, spiritual and civic communities, and brought critical federal and state dollars to the city.[20] In the midst of several ongoing investigations by the media, the FBI, and other government agencies, he revived Detroit's riverfront, defused potential riots, and confronted his critics.

A constant warrior for racial and social justice, Young was elected mayor for five terms. Known for his colorful language and controversial nature he let any and everyone know he could not be intimidated. In his inaugural address he told all pushers, rip-off artists, and muggers, "It's time to leave Detroit; hit Eight Mile Road! And I don't give a damn if they are black or white, or if they wear Superfly suits or blue uniforms with silver badges. Hit the road."

For his efforts Young was awarded the NAACP Spingarn Medal in 1981, and received the "Mayor of the Year" award from the National Urban Coalition in 1984. Married and divorced twice, his marriages did not bear any children. After retirement from the mayoral office he wrote an autobiography, *Hard Stuff: The Autobiography of Coleman Young,* published in 1994. He was also a professor at Wayne State University. Wayne State, which previously denied him a scholarship, honored him with an endowed chair in urban affairs in his name.

Fighting to the end, Coleman A. Young lost his battle with emphysema and died November 29, 1997 of respiratory failure at age 79. A son, Coleman Young, Jr., sisters Bernice Grier and Juanita Clark, sisters-in-law Elizabeth Young and Muriel Young, cousins Dr. Claud Young and Esther Walker, and his companion, Barbara Parker, survive him.

MAYOR MARION S. BARRY, JR.

(1936-) • ELECTED 1978

Sworn in by the late Supreme Court Justice Thurgood Marshall in 1978, Marion Barry became the District of Columbia's second mayor and its first African-American mayor.

A Mississippi Delta native, Barry was born March 6, 1936 in Itta Bena, Mississippi to Marion Barry, Sr., a sharecropper, and Mattie Barry. Without his father, his mother and sister moved to Memphis, Tennessee when Barry was a young child. In Memphis Barry graduated from Booker T. Washington High School where he was predominately an "A" student and an accomplished basketball and football player. On a full scholarship he attended Le Moyne College, a Historically Black College and University (HBCU) in Memphis, and earned a bachelor's degree. On another full scholarship he earned a master's degree from Fisk University in Nashville, Tennessee.

Photo courtesy of the Executive Office of the Mayor, Office of Communications, Washington, D.C.

Three years into a doctoral program in chemistry at the University of Tennessee he engaged himself in the civil rights movement. After participating in sit-ins at segregated Memphis lunch counters and voter registration drives in Mississippi, he became the first chairman of the Student Non-Violent Coordinating Committee (SNCC). He relocated to Washington, D.C. in June of 1965 to establish a SNCC office, and amidst campaigns that benefited poor blacks, he rose to prominence.

Within a few years, Barry was elected to D.C.'s first school board (1971). Receiving the highest number of votes in 1974, he was elected to the D.C. City Council. He became chairman of the council's finance committee. and he pioneered innovative property tax legislation, cut taxes for seniors, established an equitable income tax system, and reigned in the city's budget and finances.[21]

Building a coalition of blacks, women, liberal and gay whites, and other minority groups, Barry was successful in his 1978 mayoral bid. He served three terms until 1990. Under his administration the city's budget was balanced, downtown construction increased, and thousands of jobs were created. It was Barry's District Youth's Employment Act of 1979, which guaranteed a summer job for every young D.C. resident, regardless of their economic status, that earned him lasting and loyal support. Today, he is still remembered by countless individuals who received their first summer job under his program.

Unfortunately, Barry's personal problems affected his ability to govern. Further, during his administration the District's economic problems came to a head when the construction boom ended during the late 1980s. Even though there had been an increase in downtown office development, the revenue impact proved temporary. Much of the economic growth was in the suburbs, and therefore, local jobs and accompanying revenues slowed. Washington, D.C. was near bankruptcy. Instead of running for reelection in 1990, Barry ran for an at-large council seat. It was at this time that he lost his first election.

In 1992, Barry reloaded his political weaponry and moved to Ward 8 and ran for City Council. To the surprise and dismay of his critics, he was reelected mayor in a landslide victory in 1994. With the city in a major fiscal deficit before he took office, Barry had his work cut out. In 1995 Congress stepped in and established a financial control board, giving it authority over the city's budget. In 1997 Congress took further control of other mayoral responsibilities with the power to overrule the mayor and City Council. Despite his lack of congressional support and constant media battering, Barry was able to reduce the District's deficit. Although not given credit by the media or his critics, he successfully made the cuts required by Congress. He left office with a $400 million surplus, and a $1.1 billion turnaround from the time he began his last term in office. [22]

In the face of personal weaknesses that surfaced during his administration, Barry's popularity with a portion of D.C. residents remains. After leaving the mayor's office he reentered politics. Against the odds and predictions, in November of 2004 he once again trounced an incumbent for the Ward 8 council seat, receiving 96 percent of the vote. Marion Barry remains a very popular icon and champion of disenfranchised people within the District's African-American community.

MAYOR HAROLD WASHINGTON

(1922-1987) • ELECTED 1983

Born April 15, 1922, to Roy Lee Washington, Sr. and Bertha Washington, Harold was the youngest child of their union. His parents divorced in 1928 and his politically, spiritually and civically active father raised him. Roy Washington was a part-time African Methodist Episcopal minister, an attorney, and a precinct captain in the Cook County Democratic Organization. Being raised and living on Chicago's South Side for most of his early life proved to be the perfect place for an African American with leadership skills like Harold. After all, it was the South Side that gave rise to the first black elected U.S. Congress representative from a northern district and from the state of Illinois in 1928. Oscar S. DePriest (R) served during the 71st-73rd Congresses from 1929-1935.[23]

**Mayor Washington with his successor, Eugene Sawyer.
Photo courtesy of the Chicago Historical Society**

Roy Washington had been involved with the Democratic Party from the early 30s, and it was only natural that he became Harold's political mentor. His mentoring was effective as Washington succeeded his father as South Side Ward precinct captain when he died in 1953.

Washington established a private practice in Chicago before working as an assistant city prosecutor (corporation counsel) from 1954 until 1958. His legal career also included a position as arbitrator for the Illinois Industrial Commission from 1960-1964.

During his early legal career he also organized the Young Democrats, which became an effective political organization for minorities. His organizing skills were rewarded when he was elected to the Illinois House of Representatives in 1964, representing the 26th District. He served for eleven years from 1965-1976. There, he was responsible for sponsoring anti-discrimination bills and played a key role in having Dr. King's birthday recognized as a holiday in the state of Illinois.

Like other metropolitan cities, blacks in Chicago experienced unchecked police brutality. While a legislator, Washington directly confronted then Mayor Richard J. Daley about this issue. After Daley's death in 1976, Washington ran for mayor, but only garnered eleven percent of the vote.

A 1976 bid for state senator proved successful, and he was later elected to the U.S. House of Representatives in 1980. He used this position to assist in extending the 1965 Voting Rights Act and served in the House until 1983. After being persuaded by Chicago's black leadership to run for mayor, Washington entered a race where the odds were solidly not in his favor. In the Democratic primary he ran against incumbent Jane Byrne and Richard M. Daley, son of the former four-term Mayor Richard J. Daley. Both Daley and Byrne attempted to be strategic with black voters by not attacking Washington during the primary. By the time Byrne realized that Washington was actually a viable candidate it was late in the primary race. Additionally, a failed racial tactic by the Democratic Party chairman Ed Vrdolyak to swing white voters to Byrne failed. Byrne and Daley split the white vote almost in half and, as a result, Washington carried the primary with 36 percent of the total primary vote. In the black community with increased voter registration, Washington received 85 percent of a 70 percent turnout.[25] He narrowly defeated Bernard Epton (R) in the general election to become the city's first African-American mayor in 1983.

Washington dropped out of high school in his junior year. He took a job at a meat packing company and then joined the Army in 1942. Called to active duty in February of 1943, he was assigned to the 1887th Engineer Aviation Battalion, rising to the rank of first sergeant. His unit received the Meritorious Service Unit Award for building a bomber landing strip on the Pacific island of Anguar in a mere 20 days. Washington was decorated for bravery and received an honorable discharge in 1946. That same year he was awarded his high school diploma. [24]

Washington enrolled in Roosevelt College (now Roosevelt University), was elected class president in 1948, and graduated in 1949 with a bachelor's degree in political science. He went on to the Northwestern University School of Law and earned a juris doctorate in 1952.

Washington is credited with increasing employment diversity for women and minorities within the City of Chicago's administration and ending city patronage. He issued an Executive Order increasing minority business contracts, and opened the city's process to the public. Washington experienced enormous difficulty, however, in trying to implement other programs because of bitter opposition from the white majority (29 of 50 council votes). They controlled the powerful and patronage-rich council committees and would not approve hundreds of Washington's appointments, which would threaten the status quo within city agencies.[26] As a result of his initiative, in 1985 a federal court ordered redistricting of several ward boundaries, and in 1986 new elections gave Washington control of council with increased black and Hispanic representation. His executive appointments were approved as well as a new ethics ordinance and a Tenant's Bill of Rights. Washington also gained control of key city agencies.

Washington won an easy second term in 1987, but shortly thereafter he died of a massive heart attack at his City Hall desk on November 25, 1987. Although married and divorced to Nancy Dorothy Finch, their marriage produced no children. At the time of his death, Washington was engaged to Mary Ella Smith.

MAYOR DAVID N. DINKINS

(1927-) • ELECTED 1989

At the time of his election, New York City was divided by racial tensions and faced with uncontrolled crime and a challenged infrastructure. Moreover, the city carried a huge budget deficit of $1 billion passed on by the Koch administration. Not more than 25 percent of New York City's electorate was African American. However, in November of 1989 Dinkins triumphed over several candidates including former Mayor Ed Koch and Rudy Giuliani to become the City's 106th and first African-American mayor. He campaigned on the need for unity and reconciliation, and served one term from 1990-1993 as mayor of the largest city in the United States.

Born in Trenton, New Jersey on July 10, 1927, his family moved to Harlem during the Depression. His father was a barber who later became a real estate broker in Trenton.

Dinkins, after enlisting twice and being rejected because of racial quotas, served as a Marine during World War II from 1945 through 1946. He earned a bachelor of science degree in mathematics from Howard University in 1950, and an L.L.B. from Brooklyn Law School in 1956.

Dinkins married the former Joyce Burrows in 1953 and went into private law practice from 1956-1975. During that time he was active in Harlem's Carver Democratic Club, and in 1966 he was elected to the New York State Assembly. There, he created the Search for Education, Elevation and Knowledge (SEEK) program, which provides grants and educational assistance to low-

Mayor David N. Dinkins

AMERICA'S BLACK MAYORAL LEGACY

income students. Additionally, from 1972-1973 he was president of the New York City Board of Elections. In this capacity he established guidelines that stimulated increased voter registration. Dinkins was appointed to the position of city clerk in 1975 and held that post for ten years. Thereafter, in November of 1985 he was elected president of the Borough of Manhattan.

Dinkins was elected mayor in 1989 despite the fact that African Americans comprised no more than 25 percent of the electorate. With his quiet demeanor, he campaigned against the stronger personalities of former mayor Ed Koch and the then current mayor, Rudolph Giuliani. At the time of his election the city's tax revenues were down due to the stock market crash of October 19, 1987. Federal assistance had been reduced from 17.9 percent to 9.3 percent, a loss of $1.2 billion. Seventy-five thousand were counted as homeless, and of that figure only 35,000 were able to secure shelter on a nightly basis. Twenty-five percent of New York residents were classified as poor, and inadequate educational, healthcare and social service resources exacerbated the city's problems. Deep wounds of racial tensions further plagued the city including the rape and beating of a white jogger in Central Park, and the murder of a black 16-year-old who was visiting the Italian neighborhood of Bensonhurst to inspect a used car.

Dinkins' fiscal problems remained with him throughout his administration despite his efforts. New York's municipal workforce and accompanying payroll was much higher than cities of similar size. For example, public school custodians earned an average salary of $57,000, when, at the time the national average was $36,000.[27]

Similar to other black mayors elected by a diverse constituency as well as those within his own community, Dinkins had the challenge of balancing his response to each group's expectations. New York's Latino population was slightly less than the African-African population, and after his election they shared their dissatisfaction with the low numbers of professional and managerial positions held by members in their community.

Dinkins was also criticized for the pace and manner in which he handled the boycott of a South Korean-owned store in East Flatbush, which lasted more than a year. Often mixed with violence, the boycott divided the black and Asian communities. In August of 1991, an out-of-control car driven by a Hasidic Jew in the Crown Heights section of Brooklyn accidentally killed a seven-year-old black boy and injured his cousin. Rumors spread that ambulances responded and took the whites while leaving the children. In response, blacks stabbed a Hasidic divinity student from Australia who was walking in the area. Rioting broke out and Dinkins was judged for not acting quickly or forcefully.

Dinkins is, however, credited with initiating the Safe Streets, Safe City: Cops and Kids campaign, which reduced crime and offered opportunities for the city's children. Further, he instituted the first needle exchange program to reduce the spread of AIDS, promoted housing and education, and assisted small companies with a program to increase minority- and female-owned business participation in city projects. Internationally, he limited New York's investment in apartheid in South Africa and welcomed Nelson Mandela's visit to the city after his release from imprisonment by the Pretoria African government. Mayor Dinkins successfully constructed the National Tennis Center in Flushing Meadow-Corona Park with private funds. Open to the public, the tennis center generates millions for the city.

Dinkins now serves as a professor in the Practice of Public Affairs at Columbia University School of International and Public Affairs. There, he also hosts the David N. Dinkins Leadership & Public Policy Forum. He is a senior fellow at the Center for Urban Research and Policy, and hosts *Dialogue with Dinkins*, a public affairs radio program. Dinkins holds honorary degrees from Brooklyn Law School, St. Francis College, the New York Institute of Technology, Hofstra University School of Law, New York Law School, General Theological Seminary, the College of Human Services, and Pace University. He is a member of the Council on Foreign Relations and the Board of Governors of the American Stock Exchange. An active tennis player, the former mayor also serves organizations that assist children and young people. Dinkins and his wife, Joyce, have two children, David, Jr. and Donna.

MAYOR SHARON PRATT KELLY

(1944-) • ELECTED 1990

Sharon Pratt Kelly was the first African-American woman to be popularly elected mayor of a major U.S. city. Winning the 1990 election, she succeeded Marion Barry, Jr. as mayor of Washington, D.C., and was sworn in January 2, 1991.

A native of Washington, Pratt was born January 30, 1944. In 1965 she earned a bachelor's degree and in 1968 she received a law degree, both from Howard University. She entered private law practice in 1971 and was a professor of law at Antioch College. Pratt returned to Washington in 1977.

In 1982 she headed an unsuccessful D.C. mayoral campaign for Patricia Robert Harris to oust Marion Barry. That same year she also married Arrington Dixon a Democrat on the D.C. City Council. In 1983, she was named vice president of community relations at Pepco, a regional power utility. There, she was the first woman and African-American to serve in that role and was responsible for community relations and public policy.

During this time, her political ambitions were primarily on a national level. From 1977-1990, she was a member of the Democratic National Committee (DNC) from the District, and was the first female in that position. She held the position as the organization's treasurer from 1985-1989.

Dismayed with the condition of her native Washington, D.C. under Marion Barry's governance, Pratt Dixon announced her intentions to challenge him at the 1988 Democratic National Convention in Atlanta. Promising to "clean house with a shovel, not a broom," she came after Barry and his administration without hesitation. Virtually unknown and perceived as part of the District's black aristocracy, no one really thought she could win. However, with an endorsement from the *Washington Post*, and Barry bowing out of the election after his drug conviction, she easily won. Within the first year of her administration, she married businessman James R. Kelly, III and changed her name to Sharon Pratt Kelly.

Kelly's first year as mayor was turbulent and one of loss. In addition to losing her grandmother, a trusted friend and advisor died when the city ambulance went to the wrong address. Professionally and politically, Kelly was not able to implement

Sharon Pratt Kelly
Photo by Lateef Mangum, Washington, D.C.

the promised campaign reforms in city government. Her commitment to reduce the number of city employees went unsupported at the same time city services were not meeting the voters' needs. In addition, Congress questioned city accounting practices based on false or lacking financial data, and the D.C. crime rate increased. Kelly was eventually able to reduce crime by strengthening relationships between neighborhoods and the police department.

In her second year, Barry and his loyal supporters launched a recall to remove her from office. Albeit unsuccessful, it left her administration weakened and Kelly never implemented the tough reforms she proposed. She turned her attention to attacking Congress for the city's financial problems and became an advocate of D.C. statehood. Disillusioned voters backed Barry in the 1994 primary paving the way for his return. Kelly finished a distant third.

Kelly is now a fellow at the Institute of Politics. She has two daughters, Aimee and Drew, from her first marriage to Arrington Dixon.

ATLANTA'S LEGACY

Ambassador Andrew Young

Of all the major U.S. cities, Atlanta has a lasting place in history by giving us a strong lineage of successive African-America mayors. Maynard Jackson's two terms in office were from 1974 through 1982, followed by Ambassador Andrew Young, who also governed two terms from 1982 through 1990. It was Ambassador Young's foresight that embraced the idea of hosting the 1996 Centennial Olympic Games, of which he served as co-chairman. A top aide to Dr. Martin Luther King, Jr. during the civil rights movement, Young served three terms in the U.S. Congress from Georgia's 5th District. President Jimmy Carter named him Ambassador to the United Nations.

Maynard Jackson followed Young in office, serving from 1990-1994. His successor, Bill Campbell, governed Atlanta from 1994 through 2002. Current mayor, Shirley Franklin, followed him with her election as Atlanta's 58th mayor. Another history maker, Franklin is Atlanta's first woman mayor and the first African-American woman to serve as mayor of a major southern city.

Known as a strategic city during the Civil War and the civil rights movement, in the 1960s the citizens of Atlanta decided it would be "the city too busy to hate." As a result, the city's leadership has exemplified what it takes to guide a major diverse city in unprecedented growth for more than 30 years.

LOOKING AHEAD

This new millennium is clearly bringing fresh challenges to African-American chief executive officers who lead our cities, towns and villages. Gentrification, competitive shifts in the global marketplace, an aging population, and challenged healthcare and public school systems now afford them opportunities to create new paradigms for program and policy development. For some, patterns of effective government are inherited from those who went before them. Others must become visionaries, charting new paths that meet the needs of their constituents and move their communities to places of security, prosperity, and peace. It is our hope that African-American mayors emerge as strong and effective leaders who leave legacies of honorable service for the generations that will follow.

[1] Dick Case, "A Place in History for Ned Sherman," www.jubileeinitiative.org/Americans FirstBlackMayor.htm (February 22, 2003), accessed on February 2, 2005.

[2] Carl B. Stokes, *Promises of Power: A Political Autobiography* (New York: Simon and Schuster, 1973), pp. 23-25.

[3] *Cleveland Press*, November 10, 1967.

[4] Leonard N. Moore, "Carl Stokes: Mayor of Cleveland," *African-American Mayors: Race, Politics and the American City,* (Detroit: Wayne State University Press, 1989), p. 101.

[5] James B. Lane, "Black Political Power and Its Limits: Gary Mayor Richard G. Hatcher's Administration, 1968-1987," *African-American Mayors: Race, Politics and the American City,* (Detroit: Wayne State University Press, 1989), p. 58.

[6] Gregg Mayor, "The Changing Face of Jackson," *The Clarion Ledger*, October 5, 2003.

[7] "Richard Hatcher, A Pioneering Urban Mayor," *The African American Registry,* www.aaregistry.com/african_american_history, accessed on February 14, 2005.

[8] Albert Greenstein, "Tom Bradley," www.socalhistory.org/Biographies/bradley.htm (1999), accessed on February 4, 2005.

[9] Bradley interview, cited by Heather R. Parker, "Tom Bradley and the Politics of Race," *African-American Mayors: Race, Politics and the American City,* (Detroit: Wayne State University Press, 1989), p.159.

[10] Heather R. Parker, "Tom Bradley and the Politics of Race," *African-American Mayors: Race, Politics and the American City,* (Detroit: Wayne State University Press, 1989), p.159.

[11] Dave Greenwald, "Spotlight: Tom Bradley, Mayor of Los Angeles," www.ucla.edu/spotlight/archive/html_2000_2001/alumn_0201_bradley.html, (February 2001), accessed on February 7, 2005.

[12] Heather R. Parker, "Tom Bradley and the Politics of Race," *African-American Mayors: Race, Politics and the American City,* (Detroit: Wayne State University Press, 1989), p.172.

[13] Dave Greenwald, "Spotlight: Tom Bradley, Mayor of Los Angeles," www.ucla.edu/spotlight/archive/html_2000_2001/alumn_0201_bradley.html, (February 2001), accessed on February 7, 2005.

[14] "Maynard Jackson: Atlanta's First Black Mayor," *Black History Daily,* www.blackseek.com/bh/2001/07_MaynardJackson.htm (1999), accessed on February 8, 2005.

[15] Art Harris, "Atlanta's First Black Mayor Dies," CNN.com (June 23, 2003).

[16] *The Detroit Free Press*, "A Life Remembered," 1997.

[17] Coleman A. Young Foundation, "Coleman A. Young Bio," www.cayf.org/bio_cay.htm (2001), accessed on February 3, 2005.

[18] Ibid.

[19] Wilbur C. Rich, *Coleman Young and Detroit Politics,* (Detroit: Wayne State University Press, 1989).

[20] Coleman A. Young Foundation, "Coleman A. Young Bio," www.cayf.org/bio_cay.htm (2001), accessed on February 3, 2005.

[21] "Councilmember Marion Barry," www.dccouncil.washington.dc.us/123104web/barry.html, accessed on February 15, 2005.

[22] Howard Gillette, Jr., "Protest and Power in Washington, D.C.: The Troubled Legacy of Marion Barry," *African-American Mayors: Race, Politics and the American City,* (Detroit: Wayne State University Press, 1989), p. 218.

[23] Mildred L. Amer, "Black Members of the United States Congress 1870-2004, Congressional Research Service, The Library of Congress (July 28, 2004).

[24] "Facts About Harold Washington, 42nd Mayor of Chicago," Chicago Public Library, www.chicagopubliclibary.org/008subject/012special/harold-washingtonfacts/factsaboutw.html, accessed on February 8, 2005.

[25] Arnold R. Hirsch, "Harold and Dutch Revisited: A Comparative Look at the First Black Mayors of Chicago and New Orleans," *African-American Mayors: Race, Politics and the American City*, (Detroit: Wayne State University Press, 1989), p. 113.

[26] Ibid., p.115.

[27] Roger Biles, "Mayor David Dinkins and the Politics of Race in New York City," *African-American Mayors: Race, Politics and the American City,* (Detroit: Wayne State University Press, 1989), p.140.

SOMETIMES THE NAME IS EVERYTHING
★macy's
way to shop™

Rolls-Royce Motor Cars Atlanta
3040 Piedmont Road
Atlanta, GA 30305
866.812.9927

www.rollsroycemotorcarsatlanta.com

Serving GA, TN, SC, AL & MS
Visit RollsRoyce.com for
Dealers Serving Other Locales.

Well Done.

PolicyWorks is proud to salute
the commemorative edition of
Black Mayors In America.

STRATEGY   COMMUNICATION   DIVERSITY

83 PARSONS AVENUE SUITE C, COLUMBUS, OH 43215 | EMAIL: COLSPOLICYWORKS@AOL.COM

PHONE 614.469.7886 | FAX 614.469.5017
DANNETTE PALMORE, PRESIDENT & CEO

BIG CITY *Mayors*

Big City Mayors includes U.S. cities with more than 50,000 residents, and are listed from greatest to least population.

Source: National Conference of Black Mayors, Inc.(NCBM); 2004 • www.ncbm.org

THE *HONORABLE*

JOHN F. STREET

**MAYOR OF
PHILADELPHIA, PENNSYLVANIA
POPULATION: 1,517,550**

The Honorable John F. Street is mayor of Philadelphia, Pennsylvania. He is a graduate of Conshohocken High School; Oakwood College in Huntsville, Alabama, where he studied English; and Temple University, where he earned his juris doctorate degree in 1975.

Mayor Street served clerkships with Common Pleas Court Judge Matthew W. Bullock, Jr. and with the U.S. Department of Justice. He taught English in an elementary school and job training at the Philadelphia Opportunities Industrialization Center, a program started by Reverend Leon H. Sullivan. He has also practiced law privately.

Street was elected to Philadelphia City Council in 1979 and assumed office in 1980, representing the Fifth Councilmanic. He held the council seat for 19 years. In 1992, and again in 1996, he was chosen unanimously by members of council to serve as council president. As president, he worked to promote community policing, fought for tougher gun laws, promoted Townwatch organizations, and education and youth programs. He sponsored a liquor-by-the-drink tax that resulted in an additional $23 million per year for Philadelphia public schools.

In 1999, Street was elected mayor, and he was elected to a second term in 2003. He has targeted five key areas that will lead to the fulfillment of his vision for Philadelphia. They are education, neighborhood revitalization, public safety, economic development, and information technology communication.

Street is married to Naomi Post Street, an attorney and children's rights advocate. They have nurtured and raised four children: Sharif, a lawyer, Rashida, an architect, Lateef, a graduate of the University of Maryland, and Akeem, a high school senior.

Street, a fitness advocate, exercises five days a week. His goal is to run-walk 15 miles and bike 50 miles per week. He has taken a leading role in helping to "shape up" Philadelphia's standing as a physically fit city.

THE *HONORABLE*

KWAME M. KILPATRICK

**MAYOR OF
DETROIT, MICHIGAN
POPULATION: 951,270**

Since taking office in 2002 as the youngest mayor of any major U.S. city, the Honorable Kwame M. Kilpatrick has led tremendous growth in the City of Detroit. He has led the biggest housing and commercial construction boom in 50 years, the largest road and infrastructure improvement program in decades, and a $2 billion overhaul of Detroit's riverfront.

After decades of decline, Detroit is experiencing a revival thanks to Mayor Kilpatrick's leadership that has been recognized by media including the *New York Times, USA Today*, the *Los Angeles Times*, and the *Financial Times of London*. He has dramatically streamlined the economic development process while forming groundbreaking partnerships with the private sector and community organizations.

Through several volunteer initiatives, including Angels' Night and Motor City Makeover, Kilpatrick has mobilized more than 200,000 volunteers to create stronger, safer, and cleaner neighborhoods.

Before his election as mayor in 2001, Kilpatrick was the first African American to lead any party in the Michigan legislature. He played a key role in designing the $675 million Clean Michigan Initiative, and secured $7 million to address the problem of lead poisoning in Detroit. In addition, he forged a bipartisan coalition to preserve $45 million for hospitals that serve low-income patients.

A lifelong resident of Detroit, Kilpatrick attended Pelham Middle School and Cass Technical High School. He graduated with honors, earning a bachelor of science degree in political science as well as his teacher certification from Florida A&M University, where he was captain of the football team. Before his election as a state representative, Kilpatrick was a middle school teacher in Detroit. He earned his juris doctorate degree from the Detroit College of Law.

Mayor Kilpatrick and his wife, Carlita, have twin nine-year-old boys, Jelani and Jalil, and a three-year-old son, Jonas.

THE *HONORABLE*

MICHAEL B. COLEMAN

**MAYOR OF
COLUMBUS, OHIO
POPULATION: 711,470**

The Honorable Michael B. Coleman was elected in 1999 as Columbus, Ohio's first African-American mayor. He was also the first Democrat to hold the office in nearly 30 years. Prior to becoming mayor, Coleman served as president of Columbus City Council. He grew up in Toledo, Ohio, graduated from the University of Cincinnati in 1977, and earned a law degree from the University of Dayton Law School in 1980.

Coleman took office with a commitment to improving the quality of life for families in Columbus' neighborhoods. Working with businesses and community groups, he has increased the development of new homes for families with more than 12,000 new housing units. He has also worked with partners to drive urban development deals to lift up long neglected neighborhoods, including Four Corners, where there is currently $20 million of new investment and approximately 400 people working at South Linden's new village square; and the West Edge Business Center, a new $60 million office/light industrial park that will bring 1,000 jobs to the economically-challenged Franklinton area.

Coleman initiated Neighborhood Pride, a proactive initiative to engage residents and businesses as partners in revitalizing their homes and neighborhoods.

He has a proven record of balancing budgets, and Columbus is the only major U.S. city to maintain a AAA bond rating despite the impact of a national recession. Residents of Columbus also pay the lowest taxes and fees of any major city in Ohio.

THE *HONORABLE*

WILLIE W. HERENTON, PH.D.

MAYOR OF
MEMPHIS, TENNESSEE
POPULATION: 650,100

On October 3, 1991, the Honorable Willie W. Herenton, Ph.D., made history as the first African American to be elected mayor of Memphis, Tennessee. Twelve years later, he made history again as the first Memphis mayor to be elected to four consecutive terms in office.

This stamp of voter approval was a testament to Herenton's myriad of accomplishments as mayor. During his tenure, he has been the catalyst for significant change to the city's social, economic, and physical landscape. Under his leadership, Memphis realized a 30-year dream and secured its first major professional sports franchise, the Memphis Grizzlies. Downtown Memphis has morphed into the Mid-South's entertainment Mecca with the openings of such state-of-the-art sports and entertainment facilities as the FedExForum, AutoZone Park, and The Cannon Center for the Performing Arts.

Additionally, Memphis has garnered billions of dollars in downtown investment over the past decade, while affordable housing facilities and opportunities in the inner city have significantly improved. Minority and women-owned businesses have also flourished. Major corporations such as FedEx and International Paper have reinvested in the city with new jobs and facilities.

A former superintendent of Memphis City Schools, Herenton is a graduate of LeMoyne Owen College and the University of Memphis. He earned his doctorate at Southern Illinois University. He has received numerous awards for his outstanding public service, including the Horatio Alger Award in 1988, and honorary doctor of humanities degrees from Rhodes and Christian Brothers Colleges. *American City & County* magazine named Herenton the 2002 Municipal Leader of the Year. Herenton has served on the national board of directors for the Urban League and Junior Achievement; the national executive board of the National Conference of Christians and Jews; and on several corporate boards.

He has four children, Errol, Rodney, Andrea, and Michael.

THE *HONORABLE*

ANTHONY A. WILLIAMS

MAYOR OF
THE DISTRICT OF COLUMBIA
POPULATION: 572,059

The Honorable Anthony A. Williams began serving as the fourth mayor of the District of Columbia on January 4, 1999, 25 years after the city was granted home rule. Mayor Williams is serving his second term in office.

Williams and his administration have consistently produced a balanced budget, while generating economic stability and affordable housing. One of the cornerstones of his tenure has been creating a friendly government that listens to citizens through town hall meetings and citizen summits.

In December 2004, Williams was elected president of the Washington, D.C.-based National League of Cities, the oldest and largest national organization representing municipal governments throughout the United States. He was elected vice chair of the Metropolitan Washington Council of Governments in January 2005.

In 1995, D.C. Mayor Marion Barry appointed Williams as District of Columbia chief financial officer (CFO). Before joining District government, he was appointed by President Clinton and confirmed by the Senate to serve as the first CFO for the U.S. Department of Agriculture. He previously served in several other executive and government positions.

Born on July 28, 1951, in Los Angeles, California, Williams is the adopted son of Virginia and the late Lewis Williams, and is one of eight children. He graduated magna cum laude with a bachelor of arts degree in political science from Yale College, earned a juris doctorate degree from Harvard Law, and earned a master's degree in public policy from the Kennedy School of Government at Harvard University. He also served in the U.S. Air Force.

Mayor Williams is a member of St. Augustine Catholic Church and several social service organizations, including 100 Black Men, Leadership Washington, and the Washington Urban League. He and his wife, Diane, live in the Foggy Bottom neighborhood of the District. They have one daughter, Asantewa Foster.

THE *HONORABLE*

C. RAY NAGIN

**MAYOR OF
NEW ORLEANS, LOUISIANA
POPULATION: 484,674**

The Honorable C. Ray Nagin has defied conventional wisdom since he was elected in May of 2002 with a promise to fan the flames of renaissance in New Orleans.

Before becoming mayor, Nagin served as the vice president and general manager for Cox Communications in Southeast Louisiana.

As a native New Orleanian, Nagin is committed to economic development and raising the quality of life for all citizens. He moved aggressively to open the city for business and dispel the notion that graft is part of the city's old-world charm. He led the passage of a $260 million bond issue, revived the Disadvantaged Business Enterprise system and opened JOB1 satellite centers throughout the city. With burgeoning industries like Hollywood South, a second cruise ship terminal, and a 50 percent increase in building permits in Nagin's first two years in office, New Orleans now ranks 18th among the top 25 cities to do business in America, according to *Inc.* magazine.

Protecting citizens is priority number one for Mayor Nagin. He budgeted for more officers on the New Orleans Police Department, back-to-back pay raises for officers, and state-of-the-art crime cameras – resulting in a falling crime rate every year since he took office.

With a businessman's emphasis on customer service, Nagin has used technology to make City Hall more efficient, user-friendly, and transparent.

New Orleans is a city enriched by its unique neighborhoods. Mayor Nagin introduced Neighborhood 1, a comprehensive community plan to help residents build their neighborhoods with the coordinated support of city agencies.

Mayor Nagin earned a bachelor of science degree in accounting at Tuskegee University in 1978 and received a master of business administration degree at Tulane University in 1994.

He is married to Seletha Smith Nagin. They are the proud parents of three children, Jeremy, Jarin, and Tianna.

THE *HONORABLE*

SHARPE JAMES

**MAYOR OF
NEWARK, NEW JERSEY
POPULATION: 273,546**

The Honorable Sharpe James was elected the 35th mayor of Newark, New Jersey in May of 1986. He was reelected to an unprecedented fourth term in 2002, making James the only civil rights veteran still serving as a mayor in America.

While helping the City of Newark win the Most Livable City, the All-American City, and the Environmental Protection Administrator's Awards, Mayor James inspired the creation of the public/private partnerships largely responsible for the city's growth and revitalization.

During the James administration, bond rates and housing stock numbers have risen, as well as city revenues. Cultural revitalization has received a tremendous boost, with Mayor James leading the campaign for a $185 million Performing Arts Center in 1997. His recent vision will bring a new $310 million Sports Arena complex, hotel, and upscale residential community to Newark through the Downtown Core Redevelopment initiative.

James is a recipient of numerous awards. In 1999, he was inducted into the New Jersey Elected Officials Hall of Fame. In 2001, he was voted Mayor of the Year by the New Jersey Conference of Mayors. In 1992, James was named Most Valuable Public Official in municipal government by *City & State* magazine.

He serves on several boards including the U.S. Conference of Mayors. James is vice president of the New Jersey Conference of Mayors, and a past president of the National League of Cities.

James earned an undergraduate degree from Montclair State University, and a master's degree from Springfield College, where he also received the 1961 Department of Physiology Award. He has completed advanced studies at Washington State, Columbia, and Rutgers Universities. He holds an honorary doctor of laws degree from Montclair State University, and an honorary doctorate from Drew University. James also served with the U.S. Army in Europe.

THE *HONORABLE*

BERNARD KINCAID

MAYOR OF
BIRMINGHAM, ALABAMA
POPULATION: 242,820

The Honorable Bernard Kincaid, mayor of Birmingham, Alabama, was born in Birmingham (Pratt City) on June 5, 1945. The son of a coal miner and a housewife, he is married to the former Alfreda Harris, a special education teacher. He has one daughter, Amy.

Mayor Kincaid attended Birmingham Public Schools and received a bachelor of arts degree from Miles College. He holds a master of arts degree from Miami University in Oxford, Ohio and a doctorate of philosophy degree from the University of Alabama in Tuscaloosa. He received a juris doctorate degree from Birmingham School of Law.

A member of Metropolitan C.M.E. Church in Ensley, Kincaid is also a member of the W.A. Baskerville Gospel Chorus. He served in the United States Air Force from 1962 to 1966 and received an honorable discharge.

Kincaid serves as an educational consultant. A retired educator, he served as an assistant professor and assistant to the dean for cultural diversity and minority affairs at the School of Health Related Professions at the University of Alabama at Birmingham (UAB).

Kincaid is a member of the Sister City Commission, City of Birmingham. He is also a member of the Miles College Alumni Association, Omega Psi Phi Fraternity, Inc., the Jefferson County Progressive Democratic Council, Inc., and the Sigma Delta Kappa Intercollegiate Law Association.

Kincaid is the past president and vice president of the Ensley Highlands Neighborhood Association. He formerly served on the board of directors of Glenwood Mental Health Services, Inc. and the Birmingham Urban League. He was the charter president of the Pratt-Ensley Kiwanis Club, and a past member of the Birmingham Partnership (1985-86) and the Metropolitan Planning Organization.

THE HONORABLE
WILLIAM A. JOHNSON, JR.

MAYOR OF
ROCHESTER, NEW YORK
POPULATION: 219,773

In November of 1993, the Honorable William A. Johnson, Jr. was elected the 64th mayor of Rochester, New York. He received more than 72 percent of the votes in his first run for political office. In 1997, he was reelected without opposition in either the primary or general election. In 2001, he was reelected to a third term with more than 78 percent of the vote, and announced at that time that he would not seek a fourth term.

During his years in office, Johnson has launched several innovative initiatives including the nationally-recognized Neighbors Building Neighborhoods process of citizen empowerment; Neighborhood Empowerment Teams, which provide a rapid response to neighborhood quality of life issues; the first zoning code in the nation based on design; the establishment of downtown entertainment districts (including an annual music festival); comprehensive youth violence prevention programs; community-oriented policing; and a Good Grades Pay program tied to youth employment.

Under his leadership, Rochester was designated an All-America City in 1998, and one of America's Most Livable Cities in 2000 by Partners for Livable Communities. In 1999, *Governing* magazine named Johnson one of the Top Ten Public Officials in America.

Johnson earned a bachelor of arts degree and a master of arts degree in political science from Howard University. Before becoming mayor, he was president and CEO of the Urban League of Rochester for 21 years. Throughout his career, Johnson has served on numerous boards and committees, both nationally and locally. He has received more than 100 awards, citations, and honors from educational, civic, and fraternal organizations. He holds honorary doctoral degrees from Keuka College, St. John Fisher College, and the Rochester Institute of Technology.

Johnson is married to Sylvia McCoy, an assistant U.S. attorney. He has three daughters, a stepdaughter, and four grandchildren.

THE *HONORABLE*

L. DOUGLAS WILDER

**MAYOR OF
RICHMOND, VIRGINIA
POPULATION: 197,790**

Former Virginia Governor L. Douglas Wilder was elected the 61st mayor of Richmond with more than 80 percent of the vote and took office on January 2, 2005.

Wilder is the grandson of slaves. A Richmond native, he was the first African American to be elected governor in the U.S., leading Virginia from 1990 to 1994. As governor, he was commended for his sound fiscal management and balancing the state budget during difficult economic times. He served as lieutenant governor from 1986 to 1990.

Wilder was also the first African-American state senator in Virginia since the Reconstruction, and represented Richmond from 1969 to 1985. During his five terms as a state senator, he chaired committees on transportation, rehabilitation and social services, privileges, and elections.

He was appointed chairman of Governor Mark Warner's Commission on Efficiency and Effectiveness in 2002. Also that year, he co-chaired the Wilder-Bliley Charter Commission, which advocated the at-large election of mayor.

In addition to currently serving as mayor, Wilder is a distinguished professor at Virginia Commonwealth University, a radio commentator, a newspaper columnist, and the driving force for establishing a national Slavery Museum in Fredericksburg, Virginia.

As an attorney, Wilder gained recognition as a leading criminal trial lawyer. He graduated from Howard University Law School in 1959. He later established the legal firm of Wilder, Gregory & Associates, one of the few minority-owned businesses in Virginia at the time. Prior to his law degree, he graduated from Virginia Union University with a bachelor of science degree in chemistry.

He was awarded the Bronze Star for heroism in combat while serving in the U.S. Army during the Korean War.

Wilder is the father of three grown children, Lynn Diana, an artist; Lawrence Jr., an attorney; and Loren Wilder-James, a market and finance analyst.

THE HONORABLE

WILLIAM V. BELL

MAYOR OF
DURHAM, NORTH CAROLINA
POPULATION: 187,035

The Honorable William V. "Bill" Bell became the 43rd mayor of Durham on November 6, 2001. He retired from the IBM Corporation as a senior engineer.

Bill cares about the City of Durham and extends himself daily to the many citizens with their concerns. He truly stands for the motto for the City of Durham, "Good Things are Happening in Durham."

The basic precepts of Bill's political philosophy about representative government include his strong belief that its elected officials are public servants who are obligated to serve with integrity:

"As public servants, they must acquire sufficient knowledge and understanding of all matters subject to their jurisdiction; be open to the ideas of others, especially those of their colleagues, staffs, and constituents. They should be honest and scrupulous in carrying out their duties and remain ever cognizant of the fact that politics, according to Otto von Bismarck (1867), 'is the art of the possible.' Elected officials should strongly support the rule of law, always applying it justly and fairly. They also should encourage their constituents to participate actively in their government. Finally, all elected officials should bear in mind that, according to the Declaration of Independence (1776), '...all men are created equal, that they are endowed by their Creator with certain unalienable Rights, that among these are Life, Liberty, and the pursuit of Happiness...[and that they govern with] the consent of the governed...'"

Bill earned his bachelor of arts degree in electrical engineering from Howard University in Washington, D.C., and his master of science degree from New York University.

Bill's distinguished character, outstanding leadership skills, energy, and enthusiasm have been a great asset in helping the City of Durham to grow to higher heights.

THE HONORABLE

HARVEY JOHNSON, JR.

MAYOR OF
JACKSON, MISSISSIPPI
POPULATION: 184,256

The Honorable Harvey Johnson, Jr. is currently serving his second term as mayor of the City of Jackson, Mississippi. He became Jackson's first African-American mayor in June of 1997.

Johnson has always promoted economic development in Jackson, and there is currently more than $400 million of development planned or underway for the downtown area alone. He continually gives back to the community by serving as a mentor at Rowan Middle School, and as a positive role model to inner-city children.

Johnson has more than 25 years of experience in the field of planning and community development. He has served as an assistant professor of political science at Jackson State University, a captain in the United States Air Force, and a member of the Mississippi State Tax and Gaming Commissions.

In April of 2003, Johnson was elected the 15th president of the National Conference of Black Mayors, Inc. He is also a member of the U.S. Conference of Mayors and the National Conference of Democratic Mayors. He serves on the boards of directors of the Mississippi Municipal League, the Metro Jackson Chamber of Commerce, and the National Urban Fellows, Inc.

Johnson is a member of Sigma Pi Phi Fraternity, Inc. and a charter member of 100 Black Men of Jackson, Inc. He has held local, state, and regional positions with Alpha Phi Alpha Fraternity, Inc.

Born in the river city of Vicksburg, Mississippi, Johnson holds a bachelor's degree in political science from Tennessee State University, and a master's degree in political science from the University of Cincinnati. Johnson received an honorary doctor of humane letters degree from Tougaloo College.

Johnson is married to Kathy Ezell Johnson, and they have two adult children, Harvey, III and Sharla. He is a member of Hope Spring Missionary Baptist Church.

THE *HONORABLE*

RHINE MCLIN

**MAYOR OF
DAYTON, OHIO
POPULATION: 166,179**

The Honorable Rhine McLin was sworn in as Dayton's 67th mayor on January 7, 2002. She became Dayton's first female mayor.

Mayor McLin is working diligently to improve neighborhoods, create a safer and cleaner community, create more jobs for residents, provide greater care for senior citizens, and promote quality education for all children.

Mayor McLin earned her bachelor of arts degree from Parsons College and her master of education degree from Xavier University.

Before becoming mayor, McLin served in the Ohio House of Representatives from 1988 to 1994. While in the Senate, she was elected to serve in leadership as minority whip in 1998. She was elected minority leader in 2000.

Rhine McLin is also a licensed funeral director and embalmer for McLin Funeral Home.

THE *HONORABLE*

WILLIAM D. EUILLE

**MAYOR OF
ALEXANDRIA, VIRGINIA
POPULATION: 138,000**

The Honorable William (Bill) D. Euille made history for Alexandria, Virginia in May of 2003, when he was elected as the first African-American mayor in the 254-year history of the growing and diverse city of 138,000. He is also president of Wm. D. Euille & Associates, Inc., a construction services firm.

Bill was elected on the theme, "One Alexandria." He seeks to unite all citizens, Democrats, Republicans, Independents, businesses, faith-based and non-profit agencies to work in collaboration in moving Alexandria forward as "A Caring Community With A Bright Outlook."

A native Alexandrian, Bill previously served three terms on the City Council from 1994 to 2003, and on the Alexandria School Board from 1974 to 1984. On the City Council, he served as vice mayor from 1997 to 2000.

Bill earned his bachelor of science degree in accounting from Quinnipiac College in Hamden, Connecticut.

Additionally, Bill has received many awards, including Outstanding Business Leader of the Year 2002; Philanthropist of the Year 2001; and the Outstanding Community Service Award 2000, just to name a few.

Bill is strong leader and believes that "service to humanity is the best work of life."

THE HONORABLE

OTIS S. JOHNSON

MAYOR OF
SAVANNAH, GEORGIA
POPULATION: 137,560

The Honorable Otis S. Johnson is the 64th mayor of the City of Savannah. He was sworn in as the city's second African-American mayor on January 3, 2004. He is nationally known in the field of community building and youth development.

Johnson is currently a member of the Pathways to Collaboration Workgroup, funded by the W. K. Kellogg Foundation. He serves on the boards of directors of the Mary Reynolds Babcock Foundation, the Georgia Partnership for Excellence in Education, and the Georgia Municipal Association. He is a member of the National League of Cities' Council on Youth, Education, and Families; and the national advisory committee for the Urban Health Initiative, funded by the Robert Wood Johnson Foundation.

In addition, Johnson served on the board of the Georgia Family Connections Partnership. He was a founding member of the Aspen Institute Roundtable on Comprehensive Community Initiatives in 1992, and the National Community Building Network in 1993. He was a member of the founding board of directors of the Georgia Campaign for Adolescent Pregnancy Prevention in 1995. Johnson also served as an elected official on Savannah City Council from 1983 to 1988, and on the Savannah Chatham County Board of Public Education from 1998 to 2000. He was executive director of the Chatham-Savannah Youth Futures Program, funded by the Annie E. Casey Foundation, for ten years (1988-1998). He retired from the position of dean of the College of Liberal Arts and Social Sciences at Savannah State University in 2002.

Johnson earned undergraduate degrees in liberal arts from Armstrong Atlantic University, and history from the University of Georgia. He went on to receive a master of social work degree from Clark Atlanta University, and a doctor of philosophy degree in social welfare from the Heller School of Social Policy and Management at Brandeis University.

THE HONORABLE

MARSHALL B. PITTS, JR.

MAYOR OF
FAYETTEVILLE, NORTH CAROLINA
POPULATION: 121,015

At the time of his election, Fayetteville, North Carolina was one of only 29 cities in the United States with a population of more than 100,000 that had an African-American mayor. The Honorable Marshall B. Pitts, Jr. entered politics in 1997, bidding for an at-large seat. He lost by 66 votes but bounced back to convincingly win the seat on City Council in 1999. He was elected mayor pro tempore (vice mayor). Two years later, he made history by becoming Fayetteville's first African-American mayor.

Marshall has focused his efforts on making city government more user-friendly and inclusive, improving the city's image and visibility, and enhancing city services such as parks and recreation and transportation. He also works hard to foster regionalism that will diversify and improve the economy.

Marshall earned a bachelor of science degree from Appalachian State University in 1987. He excelled in athletics and academics and earned the distinction of All-Academic Student Athlete. He earned a juris doctorate from North Carolina Central University in 1990.

Marshall practices law in Fayetteville, and from 1993 to 2000 he taught courses in the criminal justice program at Fayetteville State University. While there, he published an article entitled "The Supreme Court: Forging the Way for Upheaval in the Oval Office" in the *Communication and Law Journal* in 2000.

Marshall is a member of numerous legal, business, and civic organizations. He has been featured in *Jet*, on talk shows, and in newspapers across the country. He is licensed to practice law in North Carolina and Pennsylvania, and he is a partner in the law firm of Washington & Pitts, P.L.L.C. in Fayetteville.

THE *H*ONORABLE

ROOSEVELT F. DORN

MAYOR OF
INGLEWOOD, CALIFORNIA
POPULATION: 112,580

The Honorable Roosevelt F. Dorn, mayor of Inglewood, California, was elected with more than 60 percent of the vote in April of 1997. He is serving his second full term after being reelected in November 2002.

Inglewood has been rejuvenated during Mayor Dorn's term in office. Major economic and housing development is occurring, crime has been reduced by 40 percent and residents have greater access to their municipal government.

Dorn formerly served as a Los Angeles County Superior Court judge, appointed by Governor Jerry Brown in July 1980 and elected in 1982, 1988, and 1994. Previously, he was Brown's appointee in the municipal court of the Inglewood Judicial District in Los Angeles County, an assistant Los Angeles attorney, and a deputy sheriff for Los Angeles County, where he served as a Superior Court bailiff. His career began with the U.S. Air Force.

Dorn completed the California Judicial College from the University of California School of Law at Berkeley, and the Earl Warren Legal Institute. He received a juris doctorate degree from Whittier College School of Law, and was admitted to the California Bar. Most recently, he received a doctor of divinity degree from Southern California School of Ministry.

Active in the community, Dorn is a member of the National Conference of Black Mayors, Inc., California Judges' Association, and the California Black Lawyers and Judges Association. He is a member of the John M. Langston and American Bar Associations. A past president and member of the board of directors of the 100 Black Men of Los Angeles, Inc., he is on the board of directors of Young Black Scholars. He is an ordained minister at First AME Church in Los Angeles.

Born in Checotah, Oklahoma, Dorn married Joyce Evelyn Glosson in 1965. They have three children, Bryan, Renee, and Rochelle.

THE *HONORABLE*

SHIRLEY GIBSON

MAYOR OF
MIAMI GARDENS, FLORIDA
POPULATION: 100,800

The Honorable Mayor Shirley Gibson is one of the original incorporators and the first mayor of the newly incorporated City of Miami Gardens, Florida. Miami Gardens is the third largest municipality in Miami-Dade County, with a population of more than 100,800 people, 79 percent of whom are African Americans. This blossoming new city located in the northern portion of Miami-Dade County, is a mecca for commerce, finance, education, and recreation.

Mayor Gibson is recognized as a bold leader and trailblazer who spread her wings to fly into brave new frontiers of community building. She is a Florida League of Cities member; a trustee of the Florida Municipal Insurance Trust; and an executive board member for Miami-Dade League of Cities, Inc. and the Center for Family and Child Enrichment. In addition, Gibson has served on numerous boards and committees including the Miami-Dade County Community Council, the Miami-Dade Democratic Party executive committee, and the National Council of Negro Women. Her professional career includes 16 years as a police officer with the Miami-Dade County Police Department, in addition to 15 years as an entrepreneur.

Gibson's diligence and exemplary community service has earned her numerous awards and honors. She has been featured in many local newspapers, as well as nationally renowned magazines such as *Jet, Crisis*, and *Flavor*. She has co-hosted the *Miami Talk* radio program, and has been a guest panelist on several local television programs discussing community related issues.

Gibson earned a bachelor of arts degree in criminal justice and master of arts degree in pastoral ministry from St. Thomas University. In 2004, she completed the Institute for Elected Officials and Advanced Institute for Municipal Officers. She is a skilled motivator, community organizer, and a negotiator who uses a collaborative approach to incorporate diversity, inclusiveness, and responsibility for effective outcomes.

THE *HONORABLE*

JAMES W. HOLLEY, III, D.D.S.

MAYOR OF
PORTSMOUTH, VIRGINIA
POPULATION: 100,565

The Honorable James W. Holley, III, D.D.S. was elected mayor of the City of Portsmouth in May of 1996. He was reelected in May of 2004, without opposition, for a fourth term ending in 2008. Previously, Holley served as mayor from 1984 to 1987, and as a city councilman from 1968 to 1987.

He is a 1949 graduate of West Virginia State College with a bachelor of science degree, and a 1955 graduate of Howard University College of Dentistry.

He has subsequently been honored by both his alma maters. He received an honorary doctor of laws in 1996 from West Virginia State College, the Howard University Dental Alumni Award in 1975, and the Howard University Tidewater Alumni Service Award in 1986.

Holley has been selected as Man of the Year and Citizen of the Year by Omega Psi Phi Fraternity, Inc., and Dentist of the Year by the National Dental Association. He also holds life membership in the NAACP, the National Dental Association, the American Dental Association, and Omega Psi Phi Fraternity, Inc.

In addition to his duties as mayor, Holley has served as a dental surgeon for 45 years. He is a World War II veteran and a member of American Legion Post 190.

He is married to Mary, a retired ombudsman with Norfolk Public Schools. Holley has two children, Robin, a partner with the Holley and Massie Law Firm, and James, IV, D.D.S., an associate in private family dentistry.

THE HONORABLE

C. JACK ELLIS

**MAYOR OF
MACON, GEORGIA
POPULATION: 97,255**

The Honorable C. Jack Ellis is the 40th mayor of the City of Macon, Georgia. He was elected mayor in July of 1999, becoming the first black mayor in the 176-year history of the city. In 2003, he was elected for a second term, the first mayor to be reelected in 20 years.

Ellis' administration focuses on improving the quality of life for every family in Macon, enhancing the economic vitality of neighborhoods, reducing illiteracy and crime, and investing in the city's youth.

Ellis is a retired United States Army senior non-commissioned officer. He served two years of combat duty in Vietnam as a paratrooper platoon sergeant with the 101st Airborne Division. He was awarded three Bronze Stars, the Army Commendation Medal for Valor and Heroism, and the Purple Heart for wounds received in combat. Ellis is a former cable television executive and an executive with the United States Census Bureau. He is the former host and producer of a local community affairs television program, *Community Forum.*

A member of the United States Conference of Mayors, Ellis serves that organization on the economic development and smart growth committees and as co-chairman of the advisory board to Amtrak. He is also a member of the Black Conference of Mayors and the Governor's Greenspace Commission. He was one of the speakers at the 2000 Democratic National Convention in Los Angeles, California. *Georgia Trend* magazine named Ellis one of the 100 Most Influential Men in the state of Georgia.

Ellis earned a bachelor of arts degree from St. Leo College in Florida, and he is the father of four children.

THE *Honorable*

ERIC J. PERRODIN

**MAYOR OF
COMPTON, CALIFORNIA
POPULATION: 93,493**

The Honorable Eric J. Perrodin has committed his life to public service. After graduating from California State University Dominguez Hills in 1982 with a degree in business administration, Eric was hired as a police officer in the City of Compton. Eric was one of the youngest officers promoted to the position of sergeant in the history of the Compton Police Department, and he served as president of the Compton Police Officers Association. He has never left the Compton community, and was practicing the community-based policing concept before it became vogue. He also participated in several Christmas variety shows, which raised funds to purchase food and gifts for needy families.

Eric attended Loyola Law School at night while working as a police officer during the day. In 1995, after 12 years of service, he left the Compton Police Department and became a deputy district attorney with the Los Angeles County District Attorney's Office.

It was always Eric's desire that the City of Compton be the best city it could be. Several citizens asked him to run for mayor, but he faced tremendous odds. In his first attempt to run for a political office, he ran against five political veterans including the incumbent. However, on June 5, 2001, he was elected mayor of the City of Compton.

There are several things he would like to achieve for the city. First and foremost, he wants to change the city's image, by cooperating with the Compton Unified School District to improve the quality of education. Additionally, Eric wants to bring first-rate businesses to Compton. He is also committed to working with the Los Angeles Sheriff's Department to reduce crime and make the city safe.

Eric knows all things are possible, and with the citizens working together, Compton can be the diamond it should be.

THE HONORABLE

DOUGLAS HAROLD PALMER

MAYOR OF
TRENTON, NEW JERSEY
POPULATION: 85,403

The Honorable Douglas Harold Palmer was born in Trenton, New Jersey on October 19, 1951. He earned a bachelor of science degree in business management from historic Hampton University. He played football and was an all-conference baseball player at Hampton for three years. In 1993, he received Hampton's Outstanding Alumnus Award for contributions to Trenton, where he was elected the first African-American mayor in 1990.

Palmer has orchestrated several plans that will help move Trenton toward its vision of rebirth. He is producing more than 1,400 new and rehabilitated homes for working families, and attracting market rate housing back to the city. Palmer is creating a Youth Advocacy Cabinet of local leaders to leverage resources for holistic youth development, and he is launching the nation's first federally funded anti-drug program. He is attempting to improve health care and prevention for the underserved, opening the state's first comprehensive drug treatment, research, and education facility, and ensuring that preschoolers are immunized against childhood diseases. Palmer also seeks to help Trenton become the nation's leader in cleaning up brownfields and converting land for redevelopment. Ultimately, Palmer would like Trenton to win its first national City Livability Award from the U.S. Conference of Mayors for improving people's quality of life.

Palmer has received numerous honors, including the Equal Justice Medal from Legal Services of New Jersey for his leadership on the issues of working families, and the State of Israel Peace Medal Award for improving community relations.

The mayor is president of the National Conference of Democratic Mayors and the New Jersey Urban Mayors Association; president-elect of the New Jersey Conference of Mayors; and a trustee of the U.S. Conference of Mayors.

Palmer and his wife, Christiana Foglio-Palmer, celebrated the birth of their first child, Laila Rose Palmer, on November 12, 2002.

THE HONORABLE

GWENDOLYN A. FAISON

**MAYOR OF
CAMDEN, NEW JERSEY
POPULATION: 79,904**

The Honorable Gwendolyn A. Faison, a native of Clinton, North Carolina, is a graduate of Sampson High School and has studied at Shaw, Temple, and Rutgers Universities. She was first elected to Camden City Council in the early 1980s and retired in 1995 after serving 12 years. Faison was reelected in 1997 and served as the first woman council president. She was appointed the city's first woman mayor in December of 2000.

Faison's political and community involvement spans many years. She has served as a member of the Camden County Board of Chosen Freeholders, the New Jersey Network of Women, and Camden County Women's Commission. She has been co- or vice-chairperson for the legislative committee of the New Jersey Democratic Women, the Affirmative Action Council, and the New Jersey State Martin Luther King, Jr. Commission. She has also served on the board of trustees for the Camden Friends of the Park, Lakeland Youth Center, Our Lady of Lourdes Medical Center Home Health Care, and the Camden County Board on Aging.

Faison's accomplishments and commitments are also reflected in her personal life. She is a youth advisor in her church, Tenth Street Baptist of Camden, and has sponsored a Little League team. Instrumental in organizing Whitman Park United Neighbors, We Care About Centerville, and the Save Our Youth Program in Centerville, she has been involved in raising money for scholarships for more than 25 years. She is currently president of the Eugene Waymon Jones Cultural Center of Philadelphia and a member of the National Political Congress of Black Women and the National Hook-up of Black Women.

In her vision of the rebirth for the City of Camden, Faison will focus on healthcare, housing, public safety, and economic development as priorities in her government stewardship.

THE *HONORABLE*

BRENDA L. LAWRENCE

**MAYOR OF
SOUTHFIELD, MICHIGAN
POPULATION: 78,296**

The Honorable Brenda L. Lawrence is a native of Detroit, born and raised in the metropolitan area. She has resided in City of Southfield for the last 15 years and was elected mayor of the City of Southfield in November of 2001. She is the first African American and woman mayor of Southfield, a city with a residential population of more than 78,000, a daytime business population of almost 175,000, and more than 100 Fortune 500 companies. Lawrence is committed to diversity, fiscal responsibility, education, and keeping Southfield a clean and safe city.

Since becoming mayor, Lawrence has initiated several community programs including Mayor's Walks: A Strong City is a Healthy City, a summer walking program where residents walk and talk with the mayor and other city officials; Mayor's Roundtables, a citizen-driven discussion forum; Southfield Reads!, a literacy and learning program; and *Today's Women,* a cable show featuring respected women in and around Southfield.

Lawrence volunteers in various capacities on the Parent Youth Guidance Commission, the Oakland County United Way Advisory Committee, and the Oakland County AIDS Council. She is a recipient of numerous awards, including the Jewish War Veterans' State of Michigan 2002 Brotherhood Award; Leadership Detroit's Challenging the Process Award; the American Business Women's Association Woman of the Year Award; and the Woman Achiever Award from the National Association of Negro Business and Professional Women's Club, Inc.

Lawrence is a member of the American Business Women's Association, the Oakland County chapter of the NAACP, the U.S. Conference of Mayors, the Advisory Council of the Birmingham YMCA, and the Board of Governors of the Renaissance Club.

Lawrence and her husband, McArthur Lawrence, have been married for 30 years. They are the proud parents of Michael and Michelle, both graduates of Southfield Public Schools, and have a granddaughter, Asya.

THE HONORABLE

ROBERT B. JONES

**MAYOR OF
KALAMAZOO, MICHIGAN
POPULATION: 77,145**

The Honorable Robert B. Jones, reelected in November of 2003, is serving his fourth term as mayor of the City of Kalamazoo, Michigan. Jones brings to the city more than 28 years of professional experience in supervision with Pharmacia & Upjohn Chemical Production, four years as a research chemist, and two years as a research chemist at Fort Valley State University.

Jones' personal goals include stimulating economic development in the City of Kalamazoo; focusing on building and maintaining strong neighborhoods; building a consensus to get diverse groups to adopt win-win agendas; and leading the city into a prosperous new millennium.

He was a member of the Community Development Block Grant Advisory Committee for six years, and chairman for three years. As a member of 100 Concerned Men of Kalamazoo, he was a mentor for students at Kalamazoo Public Schools and Comstock Public Schools. Jones is a volunteer with the Greater Kalamazoo United Way, and has received Outstanding Volunteer recognition from the City of Kalamazoo three times. He is a member of Mount Zion Baptist Church.

Jones is a member of the National League of Cities; state president of the National Brownfield Association; a member of the U.S. Conference of Mayors; co-chair of the Urban Core Mayors; and a trustee of the Michigan Municipal League. Appointed to the executive committee of the Michigan Economic Development Corporation by Governor Jennifer Granholm, Jones is a recipient the 2003 NAACP Humanitarian Award.

Born on April 22, 1944 in Jeffersonville, Georgia, Jones holds a bachelor of science degree in chemistry from Fort Valley State University, and a master's degree in chemistry from Clark Atlanta University.

Jones is married to Callie Baskerville-Jones and has six children, two sons at Fort Valley State University. He also has one grandson.

THE HONORABLE

LORRAINE H. MORTON

MAYOR OF
EVANSTON, ILLINOIS
POPULATION: 74,239

The Honorable Lorraine H. Morton's life in Evanston has followed two paths, one as an educator, and another in city government. Her educational career began in Evanston as an elementary teacher, and later as a junior high teacher, followed by becoming a team leader at Chute Middle School, and ending as principal of Haven Middle School.

Mayor Morton's government career began as an alderman of the Fifth Ward, serving nine years in that capacity. She was first elected mayor in 1993.

While in the educational field, Morton wrote curricula used in the Evanston schools, and served as a consultant on school desegregation, team teaching, and individualized instruction in Illinois, Michigan, and Mississippi. She was a member of a state evaluation team to assess educational practices in Chicago and Skokie and served as president of the Junior High School Association of Illinois.

As an alderman, Morton supported the Research Park agreement with Northwestern University, which resulted in tremendous growth, commercial development, and residential development in downtown Evanston.

Morton is a member of the advisory committee to the Public and Nonprofit Management Program at the Kellogg Graduate School of Management, Northwestern University; a member of the District #65 Foundation Committee; and honorary chair of several not-for-profit organizations. She is a deacon at Second Baptist Church in Evanston and a lifetime member of the NAACP. She is a member of The Links, Inc. and Alpha Kappa Alpha Sorority, Inc.

Morton holds a bachelor of science degree from Winston-Salem State University, a master of arts degree in education from Northwestern University, and an honorary doctorate for public service from Kendall College.

Mayor Morton was born in Winston-Salem, North Carolina and was married to James T. Morton, Ph.D. (deceased). She has one daughter, Elizabeth M. Brasher, and two granddaughters, Elizabeth Keziah and Constance Mariah Brasher.

THE *HONORABLE*

JAMES M. BAKER

**MAYOR OF
WILMINGTON, DELAWARE
POPULATION: 72,664**

James M. Baker's second term as Wilmington, Delaware's 54th mayor continues a long and distinguished career in public service. The mayor's career of service to citizens began in the mid-1960s, when he was assigned to Wilmington as a volunteer with the VISTA national community service organization.

Mayor Baker initially worked with youth groups, among them the Wilmington Youth Emergency Action Council, as a VISTA volunteer. He then held staff and executive positions with a number of private and governmental agencies, including the Model Cities Program, the Northeast Federal Credit Union, the Governor's Office, and Community Action of Greater Wilmington.

Before beginning his first term as mayor in 2001, Baker served as president of the Wilmington City Council, the first African American elected to that post, and had been a member of City Council since 1972. His first term as mayor was marked by an emphasis on strong fiscal management and initiatives to stabilize and strengthen Wilmington's neighborhoods.

These focused on increased homeownership, new and expanded business development throughout the city, and continued development of the city's riverfronts.

Born in Fostoria, Ohio in 1942, Baker completed high school there and enlisted in the Air Force. He was honorably discharged in 1966 and joined VISTA, the domestic Peace Corps program.

His volunteer activity record reflects his commitment to partnerships between government and the private sector. Baker helped to organize the Midtown, Upper Eastside, and Quaker Hill Neighborhood Associations, as well as the West Center City Neighborhood Planning Advisory Committee and the Afro-American Arts and Science Society.

Reflecting Baker's belief in the value of history and culture, he has played a key role in a number of projects to preserve and promote the city's heritage. He is also the author of *The Genuine American Music*, a two-volume encyclopedia of black musicians.

THE *HONORABLE*

ROBERT L. BOWSER

**MAYOR OF
EAST ORANGE, NEW JERSEY
POPULATION: 69,824**

The Honorable Robert L. Bowser, a civil engineer and surveyor by profession, was born and raised in the City of East Orange, New Jersey. Since he took office in January of 1998, Mayor Bowser, the 12th mayor in the city's history, has been chiefly responsible for fostering policies that have spawned an economic resurgence, and revitalized civic pride and a new spirit of cooperation and teamwork with the members of the City Council and the business community. He has also helped to shape a new destiny and image of progress and prosperity for the City of East Orange.

Bowser is a man on a mission, who made history as the first African-American starting quarterback on the East Orange High School varsity football team. The mayor has an abiding faith in the city's youth and has supported many cultural, educational, and sports enrichment programs. He has also been a champion of a broad range of issues that affect the city's large senior citizen population from healthcare to housing and finances.

Bowser has eyes firmly focused on an agenda to rebuild the City of East Orange and restore it to its primary and rightful place as one of the preeminent communities in the nation. Millions of dollars of commercial and new housing construction, auctions of city-owned properties, removal of blighted properties, streetscape improvements, street paving, and seven areas designated for redevelopment have happened on his watch. The City of East Orange, under Bowser's leadership, is poised for the future.

A devoted family man, Mayor Bowser is married to Marilyn K. Bowser and is the proud father of David, Lisa, and Leslie.

THE HONORABLE

EARNEST D. DAVIS

**MAYOR OF
MOUNT VERNON, NEW YORK
POPULATION: 68,381**

The Honorable Earnest D. Davis, the 19th mayor of Mount Vernon, New York, served six consecutive two-year terms as a Westchester County legislator before he was elected as mayor on November 7, 1995. He was reelected to a third term of office in November of 2003.

During his tenure as county legislator, Mayor Davis understood the problems of local communities and fought for solutions. His philosophy is based on the understanding that if the cities fail, then communities fail.

Davis, an architect by profession, formerly headed a firm based in Mount Vernon, E. Daniel Davis Architects, and designed many versatile buildings, including residential housing, churches, day care centers, and government projects.

For many years, Davis has been involved in community and civic organizations. He is a life member of the NAACP, a member of Progressive Lodge #64, and a board member of the YMCA. He is a member of the Salvation Army Service Unit, the Westchester Arts Council, the Institute for Student Achievement, and the Hoff-Barthelson Music School. Davis is a member of the African-American Men of Westchester, a lifetime member of the National Council of Negro Women, and a lifelong member of Omega Psi Phi Fraternity, Inc., where he was voted Omega Man of the Year.

Davis is the recipient of more than 60 awards, including the Lifetime Achievement Award from the Westchester Philharmonic and the Yitzhak Rabin Peacemaker Award from the Westchester Coalition for Mutual Respect.

Davis graduated from North Carolina A&T in 1960 with a bachelor of science degree in architectural engineering, and pursued his studies at New York University and City College (New York) in the master of urban design program.

Mayor Davis is married to Bettye. They have two daughters, Rene and Lisa, and two grandsons.

THE HONORABLE

WILLIE W. PAYNE

**MAYOR OF
PONTIAC, MICHIGAN
POPULATION: 66,337**

In just a three-year span, the Honorable Willie W. Payne has opened the door to more economic development, grant funding, and solutions to social issues that have been hindering progress for the City of Pontiac.

Payne's creation of partnerships and collaborative efforts have resulted in the $350 million Pontiac Woods Community project, the Target Neighborhood Initiative, the Adopt-A-Park Program, and a Junior Police Academy Program for high school students. Payne has gained unprecedented local and national media coverage through festivals, outreach, networking, and partnerships that have yielded grant dollars for programs such as Preservation Development Initiatives and Main Street for our downtown.

In 1978, Payne earned a bachelor of arts degree in journalism from Grambling State University. *The Oakland Press* recruited him as a full-time investigative reporter, a position he held from 1978 to 1985. During that time, he was assigned to the case of "The Taylor Family," involving a Pontiac family charged and convicted of shooting an officer in Montgomery, Alabama. Payne's reporting helped reveal false accusation of charges, and prevented the imprisonment of the Taylor family, and it appeared in media across the country. From his experience in that case, he authored and published *The Todd Road Incident*.

Payne has won many awards and recognition as a humanitarian, storyteller, and historian. He also served as an officer with the Pontiac Police Department for 17 years, where he received the second highest award for bravery from the police department.

Payne is a member of Newman A.M.E. Church. Some of his affiliations include The Boys and Girls Club of America, the Michigan Association for Leadership Development, the NAACP, Omega Psi Phi Fraternity, Inc., and Free and Accepted Masons, Gibraltar Lodge #19 F. & A.M. State of Michigan.

He is married to Brenda and is a father to Carra and B'Daren.

THE HONORABLE

WILMER JONES-HAM

MAYOR OF
SAGINAW, MICHIGAN
POPULATION: 61,799

The Honorable Wilmer Jones-Ham was appointed mayor in November of 2001. She redefined the history of the City of Saginaw by becoming the first female mayor and the first African-American woman to serve as mayor of Saginaw. Jones-Ham is an elected member of the Saginaw City Council serving a third term.

A devoted member of Tabernacle Missionary Baptist Church for 45 years, Jones-Ham is the minister of music. She graduated from Saginaw Valley State University with a bachelor's degree in elementary education, and a master's degree in supervision and administration. She is also the community liaison person for the City of Saginaw.

Jones-Ham currently serves on the boards of the Boys & Girls Club, SIGMA, St. John Trinity, the MBS International Airport Commission, the Municipal Employees Retirement System Pension, the Police and Fire Pension, and the Downtown Development Authority. She is a past board member of RCO and New Perspectives.

Likewise, Jones-Ham is the founder of the Saginaw Soul Children, the Mayor's Ball and Scholarship Foundation, the Saginaw Interdenominational Ministry, Saginaw International Mahogany Models, Women and Men in Praise, and the 100-voice boys choir. She is the 2004 honorary chair of Habitat for Humanity, and she received the Living Legend Award from Coleman Temple in March of 2005.

Her other affiliations include the NAACP, since 1957, and Zeta Phi Beta Sorority, Inc., since 1988. Governor Jennifer Granholm personally delivered a check in the amount of $1 million to Mayor Jones-Ham on March 8th for the development of Saginaw's East Genesee Corridor.

Jones-Ham is the daughter of Mrs. Evalena Jones and the late Wilson Jones, and she is the wife of the late Howard Leon Ham. A mother of three, DeRonnie, DeToya, and Darvin D. Ham of the Detroit Pistons, she is also a grandmother of six.

THE *Honorable*

WAYNE SMITH

**MAYOR OF
IRVINGTON, NEW JERSEY
POPULATION: 61,018**

Promoting an aggressive agenda for the rebirth of the Township of Irvington, the Honorable Wayne Smith was elected as the 20th mayor of the municipality in May of 2002. His entire slate of council candidates – known as Team Irvington – was also elected, affirming the mandate for his leadership.

Mayor Smith's tenure has been characterized by bold, innovative leadership that has yielded significant progress for the Township of Irvington. His most noted accomplishments are initiating the formation of the Anti-Crime Partnership that includes the New Jersey State Police, local, county, and federal agencies and securing the $4.4 million agreement to rebuild the Irvington Bus Terminal, which has been earmarked for completion in 2005. Smith has also demolished dozens of dilapidated, abandoned properties to pave the way for redevelopment and drastically increased code enforcement that has resulted in about $1.5 million in fines of neglectful property owners. His outstanding stewardship has delivered tangible results and high hopes for the future revitalization of Irvington.

Smith has been an active, prominent member of Irvington's civic, political, and social sectors throughout his 20 years of residence in the township. His ability to build consensus helped propel him to victory in 1996 as an Irvington Council member at-large. He was reelected two years later and unanimously chosen by his colleagues to serve as president of the seven-member legislative body.

During his political and civic careers, Smith has been covered by *The Star-Ledger*, WCBS-TV, WNBC-TV, News Channel 12, and other media outlets. In addition, his efforts have been rewarded with awards and honors from numerous organizations. His greatest reward, however, comes from the heartfelt commitment made every day to improve the quality of life for the citizens of the Township of Irvington.

THE *HONORABLE*

JOSAPHAT "JOE" CELESTIN

**MAYOR OF
NORTH MIAMI, FLORIDA
POPULATION: 59,880**

The Honorable Josaphat "Joe" Celestin, mayor of North Miami, Florida, is a native of Haiti and is the first black to be elected mayor of a large city in the State of Florida. Mayor Celestin is the 48 year-old father of two daughters, Samantha and Meghan, and a son, Joey.

Celestin is a certified land engineering contractor and a state-certified general builder. He has a master's degree in architecture and recently completed his internship. He is an associate member of the American Institute of Architects, a state-certified general line property and casualty loss consultant, a commercial and residential real estate developer, and chairman of Joe Celestin Civil Engineer and General Builder. He is also state-certified in the areas of project management, business, and finance.

Celestin has held several political appointments and has had a number of memberships in a variety of organizations, including the North Miami Board of Adjustment; the North Miami Planning Commission; and the City of Miami Finance and Budget Review Committee. He is on the United States Presidential Meritorious Rank Review Board; the governing board of Metropolitan Planning Organization; and North Shore Hospital. He was a nominee for the Florida State Senate for District 36, appointed as a member of HAVA for the commission of election reform committee, and a member of the board of directors for Miami Dade County Beacon Council and HAPAC (chairman).

THE HONORABLE

JAMES E. MAYO

**MAYOR OF
MONROE, LOUISIANA
POPULATION: 53,107**

The Honorable James E. "Jamie" Mayo was appointed interim mayor of the City of Monroe, Louisiana in June of 2001. He was elected mayor in October of 2001 and then reelected in April of 2004. Previously, he served on Monroe City Council, where he represented District Five from 1995 to 2000.

Mayo's community service is extensive. He has served on the boards of The Salvation Army and the Ouachita Enterprise Corporation. He was president of the Ouachita Council of Governments, board chairman for The Opportunities Industrialization Center, and an advisory board member for the University of Louisiana Monroe College of Business. He also served on the Letterman Club Board of the University of Louisiana Monroe, the Monroe-West Monroe Public Trust Financing Authority, and the Bancorp South Advisory Council.

Mayo serves on the president's advisory board for LAMP, Inc., and is vice president of the Louisiana chapter of the National Conference of Black Mayors. He is vice president of the Louisiana Conference of Mayors, and was nominated by Governor Mitch Landrieu to serve on the Louisiana Retirement Development Commission.

His other affiliations include the Rayville Alumni chapter of Kappa Alpha Psi Fraternity, Inc. and the Prince Hall Masonic Lodge Composite #120. He is a member of New Light Baptist Church, where Reverend James B. Johnson is pastor.

Mayo is married to the former Angela Washington and has two children, Jared, a nursing major at Grambling State University, and Ashley, a student at Neville High School.

A HISTORICAL PERSPECTIVE

One of the first meetings in Atlanta at Paschal's (left to right) Mayor Verdiacee Goston, Richwood, LA; Mayor Johnny Ford, Tuskegee, AL; Mayor Maynard Jackson, Atlanta, GA; Mayor Earl Lucas, Mound Bayou, MS; Mayor Lewis Scott, Eastover, SC; Mayor A.J. Cooper, Prichard, AL; Mayor David Humes, Hayti, Heights, MO; Mayor Nathaniel Vereen, Eatonville, FL; Mayor Ennis Humphries, Kendleton, TX. (Standing - left to right) Bernard Porsche, Executive Director, SCBM; Mayor Eristus Sams, Prairie View, TX; Charles Reid, Deputy Director

NCBM's Founding

Thirteen black mayors, newly elected in the South, were the visionaries who founded the Southern Conference of Black Mayors (SCBM) in 1974. They were elected following enactment of the Civil Rights and Voting Rights Acts of 1964 and 1965. Passage of this landmark legislation dramatically increased the number of African Americans elected to public office within a short time, especially at the local level in the South where the number of mayors multiplied fivefold.

A small group of black mayors from several southern states met informally in Fayette, Mississippi in 1972 where they discussed the possible development of programs of mutual benefit to their respective communities. A year after meeting in Fayette, a second meeting of 15 black mayors was held in Tuskegee, Alabama. Their discussions led to the founding of SCBM. In 1974, 20 black mayors gathered in Santee, South Carolina and voted to officially incorporate the organization. The group hired its first executive director and opened a headquarters office that year in Atlanta, Georgia.

By the occasion of its first annual convention in 1975 in Grambling, Louisiana, SCBM had identified various funding sources, performed several economic development and water system studies, and developed an extensive technical assistance program.

HISTORICAL PERSPECTIVE

In 1976, at the second annual convention in Atlanta, at the prompting of mayors from the Midwest who attended the meeting, the mayors voted to expand the organization's scope by changing the name to the National Conference of Black Mayors, Inc. (NCBM).

That same year, NCBM obtained tax exempt status as a 501(c)(3) organization from the Internal Revenue Service, developed and presented a series of municipal management clinics in local communities, and produced a myriad of proposals which led to a significant increase of public support to member communities.

Its Mission

Little did those mayors who came together in 1972 realize that their efforts would lay the foundation for NCBM, an organization of national and international influence now representing 532 African-American-managed cities and towns. Starting as a self-help effort, the organization continues to serve as a provider of technical and management assistance to its member mayors. NCBM embraces the mission of "Enhancing the executive management capacity of its members for the purpose of creating viable municipalities." Goals and objectives were adopted that still guide NCBM in the development of its programs over the past 30 years.

- To improve the executive management capacity and efficiency of member municipalities in the delivery of services;

- To create viable communities within which the normal functions of government can be performed with a reasonable degree of efficiency;

- To provide the basis upon which new social overhead investments in the infrastructure of municipalities might be accomplished through federal, state, local, and private resources to encourage new industry and increase employment;

- To assist municipalities in stabilizing their populations through the general improvement of the quality of life for their residents – creating viable alternatives to outward migration; and

- To serve as a vehicle through which mayors can articulate their concerns on national, state, and local public policy.

Presently governed by a 38-member mayor board of directors that meets quarterly, the organization first focused its efforts in developing programs primarily addressing infrastructure development in rural, small, and medium-sized cities and towns. As a result, millions of dollars have been generated for mostly smaller jurisdictions.

Over the years, NCBM has returned to visit its mission at strategic planning sessions of the board of directors. This ongoing planning process, coupled with membership needs assessments, assists the leadership in determining whether the organization is adequately meeting the needs of today's membership and keeping pace with the times.

One of the outgrowths of the last strategic planning session was the establishment of an Endowment Fund, which was set up in 1999 with seed monies and a plan for attracting cash, income, and assets. Based on the planning session, NCBM decided to create a presence in Washington, D.C. to monitor legislation and conduct public policy analyses. In 2002, NCBM incorporated its Corporate Advisory Council (CAC) as a 501(c)(4), based in Washington, D.C. The CAC gives corporations an opportunity to remain in dialogue with mayors on maintaining productive public-private partnerships. Another outcome of the strategic planning was the acquisition of condominium office space in East Point, Georgia for NCBM's headquarters, purchased in 2000.

www.ncbm.org

HISTORICAL PERSPECTIVE

Technical Assistance Provider

NCBM's value as a technical assistance provider has been demonstrated over the years with the awarding of grants from scores of federal agencies and foundations including the U.S. Departments of Labor, Energy, Housing and Urban Development, Transportation, Justice, and Commerce; the Environmental Protection Agency; the Ford Foundation; and more recently, the American Legacy Foundation, to name a few.

NCBM's capability as a training vehicle and supplier of technical assistance is widely recognized among black public administrators and elected officials. NCBM has also networked effectively with other national organizations of public officials in responding to national issues of mutual concern, and in forging collective approaches to problem solving.

New and innovative programs are being developed to meet the needs of NCBM membership. NCBM's premier training program, the Leadership Institute for Mayors (LIM), involving 55-65 mayors, was established in 1988 to prepare newly-elected mayors for their role as chief executive officers of local governments, and to provide in-service training for veteran mayors. Graduates of the LIM receive Continuing Education Units (CEUs) from an institution of higher learning.

International Linkages

The organization established international linkages in the late 1970s, primarily in African countries; however, in the early 1980s the formal exchanges were expanded to include countries in Asia and South America. In 1982, a delegation of mayors traveled to Japan under the auspices of the U.S. Japan Foundation and the Japanese African American Society. A similar trip was taken to Taiwan in 1983, and to Senegal, Ivory Coast, and Liberia in 1984. That same year, African-American and Chinese mayors (from the People's Republic of China) made an exchange visit. Exchange visits were also made to Guyana and Zaire. More recently, mayoral delegations visited Botswana, South Africa, and Nigeria. Recognizing the importance of maintaining international ties, the organization plans on developing mission-driven initiatives that encompass governance, health, business development, education, and cultural exchanges.

State Chapters

As the organization's numbers have increased, so has its delivery of services through the establishment of chapters in 19 states. The state chapters also address local legislative and policy issues. A state chapter manual is now available to mayors who wish to organize state chapters or enhance their existing activities.

Annual Convention

NCBM's annual convention, first held in 1975, is the organization's major fundraiser, and gives members the opportunity to publicly establish their collective opinion on issues of local governance. The convention is also the place for public officials, business and community leaders, and youth to exchange points of view on problems affecting the functioning of local government. At the close of the conference, resolutions delineating the organization's position on public policy are adopted at the Annual Business Meeting.

NCBM remains committed to its mission of promoting excellence in government. An important component of that commitment focuses on providing opportunities to uplift youth as the leaders of the future. To that end, NCBM has conducted a Youth Strategies Program that gave 500 young people an opportunity to spend a week at a resort and engage in recreation and academic enrichment programs. In 2000, NCBM launched a Scholarship Program for college-bound students, whereby 20 students receive $1,000 scholarships.

As NCBM enters its fourth decade of service, the organization intends to solidify its financial base, play a more proactive role in analyzing public policy, and improve service to its members.

BLACK *Mayors* IN AMERICA

These mayors preside over cities, towns, and villages with populations under 50,000 residents.

THE HONORABLE

JOSEPH L. ADAMS

MAYOR OF
UNIVERSITY CITY, MISSOURI

The Honorable Joseph L. Adams was elected mayor of the City of University City, Missouri in April 1996 after serving on the City Council since 1976. He was the first African American to serve on the City Council and to become mayor.

University City is one of the largest suburbs of the City of St. Louis, Missouri and will celebrate 100 years of incorporation in 2006. It is noted as one of the most successful entertainment districts in the region.

Adams' special contributions as leader of the city include overseeing a housing boom and a major expansion of the community recreation facilities. Currently, the city is embarking upon a renovation of its 100 year-old city hall, noted for its historical and architectural significance. Investment by developers in the community demonstrates their confidence in his leadership.

Adams made contributions to the region and to the nation by serving as president of St. Louis County Mayor of Large Cities 1997-1998 and the Missouri Municipal League, 1999-2000. He is a member of the governor's committees on homeland security, local government cooperation, and historic records.

A full professor of history at the St. Louis Community College until his retirement in December 2003, Adams holds both bachelor and master of arts degrees from the University of Missouri-Kansas City and has completed additional study at Washington University in St. Louis, Missouri.

THE **HONORABLE**

WILLIE ADAMS, JR., M.D.

MAYOR OF
ALBANY, GEORGIA

The Honorable Willie Adams, Jr. was born in Apalachicola, Florida and reared in Quincy, Florida. He attended the public schools of Gadsden County and currently lives in Albany, Georgia. He is married to the former Constance Lee, and they are the parents of three daughters and one son. They have four grandchildren.

After graduating from Carter Parramore High School, Dr. Adams attended Florida A&M University, where he served as president of the Student Government Association. He graduated and joined the Army as a second lieutenant. He served in that capacity for two years and retired as a lieutenant colonel in the U.S. Army Reserve.

Adams attended Meharry Medical Collage in Nashville, Tennessee, where he received his medical degree. He completed his internship at Hurley Hospital in Flint, Michigan and his residency at Emory University School of Medicine in Atlanta, Georgia.

Adams began an obstetrics and gynecology private practice in Albany, Georgia in 1973. His medical associations include the Diplomat American Board of Obstetrics and Gynecology, American College of Obstetrics & Gynecology, Governor's Council of Maternal & Infant Care, the American Medical Association, and the Georgia State Medical Society.

Adams is founder and director of the First National Bank of South Georgia, and a member of the Albany Dougherty Inner City Authority, the Dougherty County Board of Education, the Dougherty Aviation Commission, and the Georgia Chamber of Commerce. Likewise, he is a member of Phi Beta Sigma Fraternity, Inc., the advisory board of the Salvation Army, the board of directors of Mag Mutual Insurance Company, and Shiloh Baptist Church.

Adams has received numerous awards and recognitions for leadership, including honors given by Albany State University, the Department of the Army, and the Kiwanis Club.

Dr. Adams was elected mayor of the City of Albany, Georgia on February 10, 2004.

THE HONORABLE

TYRONE E. AIKEN

MAYOR OF
LINCOLNVILLE, SOUTH CAROLINA

The Honorable Tyrone E. Aiken became mayor of Lincolnville, South Carolina in April of 2000. He was elected as the 21st mayor of a town founded by freed slaves shortly after the Emancipation Proclamation and named after President Abraham Lincoln.

Before becoming mayor, Tyrone served 14 years on the Town Council, chairing various committees. He also served two years as the town's recreation director.

During his first term, Tyrone received certificates of achievement for completion of the Governor's Housing and Community Development Institute and the South Carolina Municipal Elected Officials Institute of Government.

As he begins his second term, Tyrone continues to meet challenges and accomplish the goals of a small and rural community such as building streets and sidewalks, expanding public water and sewer services, building recreation facilities, providing affordable housing, and economic development.

Tyrone is quick to point out the uniqueness of his municipality, "Lincolnville was founded and has always been governed by mayors of African descent."

Today, with a diverse population of nearly 1,000 residents, Tyrone accredits his success to his belief in the words of Hubert H. Humphrey, "The moral test of government is how it treats those who are in the dawn of life, the children, those who are in the twilight of life, the aged, and those who are in the shadows of life, the sick, the needy, and the handicapped."

Tyrone and his wife, Deborah, have three daughters, Sheri, Sherron, and Shanice, one son, Shamaal, and two granddaughters, Kailisha and Qyyara.

THE **HONORABLE**

MARY LESTEEN SUTTON AJOKU

MAYOR OF
CRUGER, MISSISSIPPI

The Honorable Mary Lesteen Sutton Ajoku took the oath of office on July 3, 2001 and holds the distinction of being the first female mayor in the Town of Cruger, Mississippi's 115-year history.

Mary earned a bachelor of science degree from Alcorn State University and a master of education degree from Howard University. She did further study at Trinity College and The Catholic University of America. Mary worked for the USDA for two years and taught in Washington, D.C. Public Schools for 33 years. After retiring, she moved back to her hometown of Cruger.

Mary was born in Cruger, a town located on the Mississippi Delta, where cotton was known as "King Cotton." Cruger received national recognition during the Depression, when the governing board exempted the town's 500 residents from paying any type of city taxes. The town treasury had enough surplus funds to run the town government without levying any taxes. The Town of Cruger Bank was one of the few banks that operated continuously during the Depression.

Upon returning to Cruger, Mary noted that the town had experienced an economic death. Cotton was no longer "king," and the town had become a ghost town. Mary's campaign slogan was "A TIME OF RESTORATION!" Her vision, and her greatest joy, is to see Cruger restored to its former status as a fine place to live.

Mary is a member of the St. James Church of God in Christ in Cruger. She has one daughter, Kristen, and one granddaughter, Kayla.

THE HONORABLE

C. LARUE ALFORD

MAYOR OF
LAKE CITY, SOUTH CAROLINA

The Honorable C. LaRue Alford is currently serving his second term as mayor of Lake City, South Carolina. In addition, he is a member of the board of directors and legislative committee of the Municipal Association.

An entrepreneur, Alford owns Pirate's T-Shirts Plus, a screen-printing and trophy company. He formerly worked as the Lake City Recreation Department athletic director, National Marine Electronics shipping and receiving supervisor, and the Coleman Company raw materials supervisor. He opened Pirate's T-Shirts Plus in 1988.

Alford is the second vice president of the South Carolina Democratic Party, as well as a member of the Private Industry Council board, the Juvenile Arbitrator Council, and the Lake City Development Corporation, where he serves on the revitalization board. He is a member of Bejilah #163 Shriner, a 32nd degree consistory, a royal arch mason, and a member of Mason Will Do Lodge #322 and Order of Eastern Star #224.

Alford was nominated as an Outstanding Young Man of America in 1992 and 1997, and attended Benedict College in Columbia, South Carolina. A member of St. Clair Baptist Church, he serves on the trustee board and is past president of the usher board.

Alford is married to Beverly Shaw Alford. He coaches and referees baseball, basketball, and football at the Lake City Recreational Department. He is the son of Helen Alford and the late Archie Alford.

THE HONORABLE

SHIRLEY STURDEVANT ALLEN

MAYOR OF
METCALFE, MISSISSIPPI

The Honorable Shirley Sturdevant Allen was born and raised in Metcalfe, Mississippi. She is the fourth of 11 children born to Thelma Sturdevant.

Mayor Allen graduated from Norma C. O'Bannon High School and Coahoma Community College. Her mentor, Rev. S.L. Lindsey, then recruited her to work within the community. She was later employed by Mississippi Action for Community Education (MACE) under the leadership of Charles Bannerman.

MACE, Friends of Education, Zeta Phi Beta Sorority, Inc., Cosmopolitan Ladies, the Metcalfe Gentlemen's Club, and the Mississippi Workers' Center for Human Rights have honored Allen for her work.

Allen was elected to public office in 1989 as an alderwoman/vice mayor in Metcalfe. In 1993, she was elected to her first term as mayor, and is presently in her third term. While she has served as mayor, the town has been awarded grants for street upgrade, housing, and the repair and restoration of the water tower.

Allen started "Metcalfe Homecoming," an annual Memorial Day celebration at the park with gospel music and fellowship. She is also mayor of the first smoke-free community in Mississippi. Former Mississippi Attorney General Mike Moore presented this award in October of 2002.

Allen served as president of the Mississippi Conference of Black Mayors, served on the board of the National Conference of Black Mayors (NCBM), and presently serves as treasurer of the Mississippi Black Caucus of Local Elected Officials.

In 2002, Allen was selected by the NCBM to travel to Nigeria as part of a delegation to participate in that country's Black Heritage Festival. The executive governor of Lagos State made her an ambassador.

Mayor Allen is the wife of Walter D. Allen, the mother of two daughters, Waukanda and Shaquita, and the very proud grandmother of two, Joseph and Elliot.

THE HONORABLE

REV. WILLIAM H. ALSTON

MAYOR OF
AWENDAW, SOUTH CAROLINA

The Honorable Rev. William H. "Bill" Alston became the first mayor of Awendaw in August of 1992, and has served unopposed for the last 12 years. In 2004, he was reelected to another four-year term. He has also served as pastor of the AME Church for more than 30 years.

Bill has offered the citizens of Awendaw the opportunity to help shape their destiny by becoming involved in the planning of the town's Comprehensive Land Use Plan. Bill worked with the Town Council and the citizens to develop the vision statement for the Town of Awendaw: "Managed growth is the key to Awendaw's future. The town should strive to maintain the existing rural character, yet grow to a moderate density residential community that has conveniences and some light industrial areas. This growth should promote compatible economic development, safeguard the environment, preserve open space, and protect the aesthetic quality while enhancing safe, healthy living conditions. Sensitivity to the rural character of Awendaw and preservation of area waterways and forest will sustain the natural environment and enhance the quality of life for our citizens."

Bill has been involved with his community long before becoming its first mayor. From the early days of the civil rights movement and the Headstart Child Development Program, Bill has provided leadership for his local community on the county, state, and national levels.

Bill earned a bachelor of arts degree from Allen University in Columbia, South Carolina. He retired from the Navy Department after a combination of military and civilian services for 30 years.

Under Bill's leadership, the Town of Awendaw has grown from less than 300 to more than 1,200 since its incorporation in 1992, according to the 2000 census.

Bill's favorite saying is, "There is no right way to do the wrong thing."

THE *HONORABLE*

FRANCES R. ANDERSON

MAYOR OF
TERRELL, TEXAS

The Honorable Frances R. Anderson began her career with the City of Terrell as an elected councilmember of District Three in May of 1984. She was elected mayor of Terrell in May of 2002, and made history as the city's first woman mayor and the first African-American woman to serve as mayor.

Anderson has held numerous other positions within the community and state. She has served on the legislative, human relations, and safety committees for the National League of Cities and the Texas Municipal League, and as a member of the Kaufman County Appraisal Board and the YMCA Board. She also served as director of the Terrell Economic Development Corporation and the Terrell Alliance for Education Arts.

She has played an active role with many organizations in Terrell including the Texas Association of Women and Youth Clubs, the 22 Marechal Neil Club, the Texas State Teachers Association/National Education Association, Alpha Kappa Alpha Sorority, Inc., and the NAACP.

She continues to be a community leader and has received numerous awards and recognitions from the community, including the Terrell Renaissance Club Community Service Award; the Phenomenal Woman of Texas Award from the Texas Association of Women and Youth Clubs; the Commitment to Excellence, Leadership, and Professionalism Award from Southwestern Christian College; and the SWCC Partnership Award.

Anderson graduated from Tuskegee University, and holds a lifetime certificate in elementary and secondary education.

She is married to Lieutenant Colonel Abbie H. Anderson (retired), and is a mother of four, all graduates of the Terrell Independent School District.

THE *HONORABLE*

MARTHA WOODARD ANDRUS

MAYOR OF
GRAMBLING, LOUISIANA

The Honorable Martha Woodard Andrus became the first female mayor of the City of Grambling, Louisiana, home of Grambling State University, in January of 2003.

Martha Andrus is working diligently to improve basic municipal services and ensure economic development. Her main project thrusts include making Grambling a safer, cleaner city, developing activities and services for seniors and challenged citizens, fostering annexations, and improving accountability in city government.

During her career, Martha has received numerous awards in education and service. They include the 2003 ExtraOrdinary Award from the Monroe-Grambling Chapter of The Links, Inc., for performance, service, dedication, and courage; the Distinguished Alumna Award from Grambling State University presented by NAFEO, 2004; the Citizen of the Year Award from the Pi Tau Chapter of Omega Psi Phi Fraternity for outstanding contributions and leadership; and Winner of the 2003 Mayor's Challenge to Buckle Up America.

Martha is a retired educator from both the public and university systems. She received a bachelor of science degree in biology from Grambling State University and a master of science teaching degree in biology from Southern University. She also completed postgraduate work at Colorado State University. She is a past president and a member of the Grambling Alumnae Chapter of Delta Sigma Theta Sorority, Inc.

Martha is the daughter of Grambling's first mayor, B.T. Woodard, Sr., and Eula T. Woodard. She has two children, Deidre Nicole and Bryan Jahmal (wife Nicole), and two grandsons, Nicolas Bryan and Naythan Jahmal. She is a member of the New Rocky Valley Baptist Church where she enjoys singing in the choir.

Mayor Andrus enjoys the challenges of city government and working for and with the citizens of Grambling – a "City on the Move."

THE HONORABLE

AMELDA J. ARNOLD

MAYOR OF
PORT GIBSON, MISSISSIPPI

The Honorable Amelda J. Arnold is a life-long resident of Port Gibson, Mississippi, located in Claiborne County. She is the eldest daughter of Lula Mae and the late Elijah Arnold. Amelda has three siblings, Melvin, Gloria, and Adrianne, and is the proud parent of Amelda Monique, who is presently a freshman at Tougaloo College in Jackson, Mississippi.

On December 7, 1999, Amelda made history when she was elected to be the first woman and first African-American mayor of the third-oldest incorporated town in the state of Mississippi. Ulysses S. Grant called the town, "The Town Too Beautiful To Burn."

Amelda graduated with a degree in elementary education from Alcorn State University in 1977 and continued graduate studies at the University of Miami Business School. From 1981 to 1992, she worked in supervisory positions with several manufacturing companies in Port Gibson. In 1992, the mayor began her own business, A to Z Electronics, Inc.

Amelda is an active member of Christian Chapel Church. She is a member of various organizations, including the National Association of Female Business Executives, the Alcorn State University Alumni Association, the Mississippi National Black Caucus of Local Elected Black Officials, and the National and Mississippi Conference of Black Mayors. A lifetime member of Delta Sigma Theta Sorority, Inc., Amelda is a board member of the Mississippi Municipal League, the Port Gibson/Vicksburg Child Abuse Prevention Center, the Traceway Development Foundation, and the executive board of the Claiborne County Democratic Party.

Since becoming mayor of Port Gibson, Amelda has brought in more than $2 million in grant money. The mayor believes that, "Nothing Great Is Ever Done Without Much Enduring."

THE HONORABLE

EARNEST O. BARKLEY

MAYOR OF
GRETNA, FLORIDA

The Honorable Earnest O. Barkley, Jr. became the first black mayor of Gretna, Florida in December of 1971. He made history by being elected as the first African-American mayor in the panhandle of Florida.

Earnest earned his bachelor of science and master of science degrees in math from Florida A&M University in Tallahassee, Florida.

A former appointee of Governor Bob Graham, from November 1979 to November 1983, Earnest is the secretary of the National Conference of Black Mayors, Inc. He is the assistant secretary general of the World Conference of Mayors, Inc. and the first vice president of the Florida Conference of Black Mayors, Inc. He has also served the Governor's Constituency of Crime Against Children.

Earnest is a member of the steward board of Springfield AME Church in Gretna.

THE HONORABLE

JAMES BATEASTE

MAYOR OF
CROSBY, MISSISSIPPI

The Honorable James Bateaste, mayor of Crosby, Mississippi, was born in Natchez, Mississippi. A lifelong resident of Crosby, he attended Stevenson Elementary School and Wilkinson County High School. He then attended Rust College in Holly Springs, Mississippi and Natchez College.

In 1979, Mayor Bateaste became the youngest black man to build a new home in Crosby. He served three terms as an alderman for the town, and he was elected mayor in 2001.

In 1988, Bateaste was selected as an Outstanding Young Man of America. Likewise, he was selected for "Who's Who of American Society" in 2001 and the "Bronze Leader for Disabled American Veterans" charity organization in 2002.

Bateaste is a member of the Mississippi Conference of Black Mayors and the National Conference of Black Mayors. He holds a Mississippi Judicial College bail agent certificate and is a member of the Mississippi Municipal League and the Mississippi Rural Water Association.

Mayor Bateaste is the father of six children, and he presently works as an automotive mechanic for Ford Motor Co. He is an active member of the Crosby Union Baptist Church, where he serves as a deacon.

THE *HONORABLE*

DEWAINE T. BELL

MAYOR OF
BARNESVILLE, GEORGIA

The Honorable Dewaine T. Bell, mayor of Barnesville, Georgia, is a family man, a community leader, and a public servant.

Educated in Georgia with a bachelor of arts degree in music from Clark College and a master's degree from Georgia State University in both music and education, Mayor Bell has always been interested in the education of young people.

Bell's professional career has followed his love for music and teaching. He began as a high school band director with the Lamar County Comprehensive High School and grew into the positions of assistant principal and principal with this institution. He later served as the director of technology and career education and pre-kindergarten with the Lamar County School System.

As a community leader, Bell has been a municipal judge, chairman of the Lamar County Tax Equalization Board, and chairman of the Lamar County Zoning Board. He serves his church in the Staff's Mill Praise Band at New Hope Baptist Church. He and his family are members of the Poplar Hill Baptist Church.

Bell serves his community through his involvement as president of Family Connection and 100 Black Men & Women, and as founder and president of the Lamar County Activity Center. A Chamber of Commerce board member and Gordon College Foundation board of trustees member, he is a member of Habitat for Humanity, Lamar Arts Council, Lamar Executive Club, and the NAACP. He was recognized as the Lamar County Citizen of the Year in 1998 and the Coca Cola Educator of the Decade in 2000.

Bell celebrates 26 years of marriage to the former Brenda Kendall of Thomaston, a retired educator. They have one daughter, Christal Bell, who is employed as the assistant project manager with U.S. Filter Construction & Engineering, currently working with the Atlanta Bio Solids Project.

THE *HONORABLE*

ROY L. BELL

MAYOR OF
GARYSBURG, NORTH CAROLINA

The Honorable Roy L. Bell has served as mayor of the Town of Garysburg, North Carolina for five two-year terms, a total of ten years. During his tenure, the town has grown from a population of 1,050 citizens to one of 1,250 citizens.

Bell's administration has also seen a dramatic improvement in the police department. It presently employs three police officers, two full-time and one part-time. A family resource center has been established, and the city limits have been extended one mile through extra territorial jurisdiction. Finally, the Town of Garysburg is building a new town hall. Expected to be completed August 2005, the new municipal building will house the town hall administrative building, the police department, and large and small conference areas for citizen use. Programs will be provided that accommodate citizens with health screening and many other needed functions.

Under Bell's leadership, the town has acquired a $305,000 Community Development Block Grant for rehabilitation of citizens' homes within the town. These are funds that assist low-income citizens who could not afford to have their home remodeled. The town has also purchased ten acres of land within the town for the purpose of bringing more economic development to the town. Citizens have expressed a desire to have a commercial center, which would house a grocery store, drug store, and many other viable businesses that would compliment the town.

It is clear to see that Garysburg is growing by leaps and bounds. It is definitely a town on the move.

THE HONORABLE

LILLIAN K. BEVERLY

MAYOR OF
NORTH BRENTWOOD, MARYLAND

The Honorable Lillian K. Beverly became the 12th mayor of North Brentwood, Maryland in 1995. North Brentwood is the oldest and first African-American municipality incorporated in Prince George's County, Maryland. The settlers arrived in 1887.

Mayor Beverly is the first female mayor of the town. She has faced many challenges, but has led her town of 540 residents to achieve many goals, including a new town hall and veterans memorial honoring the men and women that represented North Brentwood in wars from the Civil War through the conflicts. At present, the town is building the Prince George's African-American Cultural Center/Museum at North Brentwood, located in the Arts District. The goal is to make known the contributions of African Americans to the development of Prince George's County.

Beverly is very active in the county and represents the town on several boards, including the Prince George's Municipal League, Anacostia Trails Area, and Gateway Community Development Corporation.

Beverly attended Howard University, and is a member of First Baptist Church of North Brentwood, which was founded by her grandfather. In addition, she is a retired federal government administrator.

Mayor Beverly is a widow and mother of one, George, Jr. She says, "If I can help somebody along the way, then my living was not in vain."

THE **HONORABLE**

GENEVA BLEDSOE

MAYOR OF
FIVE POINTS, ALABAMA

The Honorable Geneva Bledsoe has served four terms as mayor of Five Points, Alabama. When elected in November of 1990, Mayor Bledsoe became the first female and the first African-American mayor of the small, southern Alabama town with 250 residents.

Throughout her terms, Bledsoe has secured federal grants to improve the town's water and sewer services. She is also committed to providing first class recreation for the town's citizens and is working diligently to obtain grants for this project.

Bledsoe serves on the Chambers County executive committee and is a board member of the Chambers County Enterprise Community, East Alabama Mental Health, and Chambers County Human Resources. She is affiliated with the Macedonia Missionary Baptist Church, where she is active in the teaching, mission, and choir ministries. She is also a proud member of Alpha Kappa Alpha Sorority, Inc.

Bledsoe received a bachelor of science degree in home economics from Alabama A&M University in Normal, Alabama in 1954 and worked as a home economics teacher in Chambers County before retiring. She still occasionally works as a substitute teacher in Chambers County schools.

Mayor Bledsoe is the mother of identical twin daughters and has four grandchildren and one great-grandson. She has based her life on the biblical scripture that reads: "For even the Son of Man did not come to be served, but to serve." – Mark 10:45

THE *HONORABLE*

MARY BOLTON

MAYOR OF
McLAIN, MISSISSIPPI

The Honorable Mary Bolton is the mayor of McLain, Mississippi. She is the first African American and first female to be elected to this honorable position. As mayor, Mary has placed tremendous emphasis on the growth of families and youth in an effort to build a safer and stronger community. During her term, she has established an annual youth festival, a non-profit organization, a beautification program, and a youth leadership program.

Shortly after being elected in 2001, the governor appointed Mary to the Mississippi Commission for Volunteer Service board. She was also chosen to be the guest speaker at Portsmouth New Hope Annual Martin Luther King service in Portsmouth, New Hampshire. Mary is currently affiliated with the Gulf Coast Community Action Agency, Greene County Rotary Club, and The Prisoners Advisory Council. She is the founder of the Rural Community and Youth Development, Inc., Youth-in-Action, The New Beginning Ministries, and others.

Mary has earned a bachelor of science degree in physical education, recreation, and dance at Nicholls State University. She received a master's degree in leadership administration at the University of Southern Mississippi.

Mary is the daughter of the late Dr. and Mrs. L.W. Bolton, Sr. She is the proud mother of three beautiful girls. During her spare time, Mary enjoys coaching and traveling with her sister, Ruthie Bolton. Ruthie is a two-time Olympian and a WNBA player. Growing up in a family of 20, 12 boys and eight girls, Mary's parents' philosophy, "We Need Each Other," is significantly emphasized in her position of leadership.

Mayor Bolton truly believes that she is elected by man and appointed by God.

THE HONORABLE

YOLANDA E. BROADIE

MAYOR OF
WOODMERE, OHIO

The Honorable Yolanda E. Broadie was born and raised in Cleveland, Ohio. A graduate of the Orange School System, she received a bachelor of arts degree in English from Kent State University. After graduating from Kent State University, Broadie became a senior merchandise manager for the J. C. Penney Company. She became active in politics in 1992. She was appointed to City Council in 1992, and successfully ran for two additional terms in 1994 and 1998. Broadie was council president for two years before becoming acting mayor in 2000. She was elected to her first four-year term as mayor in November of 2001.

In the past, Broadie served her community as chairperson of the finance committee, chairperson of the youth committee, and as council president.

In addition to her duties as mayor of the Village of Woodmere, Broadie is a member of the Legislative Committee, the Mayor's Association of Ohio, the Ohio Conference of Black Mayors, the Ohio Municipal League, the National Conference of Black Mayors, the National League of Cities, Women in Municipal Government, the National Black Caucus, the Cuyahoga County Mayors and Managers Association, and the Woodmere Women's Civic League. She is a founding member of the Suburban Black Caucus, and serves on the board of directors for the Wings Over Jordan Alumni and Friends. Also a trustee of Life International Ministries, Broadie is a member of the Cuyahoga County section of the National Council of Negro Women, and a Woodmere delegate of the Beach-wood/Woodmere Democratic Club.

Some of her honors include Honorable Mention in the June 2002 issue of *Northern Ohio Live's* 500 Most Influential Women, and the Spirit of Women Community Impact Award in politics from the National Council of Negro Women, Cuyahoga County section.

Broadie is the single mother of one daughter, Maya, seven.

THE HONORABLE

IRENE H. BRODIE, Ph.D.

MAYOR OF
ROBBINS, ILLINOIS

In 1989, the Honorable Irene Hale Brodie, Ph.D., was elected mayor of the Village of Robbins, a suburb of Chicago, Illinois. Brodie was the first woman mayor in Robbins; the first to get a $2.5 million HUD debt forgiven; the first to build a $403 million industrial park in Robbins; and the first village clerk elected to three four-year terms and then elected mayor of Robbins.

Some of Brodie's accomplishments include serving on one of President Clinton's environmental think-tanks in 1996 and 1997. Additionally, she was a guest lecturer in 1993 and 1994 to the Harvard University Graduate School of Business Administration (the lectures became a requirement for students). She was also a U.S. Region V Benefactor to Moraine Valley Community College in 2002, a vice-president of Illinois Municipal League, and an appointee to three transition teams for the current governor of Illinois.

Brodie holds a doctoral degree from Northeastern University in Fort Lauderdale, Florida, a master's degree from the University of Chicago, and a bachelor's degree from Chicago Teachers College, now named Chicago State University.

Determined to make a difference in Robbins, the Brodie administration was successful in getting a new healthcare center built, new water meters installed, sewer lines upgraded, streets reconstructed, and street signs and lights erected. Other improvements include an automobile sales company that relocated in Robbins, a supportive living center, a three-story senior citizen building, a new housing development, an eight-pump gasoline station with car wash and eatery, and the acquisition of three new fire engines. The entire community is especially pleased with the construction of a new Metropolitan Rail (Metra) train station and a new shelter for the cash-producing flea market.

THE *HONORABLE*

JAMES LEE BROOKS

MAYOR OF
MADISON, ARKANSAS

The Honorable James Lee Brooks was the fifth mayor elected in the City of Madison, Arkansas. He served as a council member for eight years before being elected mayor.

Born December 21, 1952, in Haynes, Arkansas, Mayor Brooks is a graduate of Lee Senior High School in Marianna, Arkansas. He attended Crowley Ridge Technical Institute and received a degree in industrial electronics. Later, he attended Jackson Theological Seminary and earned a bachelor of theology degree.

Brooks is married to the former Vhaness Kellum and they have two daughters, Jessica Brooks-Jackson and Andrea Brooks-Smith. They have three grandchildren.

Mayor Brooks is the pastor of St. John Missionary Baptist Church in Madison, where he has served for the past 16 years.

THE HONORABLE

JUSTINE THOMAS BROWN

MAYOR OF
OLIVER, GEORGIA

The Honorable Justine T. Brown became the first African American elected as mayor of the City of Oliver, Georgia in 1990. Before her election as mayor, she was the only African American to be elected to serve on a council seat. Justine's affiliation with various national and state political organizations won her the Renaissance Image Award in Politics in 1998 and 1999.

In addition to her political involvement, Justine is a pioneer for being a positive role model in the Screven County-Sylvania, Georgia area. Recently retired as a physical education/ health teacher and athletic coach at Screven County Middle School, she has touched many lives. A living legend with the respect of her colleagues and the community, Justine has earned several accolades, recognition as Teacher of the Year, and a listing in *Who's Who Among* Black *American Educators.* For years, she was a demonstration teacher for Georgia Southern University in Statesboro, Georgia.

Justine's leadership expands beyond the classroom and the city government. She has served on various committees including the System Wide Advisory Committee, the Emergency Food and Shelter Board, the Screven County Hospital Authority Board, and the Screven County Recreation Board.

A proud member of the Chi Pi Omega chapter of Alpha Kappa Alpha Sorority, Inc., Justine is continuously involved in inspiring the African-American community. She is an accomplished pianist and plays at various events and at churches.

Justine is the daughter of the late Reverend and Mrs. J.W.H. Thomas, Sr. She has been married to Willie Brown for 43 years. They have three children, Rahn, Antjuan, and Jatavier Brown.

THE HONORABLE

MICHAEL D. BROWN

MAYOR OF
RIVIERA BEACH, FLORIDA

The Honorable Michael D. Brown, mayor of Riviera Beach, Florida, grew up in Riviera Beach and West Palm Beach on a farm that was located on Military Trail just south of 45th Street.

One of eight children, Brown attended Purdue University, and studied law at Howard University. After working two years at the Justice Department in Washington, D.C., he returned to Florida, where he joined a law firm for five years before opening his own practice in 1992, which is located in Riviera Beach.

Brown's legal practice specializes in commercial, personal injury, eminent domain, and civil litigation representing a number of individuals, small local businesses, and national corporations.

He takes particular pride in being able to assist his neighbors and encouraging economic development in Palm Beach County, especially Riviera Beach.

In 1994, Brown was elected as a commissioner for the Port of Palm Beach. He chose not to seek reelection to that seat, and in 1999, he was elected mayor of the City of Riviera Beach under a "New Wave of Leadership." Brown's focus is to better the opportunities for the citizens of Riviera Beach by helping the city to develop its enormous economic potential.

THE HONORABLE

SAMUEL S. BROWN

MAYOR OF
LAUDERDALE LAKES, FLORIDA

The Honorable Samuel S. Brown was elected the fifth mayor of Lauderdale Lakes in March of 1998. He is the city's first black mayor. Under his leadership, the city has made aggressive strides in the areas of redevelopment and capital improvement. Likewise, the city is strengthening its financial position and continuing to provide quality services and programs. Notable accomplishments to date include the passage of a $15 million capital improvement bond; construction on a new elementary school; and the successful attraction of a more than 200,000 square foot Wal-Mart Superstore and Florida's premier film production studio, AGU Studios.

Samuel leads the charge in various endeavors to benefit the needy both near and far. He spear-headed efforts for an annual Thanksgiving Food Drive, Angel Tree Gift Giving Program, Caribbean Hurricane Relief Effort, and Asian Tsunami Donation Drive. In addition, he also helped establish a scholarship fund for local high school students, and a city newspaper.

Samuel graduated from Calabar College in Kingston, Jamaica, West Indies, and he enjoyed a successful career as an educator. At the age of 82, Samuel remains active in his community. He serves as a member of the Florida Medical Center board of directors, the Broward League of Cities' health and social resources committee, the Metropolitan Planning Organization of Broward County, Florida, and the Kiwanis Club of Lauderdale Lakes/West Sunrise. He also holds the rank of major in the Broward Sheriff's Office Citizen Observer Patrol of Lauderdale Lakes.

Samuel is a unifying force in the community, exemplifying the message of "Unity in Diversity" through his many civic, charitable, and philanthropic endeavors.

THE *HONORABLE*

LARRY S. BRYANT

MAYOR OF
FORREST CITY, ARKANSAS

The Honorable Larry Bryant has known since the fourth grade that he wanted to be a politician. Born on June 9, 1952 in Forrest City, Arkansas, he was elected to serve the city as mayor in 1998, and is now in his second four-year term.

Mayor Bryant started his education in Chicago, Illinois and continued at Stewart Elementary in Forrest City, which was an all-black school. He graduated from Forrest City High School, one of the first schools in Forrest City to integrate under the Freedom of Choice Plan. Bryant attended Laramie County College in Cheyenne, Wyoming while serving in the U.S. Air Force, and attended Arkansas State University, where he received a bachelor of science degree in radio and television and a master's degree in mass communication.

Bryant, a former youth counselor for Multi-County Youth Services, was employed with Arkansas Educational Television and KAIT-TV 8. Currently, he is the owner of Bryant's Photography Enterprises and LScott Plaza. He is president of the Arkansas Black Mayor's Association, an executive committee member of the Arkansas Municipal League and National Conference of Black Mayors, and a member of the St. Francis County Cancer Coalition and the St. Francis County Hometown Health Network.

Bryant is a life member of the NAACP and former president of the St. Francis chapter of the NAACP. He has served as board president, executive director, financial donor, and fundraiser for Forrest City Community Voices. He has been instrumental in the organization's work for a better community through education.

Bryant received the Leadership in Civil Rights Award from the Arkansas state chapter of the NAACP and the Impact Award from the Arkansas Regional Minority Supplier Development Council.

Mayor Bryant is married to Stephanie (Rainey) Bryant. He is the proud father of two children, Justin and LScott.

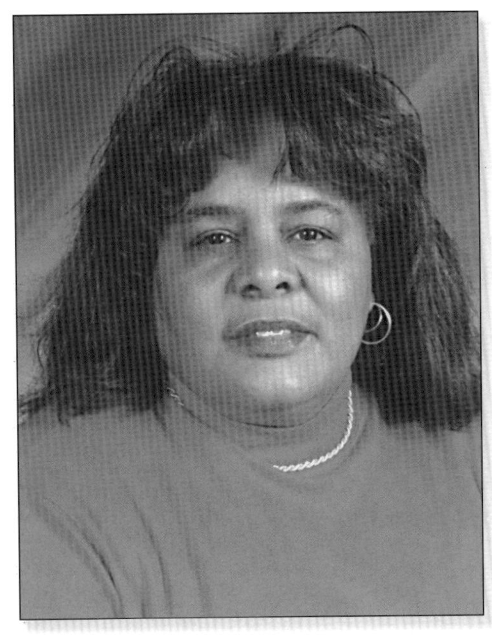

THE HONORABLE

MILDRED BURKHALTER

MAYOR OF
RENTIESVILLE, OKLAHOMA

The Honorable Mildred Burkhalter became the first African-American female to head the leadership of Rentiesville, Oklahoma, one of the remaining all-black towns in the state. She was first elected in April of 1991.

Mildred is goal-oriented, ambitious, and determined, and she has offered the people of her community a vision to preserve the heritage, life, and history of this small town. Through determination and hard work, and being driven by an inner desire to "make a difference," she has brought viability back to this small town by providing services to the elders, children, and families.

Mildred has received many awards including the Wal-Mart Outstanding Small Town Leadership Award, which rendered a monetary award for her community.

Mildred Burkhalter received her bachelor's degree from Northeastern State University (NSU) in Tahlequah, Oklahoma and later pursued her master of business administration degree from NSU. She is presently seeking her master's degree in education from the University of Phoenix in Tulsa, Oklahoma.

THE *HONORABLE*

DENAY L. BURRIS

MAYOR OF
FT. COFFEE, OKLAHOMA

The Honorable DeNay L. Burris grew up in Ft. Coffee, Oklahoma. She graduated from Spiro High School in 1986. She earned a bachelor of arts degree in accounting at Langston University, which is located in Langston, Oklahoma, in 1989. She subsequently moved to St. Louis, Missouri.

Mayor Burris then began working for Farmers Home Administration. During this time, she earned a master's degree in public administration with an emphasis in finance and budgeting from Southern Illinois University–Edwardsville. She ended her career with Farmers Home in management.

Burris moved on to become a federal agent for the Internal Revenue Service in Atlanta, Georgia. For health reasons, her career as a federal agent ended early. She relocated back home to Ft. Coffee, where she served on the board of trustees for two years before becoming mayor in 1999.

Throughout Burris' career, she has been very active in the community and has had a great concern for children. Fourteen years ago, she founded the Muhammad Robbalaa Minority Scholarship Award. The award is given annually during her former high school's graduation ceremonies. It was established to provide financial assistance to minority students registered to attend Burris' alma mater, Langston University.

She has been involved with various other organizations and committees throughout her career. She believes that the most rewarding organization that she has been involved in to date has been little league sports. Burris has coached little league baseball for eight years, basketball for two years, and soccer for one year.

Mayor Burris is the proud mother of two sons and a nephew. Her sons, Kent and Joseph, and her nephew, Samad, are growing up to become strong black men. She is thankful for her blessings from God.

THE HONORABLE

ELAINE A. CARTER

MAYOR OF
GLENARDEN, MARYLAND

The Honorable Elaine Allen Carter is the 13th mayor of the City of Glenarden, Maryland, and the first woman to be elected to that office. Mayor Carter was elected to fill a vacancy in March of 2003, and in June of that year, she was elected to a full two-year term of office.

Carter's first and most important challenge was to improve the city's financial posture and the city's level of personnel, so that Glenarden could move forward. Glenarden now has an improved computer and technical system, and the city is working to improve communications with citizens through the city newsletter and an updated cable station.

Carter was recently profiled for Black History Month in the local newspaper, the *Prince George's Gazette*. She is an active member of the Union Wesley AME Zion Church in Washington, D.C., a member of the Polish Jewels Social Club, and a member of the Book Diva's book club.

Carter was educated in the Passaic, New Jersey public school system. She is a graduate infant technician from St. Vincent's Hospital in Montclair, New Jersey, and she is a certified housing specialist.

Mayor Carter is dedicated to God through her church, Glenarden as mayor, and her family as wife to Henry Carter, and a mother and grandmother.

THE HONORABLE

JAMES CARTER

MAYOR OF
WOODLAND, GEORGIA

The Honorable James Carter became the first African-American mayor of Woodland, Georgia in January of 1983. He is also the city's first African-American municipal court judge. Mayor Carter holds the distinction of being the first mayor to become a certified clerk and finance officer through the University of Georgia Carl Vinson Institute.

Under Carter's direction, the City of Woodland has completed many public works projects, such as upgrading the citywide water system, upgrading the publicly owned gas system, and constructing a recreational complex. Carter has secured more than $3 million in grants for the Woodland community.

A true public servant, Carter serves on numerous boards and committees, including the Georgia Conference of Black Mayors, the National Conference of Black Mayors, the NAACP, and the Georgia Municipal Association. He is also a member of the Masonic Lodge, Talbot Adult Education, Talbot County Chamber of Commerce, the Lower Chattahoochee RDC board of directors, and the Talbot County Interagency Council.

Before Carter started in politics, he completed his secondary education at Ruth Carter High School. He earned a master's degree from Albany State University and will soon become a certified paralegal. Carter is a true entrepreneur. He owns a real estate sales/consultant business and works as a tax accountant.

Carter realized that he wanted to be a public servant when Woodland residents said that they needed him "uptown."

THE HONORABLE

JOHN R. CARTER

MAYOR OF
GRAY COURT, SOUTH CAROLINA

The Honorable John Robert Carter was born in Gray Court, South Carolina and attended public school in Laurens County. He is the first African American to be elected mayor of Gray Court.

Mayor Carter is a graduate of Limestone College in Gaffney, South Carolina. He holds a bachelor of science degree in business administration.

Carter has earned continuing education credits from the University of South Carolina, the University of Georgia, Clark University of Atlanta, and Florida Memorial College in Miami.

A deacon at Pleasant View Baptist Church of Gray Court, Carter is a member of Phi Beta Sigma Fraternity, a past member of the local Red Cross board of directors, and past president of the South Carolina Conference of Black Mayors. He is a member of Red Cross Masonic Lodge, Piedmont Consistory #169, Greenville, South Carolina; Azah Shrine Temple #140; and past president of the NAACP of Laurens County.

Among many others, Carter has served on the board of directors of the National Conference of Black Mayors, board of visitors for Piedmont Technical College, board of the Upper Savannah Council of Government, and the board of Safe Homes.

Carter has also received numerous awards for his untiring efforts to improve the quality of life for all citizens of America. The town has received several grants for water line updates, housing, and beautification projects. Gray Court recently received a $100,000 private donation to construct a town park.

Carter retired from the Department of Social Services as a work force consultant in Laurens, Newberry, and Saluda Counties.

He was recently elected to a fifth term as mayor of the town of Gray Court.

THE HONORABLE

ETHEL T. CLARK

MAYOR OF
SPRING LAKE, NORTH CAROLINA

The Honorable Ethel T. Clark is the first African-American female mayor of Spring Lake, North Carolina. Currently serving her second term in office, she was elected by a landslide margin in the November 2001 election.

Mayor Clark began her public service career in 1981, becoming the first, and thus far the only, African-American female elected to the board of aldermen in Spring Lake. She served continuously until her election as mayor.

As mayor, Clark's motto, "Let's make it happen," truly describes her winning attitude on making positive things happen for Spring Lake, a small town nestled between Fort Bragg Military Post and Pope Air Force Base. Her reputation is noted statewide, where she has served in many organizations including the North Carolina League of Municipalities, Mid-Carolina Council of Government, and the North Carolina Housing Trust Fund Study Commission. She is currently chair of the Sustainable Sandhills Leadership Council in partnership with Fort Bragg and the North Carolina Department of Commerce.

Clark's professional career is as exemplary as her public service. She is the office manager and financial services director at Hall Real Estate in Spring Lake. As a realtor for more than 30 years, she has served in leadership roles at local, state, and national levels.

Her commitment to Spring Lake extends to her church. Since 1975, Clark has been a devoted member of the Williams Chapel Free Will Baptist Church. She is one of the lead vocalists in the United Gospel Chorus, and has been on the board of trustees since 1998, where she is currently serving as church treasurer.

Clark is married to U.S. Air Force master sergeant (retired) David L. Clark. They have two sons, Jonathan and James, and four grandchildren, Brittany, Ashley, Amber, and Dallas. For recreation she enjoys traveling, cooking, and putting together large puzzles.

THE *HONORABLE*

KEITH L. CONWAY

MAYOR OF
KINLOCH, MISSOURI

The Honorable Keith L. Conway began serving as the tenth mayor of the City of Kinloch, Missouri's first black city, and as the city's youngest mayor on April 11, 1999. He was elected to a second four-year term, which began in April of 2003.

Mayor Conway is very active in the community and interacts with mayors and public officials of other communities, cities, and counties to promote growth and prosperity. He is also active and attends local, public, social, and civic functions representing the community.

Over the past 20 years, the City of Kinloch was devastated by a massive buyout, designed to destroy the community. The city's population dwindled from 6,000 to less than 500 because of the buyout. However, under Conway's leadership, Kinloch is well on the way to once again becoming a thriving community. Two apartment complexes that were closed because of the buyout have been reopened, and they are more than two-thirds full.

During his tenure, Conway has received several awards, which include the North County Inc. and East-West Gateway awards, and has been featured in several publications in and around the St. Louis area. Before becoming mayor, he toured the country as an entertainer.

Mayor Conway is well liked in the community, and, after being illegally taken off of the ballot to run for mayor, the residents voted him into office as a write-in candidate. He beat the incumbent mayor by a vote margin of 127 to 50, clearly a mandate. Because of the fact that Conway works with the children and knows everyone in the community, this venture has turned out to be just what everyone wanted: hope, life, and the rebirth of the great City of Kinloch.

THE HONORABLE

EMMA COOPER-HARRIS

MAYOR OF
ANGUILLA, MISSISSIPPI

The Honorable Emma Cooper-Harris became the first African-American female mayor of Anguilla, Mississippi in June of 2001. She made history in the small town and in Sharkey County, Mississippi, winning the election by ten votes from her opponent, who had 30 years of experience in municipal government.

Mayor Cooper-Harris brought vision and hope to Anguilla with the slogan, "The town with the courage to change." Her leadership led to improvements in streets, water and sewer services, safety, community services, and a new infrastructure for small-town Mississippi. During her tenure, Anguilla has been featured in the *Mississippi Rural Water Association* publication as one of the cleanest small towns in the Delta.

Cooper-Harris earned her associate of art degree from Natchez College, with further studies at Jackson State University in Jackson, Mississippi and LeMoyne-Owens College in Memphis, Tennessee. She has attended several rural leadership and development institutes and has 50 hours of study in municipal government and management.

Cooper-Harris has received numerous awards including the prestigious Harriet Tubman Award from the Mississippi Magnolia Bar Association. She says, "It matters whose hand the town is in."

THE HONORABLE

RON DAVIS

MAYOR OF
PRICHARD, ALABAMA

The Honorable Ron Davis, mayor of the City of Prichard, Alabama, is a graduate of W.P. Davidson High School in Mobile. He earned a bachelor's degree in criminal justice and social rehabilitation from Troy State University.

Mayor Davis served four years as president pro tem of Prichard City Council and 17 years as a corporal of the Mobile County Sheriff's Department.

Mayor Davis is a member and deacon of Yorktown Missionary Baptist Church. Likewise, he is a member of the Prichard Exchange Club, the Women's Federated Club advisory board, and Dragons Civic Organization. He is also a member of the Mobile County Democratic Executive Committee, the Mobile County Criminal Justice Society, Pride of the South 15-A Masonic Lodge, Eight Mile Lions' Club, and Mobile United.

Mayor Davis is married to Alisa Davis and is the father of Shannon, JaRon, and JaRhonda Davis. He is the uncle of a special niece, Ahyana Morris.

THE *HONORABLE*

WILLIE DAVIS, JR.

MAYOR OF
FARMERVILLE, LOUISIANA

The Honorable Willie Davis, Jr. was raised in Farmerville, Louisiana and Chicago, Illinois. He attended public school at Union Parish Training School in Farmerville and attended Olive Harvey College in Chicago. He served in the U.S. Army during the Korean conflict.

Mayor Davis is a retired administrator's assistant of United Blood Service and Research in Chicago. On January 1, 1993, he was inaugurated as mayor of Farmerville, Louisiana. He continues to serve and oversee the progress of the town.

A member of Zion Hill Missionary Baptist Church, Davis serves as deacon, treasurer, and Sunday school teacher. He is the president and owner of "D," Inc.; West Street Trailer Park; and West Street Day Care.

Davis is past master of Farmerville Lodge #203 Free & Accepted Masons, illustrious peer of the 33rd degree P.H.A., and past illustrious potentate of the Imperial Council Ancient Egyptian Arabic Order Nobles of the Mystic Shrine. Likewise, he is worthy patron of the Esther Grand Chapter O.E.S. Budding Rose Chapter #86.

Davis is a member of the jury commission for the Union Parish Third District Court, the Lions Club, the Farmerville Airport Authority Commission board, and the Union Parish Triad board. In addition, he is a former member of the Union Parish Tourist Commission and the Union Parish Chamber of Commerce board of directors. Davis is currently a very supportive member of the Louisiana chapter of the National Conference of Black Mayors.

Mayor Davis is married to the former Georgia West of Farmerville, and is the father of five children and grandfather of 11 children (one deceased).

THE HONORABLE

ALFRED DIXON

MAYOR OF
GREENEVERS, NORTH CAROLINA

The Honorable Alfred Dixon became the second mayor of the town of Greenevers, North Carolina in November of 1986 at the age of 30. Greenevers was established in 1969 by local community leaders and the former mayor, Alex Brown.

Mayor Dixon received a bachelor of science degree from North Carolina Central University. After receiving a master's degree in city and regional planning from Howard University, he decided to move back to North Carolina to share his knowledge of city planning with his state, county, and community.

Dixon is also the president of Multi-State Contracting Corporation, which provides general contracting services throughout the state of North Carolina.

Dixon's motto is, "Obstacles or no obstacles, there is always a way in getting something done."

THE HONORABLE

EARNESTINE DIXON

MAYOR OF
WEBB, MISSISSIPPI

The Honorable Earnestine Dixon became the second female mayor of Webb, Mississippi in June of 2001, and made history as the first African-American female mayor of Webb.

Mayor Dixon offered residents a vision and passion for making Webb a safer, cleaner, and better-constructed city for families, seniors, and children. She also provides a more open, responsive, and effective city government.

During Dixon's outstanding career she has received numerous awards. She has been a speaker at various events and had the opportunity to welcome the Honorable Ronnie Musgrove, governor of Mississippi, into Webb in June of 2004.

Dixon earned an associate of arts degree from Coahoma Community College in Clarksdale, Mississippi. She continued her education and leadership role at Tougaloo College in Jackson, Mississippi.

Mayor Dixon has been faced with some of the toughest challenges in city government, but she made it through as a firm believer that nothing easy comes on a silver platter.

THE HONORABLE

PERRY DIXON

MAYOR OF
SANDYFIELD, NORTH CAROLINA

The Honorable Perry Dixon, son of John Q. and Sallie Dixon, is a native of the Sandyfield, North Carolina community. He and his partner of 40 years, the former Rebecca J. Graham, are the parents of Tammy, Kim, Donnell, and Perry, Jr., and the grandparents of three. Dixon has eight siblings, including Willie Dixon, mayor of East Arcadia, North Carolina.

In 1963, Mayor Dixon graduated from Armour High School and moved to New Jersey, where he was trained as an automotive technician for General Motors. He opened his own business rebuilding and accessorizing cars in 1977.

In the late 1970s Dixon, the son and grandson of landowning farmers, saw the decline of the number of black farmers. He began to campaign for rural towns such as Sandyfield to get a fair share of governmental services, in order to supplement the loss of farm income.

Dixon's political career began as a community leader who successfully lobbied local and state officials for a rural activity center. He formerly served on the Ransom Activity Center board and as chairman of the advisory council of the Columbus County School Board.

In 1994, Dixon helped draft the Sandyfield town charter, and his leadership was acknowledged when he was selected as interim mayor.

Dixon served as a councilman from 1995 to 2003, and as mayor pro-temp from 1999 to 2003. He was elected mayor after a groundswell of support resulted in a write-in victory.

An ordained deacon and Sunday School superintendent, Dixon is a member of Mount Zion Missionary Baptist Church. He is also secretary for the Ministers and Deacons Union of the Middle District Missionary Baptist Association and a field representative for churches in Columbus, Brunswick, and New Hanover counties.

Mayor Dixon considers himself fortunate to be able to serve both God and his community.

THE HONORABLE

JOHNNY L. DUPREE

MAYOR OF
HATTIESBURG, MISSISSIPPI

The Honorable Johnny L. DuPree became the first African-American mayor of the City of Hattiesburg, Mississippi in July of 2001.

Mayor DuPree's civic involvement began in 1987, when he was appointed to the Hattiesburg School Board and served until 1992. He was elected three times to the Forrest County Board of Supervisors, serving from 1992 to 2001.

DuPree believes that the most effective city government is one with an active citizenry. He is working to redevelop neighborhoods within the city and improve infrastructure. One of his missions as mayor is to improve the housing conditions for the people of Hattiesburg, and he is working diligently to institute programs to address that most basic need of citizens.

Hattiesburg has received state and national recognition for two programs begun under his administration. Those are the Early Warning Weather Alert Program, which places weather radios into the homes of low-income, elderly, and disabled citizens, and the Mayor's Financial Education Initiative, which provides free tax preparation to people in the Hattiesburg area.

In addition, the Council of Neighborhoods, one of DuPree's visions when he was running for mayor, has been recognized with a second place national award for cultural diversity from the National League of Cities. The council, made up of representatives of Hattiesburg's nearly 40 organized neighborhood associations, meets quarterly to learn about things the city has planned and offer input.

Governor Ronnie Musgrove appointed Mayor DuPree to the Federal Election Reform Act Commission for Mississippi and the Tri State Southern Rapid Rail Transit Commission because of his outstanding civic work and commitment to bettering his community.

DuPree is currently pursuing a doctorate in urban studies from Jackson State University.

THE *HONORABLE*

ROLAND DYKES

MAYOR OF
NEWPORT, TENNESSEE

The Honorable Roland Dykes is the first black mayor of Newport, Tennessee. Professionally, Dykes owns a construction company, a family business that has been in operation more than half a century.

Dykes' history-making foray into public office began in 1987 when he was elected to his first term as alderman with the Newport City Council. In 1990, he was elected vice mayor, where he served until 1998 when he was appointed mayor of Newport following the death of then Mayor James Robinson. In November of 1998, Dykes was elected mayor and then reelected in 2002.

Dykes is a lifetime member of the Kiwanis Club of Newport and the recipient of the prestigious President's Award, which he received at the Kiwanis Club's first internationally held conference in Australia.

A dedicated public servant, Dykes serves on several committees and boards including the newly established Boys and Girls Club of Newport; the board of trustees for the Holston United Methodist Home for Children; Local Workforce Investment Board 2; the Newport/Cocke County Economic Development Commission board of directors; the Local Government Planning Advisory Commission; the Newport Planning Commission; and the East Tennessee Development District Board. Dykes is also president of the Tennessee Picnic Organization and a member of the Newport branch of the NAACP.

In 2001, he was named Citizen of the Century for the Senior Home Assistance. He was appointed to the Tennessee Municipal League board of directors in 2003.

His concern for the welfare of his fellow man led him on several missions to the Dominican Republic to help rebuild communities after hurricanes devastated the island in the late 1970s.

Dykes is a faithful and dedicated member of Woodlawn United Methodist Church where he has served in many capacities. He is married to Elizabeth K. Smith and they have eight adult children.

THE HONORABLE

AUDREY EDMONSON

MAYOR OF
EL PORTAL, FLORIDA

The Honorable Audrey Edmonson, a resident of El Portal, Florida since 1978, became mayor of the village in January of 1999. She served as councilperson during 2000 and 2001, and has been serving as mayor since 2002.

During the course of her exceptional career, Audrey successfully lobbied federal, state, county, and private agencies for more than $3.5 million in grant funding for village improvement projects. Her achievements include a $350,000 grant for a community outreach program; revision of the village's comprehensive plan; successful negotiation of the PBA contract; and implementation of a citizens' committee to completely revise the village charter. Likewise, Audrey successfully lobbied the state for $150,000 for a storm water master plan, as well as many other noteworthy accomplishments for her village. Under her leadership, El Portal hired a village manager for the first time.

Audrey received an associate degree from Miami-Dade Community College, a bachelor of arts degree in psychology from Florida International University, and a dual master of science degree from Barry University in marriage and family therapy and mental health counseling.

Audrey is a member of the Miami-Dade County League of Cities, a charter member of the Miami-Dade County Mayor's Roundtable, and was recently appointed to the Florida League of Cities Criminal Justice Policy Committee. She is a member of the NAACP and the board of directors of South Florida Jobs with Justice.

Audrey holds leadership and advisory roles with St. James AME Church, Delta Sigma Theta Sorority, Inc., Top Ladies of Distinction, the Just Us Social Club, and the board of directors of the Institute of Black Family Life-Gram and Me Program.

Audrey is married to Louis. She is the mother of Ebony Nicole and Louis Ivory, and the proud grandmother of Bianca Alexandria Casher.

THE *HONORABLE*

FRED ESCO, JR.

MAYOR OF
CANTON, MISSISSIPPI

On October 22, 2002, the Honorable Fred Esco, Jr. became the 21st mayor of the City of Canton, and he made history by becoming the first African-American male to be elected mayor. As mayor, Esco has a great vision for what Canton will look like in the very near future, and has implemented plans to make that vision a reality.

Esco was born on September 13, 1954 in Canton, Mississippi, to Fred Lee Esco and Ida M. Hudson. His father, now deceased, worked as a supervisor for the American Tent Company and was self-employed as a barber. His mother was a production supervisor at the Mississippi Industry for the Blind.

Esco is a graduate of the Canton Public School system, completing high school in 1972. He went on to graduate from Mississippi Valley State University with a degree in business administration and accounting, and he earned a degree from Mississippi Baptist Seminary.

Esco began his political career early. By age 24, not only was he a successful businessman, he had also been elected as alderman for Ward Five of the City of Canton. He served faithfully and achieved many prestigious accomplishments during his 18-and-a-half years in this position.

Prior to being elected mayor for the City of Canton, he was CEO of Esco's Insurance Company, a very successful entity for more than 24 years. His community involvements include the local Boys and Girls Club, and the Hispanic Outreach of Canton program. He is a Mason and a member of the Elks and the NAACP. He fondly calls Mt. Zion Missionary Baptist Church his home, where Reverend W.L. Johnson is pastor.

Esco married the lovely Fleta M. Jones in 1982, and he is the proud father of five children, four girls and one son.

THE HONORABLE

CLARENCE FIELDS

MAYOR OF
PINEVILLE, LOUISIANA

The Honorable Clarence R. Fields is a lifelong citizen of Pineville, Louisiana. He married his high school sweetheart, Rosa Ceasar Fields, in 1975. They are the proud parents of two children.

Before becoming an elected official, Mayor Fields was employed by CLECO Corp. for 22 years. While employed by CLECO Corp., he received numerous awards and certificates relating to management and supervisory roles.

In 1998, Fields felt the time had come for his generation to "give back" and make a difference in the City of Pineville and in his community. He was elected to serve as the city's District 2 council representative. In December of 1999, Fields was appointed as acting mayor. In October of 2000, he was elected to complete the unexpired term of the former mayor. In an election held in April of 2002, Fields was again chosen to serve for a full four-year term. He is the first African-American mayor elected in the City of Pineville.

Fields is an active community leader. Currently, he serves on the Rapides Regional Hospital board of directors, the Boys & Girls Club board, Salvation Army, Renaissance Home for Youth, and the LSUA Foundation board. He is vice chair of the Rapides Area Planning Commission and a member of the Louisiana Municipal Association's executive board, where he also serves as district vice president for the Central-Northeast towns and cities.

Mayor and Mrs. Fields attend Pineville First United Methodist Church, where he serves on the board of trustees. They believe God has a purpose in their lives and expects them to bless others by giving of themselves, setting the example of humility, upright living, honest leadership, and integrity. Fields knows that he has "a charge to keep and a God to glorify."

THE HONORABLE

JOHNNY FORD

MAYOR OF
TUSKEGEE, ALABAMA

The Honorable Johnny Ford was born in Midway, Alabama in Bullock County. At the age of four he was adopted by his uncle, Charlie Benjamin Ford, and was raised in Tuskegee, the home of Tuskegee University.

Mayor Ford attended elementary school at the Washington Public School and graduated in 1960 from the Tuskegee Institute High School. He received his bachelor of arts degree in history and sociology from Knoxville College and his master of public administration degree from Auburn University at Montgomery. He has received four honorary doctorate degrees.

Ford was first elected mayor of Tuskegee in 1972 and served in this position for 24 years, until 1996. He was elected in 1998 to the House of Representatives in the State of Alabama and served there until 2004, when he was reelected mayor.

Ford is the founder and director general of the World Conference of Mayors, Inc., and serves as president of Johnny Ford and Associates, Inc. He is also the president-emeritus and founder of the National Conference of Black Mayors.

Ford is a former member of the Alabama Foreign Trade Commission and the Alabama Municipal Electric Authority, and former chairman of the National Utility Alliance. He is a former U.S. presidential appointee to the Presidential Advisory Committee on Federalism and the U.S. Intergovernmental Policy Advisory Committee on Trade. President George W. Bush reappointed Ford to the policy committee in 2004. He is also a past president of the Alabama League of Municipalities.

A member of Kappa Alpha Psi, Ford is the founding president of the Tuskegee Optimist Club, and is a member of the Mount Olive Missionary Baptist Church, the home church of Dr. Booker T. Washington.

The Fords reside in Tuskegee, overlooking beautiful Lake Tuskegee. They have three children, John, Christopher, and Tiffany.

THE *HONORABLE*

ELDER FLETCHER FOUNTAIN

MAYOR OF
FORT DEPOSIT, ALABAMA

The Honorable Elder Fletcher Fountain has experienced many firsts in his life. In 1962, he became the first black male to integrate Fortex Manufacturing Company, now known as American Apparel. In 1974, Fountain was the first black male to become a full-time pastor in Lowndes County, where he also built the first modern church facility and organized the first adult day care center. He was one of the first black males to be elected to the Lowndes County Board of Education in 1974, and he is the first and only to host the World Council of Churches Conference. In 2000, Fountain became the first black male to be elected mayor of Fort Deposit, Alabama. He was reelected in 2004.

In addition to serving as mayor, Fountain is pastor of Lily Baptist Church in Letohatchee, Alabama, where he has served for 21 years. His goal is to help someone so that his life will not be lived in vain. He accepted his calling in 1970 and has served as a pastor for 34 years. He also taught school at Central and Lowndes County Middle School, but retired from teaching in 2000.

A native of Fort Deposit, Alabama, Fountain is one of nine children born to Lurlene (Thigpen) Fountain and the late Willie Robert Fountain. He received his elementary and high school education in the Lowndes County Public School System. He obtained a bachelor of science degree from Alabama State University in Montgomery, Alabama, and a bachelor's degree from Hood Theological Seminary in Salisbury, North Carolina.

He is married to Geraldine (Stiener) Fountain, and they are the proud parents of three children and two foster children.

THE HONORABLE

BETTY W. FOWLER

MAYOR OF
SUNFLOWER, MISSISSIPPI

The Honorable Betty W. Fowler is the first African American to serve as mayor of the Town of Sunflower, Mississippi since its incorporation in 1896, and the only person in history ever elected mayor of two different municipalities. She previously served as the mayor of Moorhead. Under her leadership, that city received $1.5 million in grants for housing, street improvements, and water and sewage system improvements.

Betty returned to her hometown, Sunflower, and was elected mayor in 2001. She has been featured in *Soundprint* magazine and *Pacific News Service*. The *Soundprint* article was broadcast on Public Radio of Mississippi. In 2004, she received the Harriet Tubman Award for the Northwest District of the Magnolia Bar Association.

Betty serves on the boards of the Sunflower County Economic Development District, the Mid-Delta Empowerment Zone, Rash Temple Youth Organization, and the Town of Sunflower Reunion committee.

Under Betty's administration, the mayor's office has an open door policy for all of the citizens. Her campaign, "A Woman of Action," focused on infrastructure and improving the quality of life for the citizens. In the first two years of her administration, Sunflower was awarded more than $900,000 in grants for street improvements, housing, and public facilities. In addition, the town was annexed, benefiting some 350 families who were disenfranchised by previous administrations. Betty is in the process of seeking funds to build a library, public park, and a youth recreation facility.

Betty attended Mississippi Delta Junior College and, since 1986, has been an office manager and legal assistant for the first African-American law office in Indianola, Mississippi.

She has a daughter, Taleja, a son, Kedric, and four grandchildren, Chezz, Chey, Michael, and Makail. She attends Traveler's Rest M.B. Church.

Betty's favorite quote is, "There are two sides to every story, then there is the truth."

THE HONORABLE

HELEN JOANN FOX

MAYOR OF
GRAYSON, OKLAHOMA

The Honorable Helen JoAnn Fox is the mayor of Grayson, Oklahoma. Having held this office for 12 years, she is distinguished as the first woman mayor in the 105-year history of this historically black municipality.

With degrees in human resources management and business, Mayor Fox has parlayed her academic skills and work experience into effective leadership for Grayson. She has enjoyed much success in this village of approximately 200 people, while working as a childcare specialist with the Muscogee Creek Nation.

Fox spearheaded a feasibility study to create a renewable energy utility company with Native American and African-American communities in Oklahoma, the first collaborative effort of its kind in the country. The city received a REAP grant to repair roads, drainage, and other public works issues, and money for a community center expansion.

Fox was instrumental in replacing several resident families' dilapidated homes with new manufactured housing at no cost to the residents.

As chairperson of the Grayson Development Authority, Fox successfully solicited funds for a sewer lagoon system for the city. The city has received grants from the Agriculture and Forestry Division to build a fire station; the Department of Commerce for a capitol improvement plan; and was one of 250 recipients of Wal-Mart's American Hometown Leadership Award.

The City of Grayson has received the State Arts Council's 21st Annual Governor's Art Award, the George Nigh Mayor's Award, and was the first historically black town invited to a presidential inauguration. Grayson also participated in the historically all-white Okmulgee Festival of Lights Parade.

Fox is an Eastern Oklahoma Development–Sub-State Planning District executive/board member, a Deep Fork Community Action Agency board member, and a Leadership and Pride Task Force member. She is president of the Oklahoma Conference of Black Mayors, Inc., and a Historically All-Black Town Foundation board member.

THE **HONORABLE**

MARCIA L. FUDGE, ESQ.

MAYOR OF
WARRENSVILLE HEIGHTS, OHIO

With the coming of the new millennium, history was made in Warrensville Heights, Ohio. For the first time since the city's founding, 193 years ago, an African American and a female, Marcia L. Fudge, was elected mayor.

After graduating from Shaker Heights High School, Marcia received a bachelor of science degree in business administration from The Ohio State University in 1975. She received a juris doctorate degree from Cleveland Marshall College of Law at Cleveland State University in June 1983.

Professionally, as an attorney, Marcia has had many different employment experiences, including private industry, the City of Cleveland, the City of Bedford, Cuyahoga County, the State of Ohio, and the Congress of the United States of America. Each professional position helped prepare her for her new role as mayor.

As a dedicated public servant, Marcia has developed her listening skills, sensitivity to others, ability to recognize and accept good counsel, decisiveness, flexibility, patience, and a sense of humor. She is well schooled by her previous experiences as a solo law practitioner, visiting referee, and active judge. While in these different roles, she observed, thought, and acted in accordance with her best judgment, and this helped make Marcia a success in her civic endeavors.

She currently serves on the boards of the Cleveland Public Library, Alcoa Aluminum, and the Judge Lloyd O. Brown Scholarship Committee. Marcia also gathers strength from her church, the Glenville Church of God. She has modeled her life after her mother, Marian Saffold, and she practices the principles of Delta Sigma Theta Sorority, Inc., where she is the 21st past national president.

THE HONORABLE

SARATHA A. GOGGINS

MAYOR OF
EAST CLEVELAND, OHIO

The Honorable Saratha A. Goggins is the fifth mayor of the City of East Cleveland, Ohio.

Mayor Goggins brings to the office of mayor a wealth of distinguished public service and experience. She is known statewide for her ability to mobilize constituents and her undying loyalty to the community and people that she serves.

Goggins previously held the positions of president and vice president of the East Cleveland City Council. She was first elected a member of council in 1995, and during her tenure, she chaired a number of important committees including contracts and property, general services, and administration and finance.

Most recently, she has been the driving force behind the East Cleveland 2010 Project, a collaborative of community leaders, organizations, universities, and public agencies across Cuyahoga County focused on the revitalization and rebuilding of the City of East Cleveland.

Goggins also represents her community with distinction on a national level. She is the chairman of the economic development committee of the National Black Caucus of Local Elected Officials, and was appointed to the steering committee of the National League of Cities' Economic and Community Development Initiative. In addition, she is a past president of the Cuyahoga County Section of the National Council of Negro Women.

Mayor Goggins and her husband, James, have been active residents of the City of East Cleveland for more than 30 years. She has three children, Adrian Underwood (married to Mechiel), Erica Underwood, and Rashad Goggins, and three grandchildren, Jalen, Justin, and Alexis.

THE HONORABLE

BILL GOODSON

MAYOR OF
WHITEWRIGHT, TEXAS

An elected official for 22 years, the Honorable Bill Goodson became the first black mayor in North Texas and the first black mayor of the city of Whitewright, Texas. Whitewright is comprised of 95 percent white citizens and five percent black citizens.

Mayor Goodson is involved in rural development and has concerns regarding the future of rural Texas communities. He is committed to strengthening rural communities in Texas. He was an organizer of the Highway 69 Corridor Coalition, which is made up of five cities and three county precincts.

During the course of his outstanding career, Goodson has received numerous awards from the *Dallas Morning News* and other awards including the Texas Outstanding Political Award and the Grayson County Community Development Award.

Likewise, he is the recipient of Texas Governor Rick Perry's Community Development Block Grant Award and the Floyd C. Wallace Award, the highest political award granted by the Texoma Council of Government. Only three individuals have received this award in the history of Grayson County.

Goodson earned a bachelor's degree in business and education from Bishop College, a pharmacy and business management degree from the University of San Francisco, and a business management degree from Southwest Business School.

He is a member of the Western Beauty CME Methodist Church in Whitewright.

Mayor Goodson's campaign slogan is, "Everything is Right in Whitewright; no changes needed."

THE **HONORABLE**

JANIE GLYMPH GOREE

MAYOR OF
CARLISLE, SOUTH CAROLINA

The Honorable Janie Glymph Goree is the mayor of Carlisle, South Carolina, where she made history in 1978 as first African-American woman elected to that office.

A dedicated public servant and educator, Mayor Goree taught in the Union County public school system for more than 30 years, and served as the judge of the Town of Carlisle from 1978 to 1990.

As mayor, Goree was successful in securing major grant funding to improve Carlisle's water and sewer systems, recreation areas, the fire department, and an administration building that bears her name.

Goree serves as a member of Union County's Chamber of Commerce, Department of Social Services Board, Safe Homes Network, and the World Conference of Mayors. She serves as vice chair of the South Carolina Conference of Black Mayors and continues to travel extensively to promote local government.

Goree has also served with numerous other civic, professional, and service organizations, including Delta Sigma Theta Sorority, Inc., the Grassroots Rural Development advisory board, and the Clemson Extension advisory board. She served as an executive with the Democratic Party from 1976-1982, and in the Black Women's Caucus of the National Conference of Black Mayors.

Goree has been recognized by organizations such as the Southern Christian Leadership Conference, the Metropolitan Women's Democratic Club of Washington, D.C., and the National Alliance of Business. Southern Bell's South Carolina African American History Calendar, the National Council of Negro Women, and the South Carolina Conference of Black Mayors have also honored her.

Mayor Goree graduated magna cum laude from Benedict College and earned a master's degree from the University of Colorado. She attended the University of South Carolina, The University of Wyoming, The University of Notre Dame, and South Carolina State College.

She is a member of Seekwell Baptist Church.

THE HONORABLE

GEORGE L. GRACE, SR.

MAYOR OF
ST. GABRIEL, LOUISIANA

The Honorable George L. Grace, Sr. was appointed in 1994 by Louisiana Governor Edwin Edwards as the first mayor of the newly incorporated Town of St. Gabriel. In April of 1995, he was elected to the position.

Mayor Grace was elected unopposed in 2003 for his third term as mayor of St. Gabriel. During his tenure as mayor, he has plotted a vision for the growing community. His blueprint for success has led to St. Gabriel's statewide, national, and international recognition including economic and community development, growth and development of affordable housing, and the completion of the St. Gabriel Community Center. St. Gabriel received city designation in 2001.

Grace has a bachelor of science degree in education and a master's degree in administration and supervision from Southern University and A&M College in Baton Rouge, Louisiana. He was formerly the state vocational director, a teacher, and a coach.

Grace's present affiliations include the Iberville Parish Strategic Planning Committee, the Louisiana Municipal Association, St. Gabriel Kiwanis Club, and the Black Men's Society of St. Gabriel. He also serves as the third vice president of the National Conference of Black Mayors, immediate past chairman of the Louisiana Community Development Authority, and member of the Iberville Municipal Association.

Grace coined the city slogan, "No matter where you are going, you can get there from St. Gabriel!"

THE HONORABLE

PHAEDRA GRAHAM

MAYOR OF
RIVERDALE, GEORGIA

When the Honorable Phaedra Graham became mayor of Riverdale, Georgia, she set a new standard. She became Clayton County and Riverdale's first African-American mayor. With hard work and a strong team of supporters, Graham's vision for a new Riverdale was set in motion in 2003. Her vision has the entire community excited about the new changes in Riverdale.

Graham loves being the "People's Mayor" because she enjoys direct involvement in government and the opportunity to enhance the lives of people. She lives by her own words, "As in life, and in any race, enter to win." Everywhere she goes Graham desires to win the hearts of people by empowering them to get involved in their community.

Graham participates in the Clayton County National Council of Negro Women, Toastmasters, the East Point/College Park chapter of Delta Sigma Theta Sorority, Inc., and many other community groups.

A graduate of the University of North Florida and Clark Atlanta University, Graham knows the importance of getting a good education and using that knowledge to improve the lives of people in the community. Currently, she is a high school English instructor in Clayton County, Georgia. Graham loves to read and listen to classical music, and she aspires to become an author of children's books.

THE *HONORABLE*

ANTHONY GRANT

MAYOR OF
EATONVILLE, FLORIDA

The Honorable Anthony Grant is chief executive officer of Eatonville, Florida, which has a population of 2,500. The mayor is responsible for the delivery of government services with the help of approximately 42 public employees. The chief administrative officer and the appointed division directors assist him in the day-to-day operations of town government.

A native of Orlando and a lifelong resident of Eatonville, Mayor Grant was elected to this office in March of 1994. He earned unique distinction as the youngest African-American mayor of the 388 who were elected to office in the United States in 1994. Before his election, Grant attended Edgewater High School and Seminole College.

Along with serving two successful stints on the Eatonville Town Council, Grant has received several awards for outstanding public service, including a recent nomination for the Good Government Award, presented by the West Orange Jaycees.

Grant is a member of the NAACP, Florida League of Cities, the Orange County Community Action Agency, the Local Council of Governments Florida Recreation and Parks Association, Inc., and the National Forum for Black Public Administrators. He is an honorary board member for Preserve The Eatonville Community, Inc.

Grant presently serves as treasurer for the National Conference of Black Mayors and vice president of the Florida Conference of Black Mayors. He has also devoted time to civic and service organizations including the United Way and NAACP. Grant has been instrumental in the development of Eatonville's senior citizens network efforts. He is also a proud member of Macedonia Missionary Baptist Church.

Mayor Grant is married to Lisa Grant. They have five children, Adasha, Donte, Teddy, Adrian, and Briana. His hobbies include fishing, tennis, and traveling.

THE HONORABLE

EUGENE W. GRANT

MAYOR OF
SEAT PLEASANT, MARYLAND

The Honorable Eugene W. Grant, mayor of Seat Pleasant, Maryland, was born in Los Angeles, California and lived across the United States before settling in the Washington, D.C. area. In 1989, he started a non-profit organization under the name Mid-County Youth Services, which he still runs today as Global Developmental Services for Youth, Inc. Through this international organization, based in Seat Pleasant for almost 16 years, Grant has affected the lives of well over 3,500 youth worldwide. He has worked with governors, congressmen, and presidents, both foreign and domestic, to improve the lives of youth in the United States, the Caribbean, and Africa, particularly.

Grant has been a leader in the community through various boards and commissions that he has served on, such as being appointed to President Clinton's Crime Bill Committee and the Governor's Task Force on Systems Reform. He has also served on the Prince George's Sheriff's Advisory Board, Prince George's Department of Corrections Community Advisory Board, and Prince George's Police Chief's Advisory Council, which he chaired in 2002. He has also lectured young college students on leadership skills at several universities, including Bowie State University and James Madison University.

Grant has received recognition in *Who's Who Among Global Business Leaders* and *Who's Who Among Entrepreneurs*. He has also received the Distinguished Business Leader Award from Congressman Robert Ehrlich, Jr. and the prestigious Phoenix Award from Mayor Shirley Franklin of Atlanta.

On September 13, 2004, Grant was elected by his community to serve as the 11th mayor of the City of Seat Pleasant. As mayor, he introduced a new city motto: "Seat Pleasant: A City of Excellence." He has boosted employee morale, led community cleanups, and directed the police department to increase activity, which has resulted in a significant reduction in crime throughout the city.

THE HONORABLE

ROBERT L. GRAYSON

**MAYOR OF
TUTWILER, MISSISSIPPI**

The Honorable Robert L. Grayson is the first African-American mayor of Tutwiler, Mississippi.

Born on May 10, 1941 in Tulsa, Oklahoma, Mayor Grayson is a 1960 graduate of West District High School.

Grayson is a 20-year Vietnam veteran who received the Purple Heart, Silver Star, Bronze Star with Oak Leaf Cluster, and CIB Badge. He retired from the Mississippi Department of Corrections after 30 years of dedicated service.

Active in the community, Grayson is the president of the Jerome G. Little Minor Board, the vice chairman of the Tallahatchie Housing Board, and vice chairman of the Aaron E. Henry Health Care Board. In addition, he is council on the Tutwiler Board of Aldermen, campaign coordinator for the Democratic Party of Tallahatchie County, and a member of the Minister Alliance Board and the Grafton Gray Burdy Kegler Minor Board.

Grayson has dedicated his life to helping the people in his community, and never takes no for an answer. The work that he does is not just for his family, but for all of the people he serves in Tallahatchie County and the surrounding areas.

Mayor Grayson has been married for 30 years to Rosie Hilson Grayson. They have five children, Travis, Shelia, Daven, Corey, and Jarvis.

THE HONORABLE

EMMA R. GRESHAM

MAYOR OF
KEYSVILLE, GEORGIA

The Honorable Emma R. Gresham is the first mayor of Keysville, Georgia since 1933 and the first and only black female mayor in Burke County and the Central Savannah River Area.

The town of Keysville was incorporated in 1890. White politicians disassembled the city's government in 1933, and the black residents were stripped of their right to vote. Mayor Gresham was elected in 1988, the first municipal election in 55 years. The town has since purchased land, resurfaced streets, and built a fire station and a new post office. In 2004, an open house and ribbon cutting were held for Keysville's first municipal building.

Gresham is retired from the Richmond County School System after teaching for 32 years. Her years in the classroom, with Cub Scouts, and with YPD were her training ground to become a leader, teacher, and a committed mayor.

Gresham is the secretary of the trustee board, secretary of the Lay, and devotional leader of the Missionary Society at her church, Mt. Tabor. She is a member of the National Council of Negro Women and the American Association of University Women.

Gresham is an honor graduate of Boggs Academy and Paine College, and studied at Atlanta University, Augusta State College, and the University of Georgia.

In 2000, Gresham was one of the One Hundred Eckerd Women honored by the Eckerd Organization in Washington, D.C. She was also an *Essence* Awards honoree.

Mayor Gresham is the daughter of Rev. Marvin Rhodes and Mrs. Ida B. Rhodes. She is the youngest of eight children. The wife of the late Quinten G. Gresham Sr., she is the mother of one son, stepmother of one son, and mother of three daughters. Three of her children are AME ministers, Rev. Quinten G. Gresham Jr., Rev. Laverne Comer, and Minister Lola Russell.

THE *HONORABLE*

FLOYD L. GRIFFIN, JR.

MAYOR OF
MILLEDGEVILLE, GEORGIA

The Honorable Floyd L. Griffin, Jr. has been a cadet, Vietnam helicopter pilot, Army colonel, football coach, professor, businessman, state senator, and mayor. Throughout his life of change and challenges, he has remained a dedicated public servant.

In 2000, Floyd Griffin was elected the first African-American mayor of the Old Capitol City of Milledgeville, Georgia. He did this after having distinguished himself in 1994 as the first African American in modern times to be elected Georgia state senator in a rural legislative district containing a majority of white voters.

Since taking office as the mayor of the City of Milledgeville, Griffin remains a force to be reckoned with in Georgia, where he serves as the president of the Georgia Conference of Black Mayors. He is active in a number of organizations, which include Sigma Pi Phi, the American Legion, Prince Hall of Free & Accepted Masons, Nations War College Association, Omega Psi Phi Fraternity (life member), and the 100 Black Men Organization of Milledgeville and Baldwin County. He also serves on several local, state, and national boards. In 2002 he was presented The James Wimberly Racial Barrier Breaker Award and saluted as one of the 2002 recipients of The National History Makers in Chicago, Illinois.

Griffin holds a bachelor of science degree in building construction from Tuskegee University and master of science degree in contract and procurement management from Florida Institute of Technology. He holds an associate of science degree in funeral service from Gupton Jones College. He is a graduate of the Army Command and General Staff College and the National War College.

Griffin is vice president of Slater's Funeral Home, Inc., a 40-year-old family-owned business. He is married to the former Nathalie Huffman and they have two sons and four grandsons.

THE HONORABLE

MIMS HACKETT, JR.

MAYOR OF
ORANGE TOWNSHIP, NEW JERSEY

In January 2004, the Honorable Mims Hackett, Jr., mayor of Orange Township, New Jersey, was sworn in for a second term as a member of the New Jersey Assembly, representing the 27th District.

Mayor Hackett has taken measures to improve the quality of life for residents and merchants in Orange. Under his leadership, the city abated an $8 million budget deficit, creating a more efficient government. The city also enjoys partnerships with New Jersey Transit and the New Community Corporation.

Hackett has a special interest in programs for the community's youth. In coordination with the Orange Board of Education, the city launched the Extended School Day Program for junior and senior high school students. The mayor recently established a Junior Police Academy to expose children to discipline, hard work, public safety careers, and conflict resolution.

Hackett believes that children are the products of the environment created for them. He believes citizens should see to it that children have the resources and support to achieve academically and socially. Through the Mims Hackett Civic Association, he provides scholarships to deserving students.

In addition, Hackett is a board of trustees member for the Orange Public Library, the E.O.F. Program at the University of Medicine and Dentistry of New Jersey, and the School of Pharmacy at Rutgers University. He is a member of Bethel Baptist Church and Bethel Lodge #10 F&A M Prince Hall.

Hackett holds a bachelor's degree from Paul Quinn AME College and a master's degree from Seton Hall University. He spent 32 years as a science teacher in the Union City Board of Education, where he was named Teacher of the Year.

A native of Birmingham, Alabama, Mayor Hackett has been married to wife, Bernice, for 42 years. They have lived in Orange for 36 years, and have six adult children.

THE HONORABLE

HILLIARD L. HAMPTON, JR.

MAYOR OF
INKSTER, MICHIGAN

The Honorable Hilliard L. Hampton, Jr. currently serves as mayor of the City of Inkster, Michigan. Previously, he served in a variety of capacities including sheriff deputy, city councilman, deputy, airport policeman, teacher, wastewater specialist, and owner of Hampton Security, Inc.

Professionally, Hampton has served as a commissioner of the Detroit Water and Sewage Department; a board member of the Wayne County Youth Association; a school board member of Thomas-Gist Academy; and a member of the Southeast Michigan Council of Governments. He has served on the presidential search committee of Wayne County Community College; as a trustee of the Inkster Board of Education; as chairman of the Inkster Planning Commission; as commissioner of the Inkster Building Authority; and as a presidential delegate of the Democratic National Convention. Likewise, he has served on a Charity Golf Outing Committee, on the Executive Board of Local 1659, A.F.S.C.M.E., and as steward of Local 1659, A.F.S.C.M.E. Hampton has also made charitable contributions to Goodfellows, the Optimist Club, and the Kamalaw White Foundation.

In the community, Hampton actively participates as a baseball coach in the Inkster Recreation Program. He is a member of the Inkster Goodfellows, the 13th Congressional District Democratic Party, the Optimist Club, the Kamalaw White Foundation, and the Police and Fire Pension Board. Hampton is also a founder and editor of *The Inkster Democrat* newspaper, and a commissioner on the Downtown Development Authority.

Hampton is a graduate of Robichaud High School and the Wayne County Sheriff Training Unit. He holds a bachelor of arts degree from Wayne State University, and an associate of arts degree from Wayne County Community College.

Born in Ypsilanti, Michigan, Hampton is married to Marcella Hampton, and has three children. He attends Holy Family Catholic Church in Inkster.

THE HONORABLE

CLIFTON HARRIS

MAYOR OF
ARCOLA, MISSISSIPPI

In 1986, the Honorable Clifton Harris became the first African-American mayor of Arcola, Mississippi, and the second black mayor in Washington County. His vision was to move Arcola out of its state of disrepair by building and repairing the infrastructure. In addition, adequate fire protection, housing, and a municipal building were needed.

Mayor Harris' years of service have been rewarding. Today, the citizens of Arcola have new streets, a new municipal building, a fire station, and an ongoing project to eradicate all substandard homes. Arcola is 98 percent crime-free and is a great family environment. Harris has lived up to his campaign promise, "Elect me, and I will work hard to make this a city to be proud of."

Harris has received numerous awards during his tenure, and has been featured in several publications, including *Who's Who Among African-Americans,* the *Delta Democrat Times*, the *Deer Creek Pilot*, and the *Delta Business Journal.*

A graduate of Delta Community College, Harris has continuing education credits from Clark-Atlanta University and Howard University. He is a member of Pilgrim Rest Baptist Church, where he serves as a deacon and superintendent of Sunday school.

Mayor Harris and his wife, Maxine, have three children. He enjoys golf and carpentry.

THE HONORABLE

EDWARD L. HARRIS

MAYOR OF
RICHWOOD, LOUISIANA

The Honorable Edward L. Harris is the third mayor of the Town of Richwood, Louisiana. He is currently serving his fifth term as mayor. In 1984, Harris gave up his financially rewarding nursing career to become the mayor of Richwood. At the time, Richwood was an insolvent community, financially unable to conduct business without the mayor signing his personal signature on promissory notes.

Harris' ultimate goal is to procure independence for Richwood through an established tax base, and placing a high value on education. Through his vision and participation on the East Ouachita Task Force committee, appointed by the Ouachita Parish School Board, he was instrumental in getting Richwood High School (closed in 1987) reestablished in a newly developed facility in 2001.

Harris has been recognized as Most Persistent President and Mayor while serving as president of the Louisiana chapter Conference of Black Mayors. He was also honored as an Outstanding Public Servant in Louisiana.

Harris' dedication to community development is taking the Town of Richwood to new heights.

THE HONORABLE

PATRICIA HENDERSON

MAYOR OF
EDMONDSON, ARKANSAS

The Honorable Patricia Henderson became the first woman mayor of Edmondson, Arkansas in January of 1999. This election was Henderson's start in politics. She decided that she would be most effective as mayor and not as a member of City Council. Her campaign slogan was, "If not me, then who…if not now, then when?" Edmondson is a small African-American community in the southwest of Crittenden County, Arkansas. In addition to her part-time duties as mayor, Henderson is a full-time senior programmer analyst at Methodist Healthcare of Memphis.

During her career as mayor, Henderson has been very instrumental in making Edmondson a cleaner, safer, rural community. She personally wrote and administered a fun park grant. The new park development, Lloyd Campbell Community Park, was named after a former councilman. Other notable accomplishments during Henderson's tenure include the establishment of a police department with funding from COPS, and the erection of a new four-bay fire station.

Henderson is an active member of the Crittenden County NAACP, a member of the Crittenden County Democratic Central Committee, secretary of the Arkansas Conference of Black Mayors, and a member of the National Conference of Black Mayors. She also serves as secretary of the Brilliant Light chapter of the Order of the Eastern Star.

Henderson has a wealth of new technology and computer experience, which she shares with neighbors and friends. She is a very organized, aggressive, quality-driven person who volunteers many hours assisting fellow elected officials and organizations that seek her assistance. Henderson is a member of First Baptist Church in Edmondson.

She attended Memphis State University before receiving a degree in information systems management, with high honors, from East Arkansas Community College in Forrest City, Arkansas.

Henderson is a single parent of a teenage son, Brandon, and a daughter, MyKeya.

THE HONORABLE

DONALD R. HILL

MAYOR OF
TAYLOR, TEXAS

The Honorable Donald R. Hill, mayor of Taylor, Texas, was first elected to the Taylor City Council in April of 1986, after a lawsuit to establish single-member districts. He has been reelected six times.

In 1991, Mayor Hill was elected by his fellow council members to serve as mayor. He was elected to that post again in 1992, 1993, 1997, 1998, 1999, 2003, and 2004. For three months in 1991, he was acting city manager, and again for 14 months in 1997-1999. During his 14 months as city manager and mayor, the citizens passed an $8 million bond package for major infrastructure work. A successful trip, and presentations at Wall Street, Standard & Poor, and the Moody Organization enabled the city to have a better bond rating.

Based on presentations by Hill, the Governor's Regional Review Committee ranked the City of Taylor highly enough to receive numerous grants in the 1990s (five annual grants in seven years at $250,000 per annum) and an additional planning grant of $50,000. In March of 2003, Hill gave a presentation to the Regional Review Committee that ranked first out of 28 applicants.

Hill has served on numerous boards including 12 years of service to the Regional Council of Government's executive board and nine years on the Texas Workforce Commision board. In 1993, voters approved the creation of an economic development department, and the mayor served on this board for ten years.

In 2004, Hill was given the Citizen of the Year Award. This award has only been given to one other African American, Dr. J. L. Dickey, who received this award in 1953.

Both Mayor Hill and his wife of 43 years, Leslie, are active in their church, community, and county. They have four children.

THE HONORABLE

PATSY JO HILLIARD

MAYOR OF
EAST POINT, GEORGIA

The Honorable Patsy Jo Hilliard was inaugurated as the first woman mayor of East Point, Georgia on January 5, 1993. She was reelected for a third term in November of 2001. Hilliard is the first female African-American mayor in the metropolitan Atlanta area, and the first female mayor in the 117th year of the City of East Point.

Hilliard brings a vision of leadership and passion to improve the quality of life, economic development, cultural enrichment, and national and international recognition to the citizens of East Point. She has led the city through the years of citizen emigration and the loss of business, to a great recovery that can now be seen, with an even brighter future ahead.

Hilliard has been showered with many local, state, national, and international awards for her work. She has also been elected and appointed to various local, state, and national leadership positions by her peers in other elected offices.

A native of Denver, Colorado, Hilliard earned a bachelor's degree and a master's degree from San Francisco State University. She has also found the time to provide leadership in numerous community organizations while maintaining great family relationships.

THE HONORABLE

MELVIN HOLDEN

MAYOR OF EAST BATON ROUGE PARISH, LOUISIANA

After a distinguished 20-year career in public service, Senator Melvin "Kip" Holden was inaugurated mayor-president of East Baton Rouge Parish, Louisiana on January 3, 2005. Throughout his career, Mayor Holden has worked to improve education and has been honored for his accomplishments. Providing leadership in the efforts to build better classrooms through technology was a cornerstone of his campaign, and he received the support of numerous teacher and educator associations in his election.

A coalition builder, Holden attracted a broad base of support throughout the parish, defeating the incumbent mayor-president by a margin of 54 percent to 46 percent to become the first African-American mayor in parish history.

Holden is a graduate of both Baton Rouge universities, earning a bachelor of arts degree in journalism from Louisiana State University, a master's degree in journalism from Southern University, and a juris doctorate degree from Southern University School of Law. He was also invited to study at the Oxford University Round Table in England.

With experience on the Metro Council and as a member of the Louisiana House of Representatives and Senate, Holden has taken office with extensive knowledge of East Baton Rouge Parish government.

Holden assembled a diverse team of over 100 community leaders, citizens, and university students to form his Green Light Baton Rouge Citizens Council to help develop plans to make Baton Rouge America's next great city and set priorities for his administration.

Born in New Orleans on August 12, 1952, Mayor Holden is married to Lois Stevenson Holden and is the father of five children, Melvin, II, Angela, Monique, Myron, and Brian Michael. He is a member of Greater King David Baptist Church.

THE HONORABLE

DAROLD PETER HONORÉ, JR.

MAYOR OF
LITHONIA, GEORGIA

The Honorable Darold Peter Honoré, Jr. was elected to his first term as mayor of the City of Lithonia, Georgia on November 4, 2003. Located in the far southeast corner of DeKalb County, Lithonia has a long and rich history as the "City of Granite."

A native of New Orleans, Louisiana, Darold comes from a family of craftsmen, and he is a third generation carpenter. This skill, which he learned as a child, has become invaluable. In 2000, he and his wife, Tammy, moved to Lithonia from greater DeKalb County and purchased what was the county's first library. Together, they have taken what once was a dilapidated victim of old age and neglect, devoted their time to it, and have refurbished it into a magnificent home, room by room. Darold felt compelled to do the same for the city, and in September of 2003 he placed his hat in the ring and ran for mayor. During the final days of the election, Darold and Tammy received their greatest gift from God, a newborn son, Darold III.

In addition to serving as mayor, Darold is self-employed and has served as president of Square One Mortgage L.L.C. since 1999. Prior to that, he was president and vice president of Fresh Start Mortgage Services and H & R Real Estate Services, respectively.

A graduate of Georgia State University, Darold is a member of New Birth Baptist Church and the Metro DeKalb Kiwanis Club. He is also a board member of the Greater Lithonia Neighborhood Development Corporation and the DeKalb Board of Health.

Darold ran his mayoral campaign on the theme, "Renewing the Spirit of Lithonia." He is committed to developing the City of Lithonia into DeKalb's focal point for community, cultural, and economic development.

THE HONORABLE

R. C. HORN

MAYOR OF
JASPER, TEXAS

The Honorable R. C. Horn has served as mayor of Jasper, Texas since 1997, and will serve the maximum six-year term limit. As mayor, Horn created and constructed the Jasper Airport Industrial Park, erected the new city police station, and effectively managed the crisis situation resulting from the James Byrd murder.

Prior to his service as mayor, Horn was a city councilman with the City of Jasper from 1989 to 1997. From 1991 to 2000, he served as president of the Robinson Community Funeral Home. He was a shipping manager with Visador Corporation from 1966 to 1995, where he received the Tom Bell Performance Award for Excellence. Horn also served as a sergeant first class in the U.S. Army from 1952 until his honorable discharge in 1956. He graduated with a bachelor's degree in business administration from Texas Southern University in 1958.

Horn was chairman of the board of directors for the Jasper Economic Development Corporation from 1992 to 2001. He is secretary of the Sam Rayburn Municipal Power Agency in Livingston, Texas; chairman of World Services for the Blind, District 2S-1, Little Rock, Arkansas; and a member of the Nafud Temple #80 in Beaumont, Texas. A past president of the Jasper Evening Lions Club, Horn is a 33° Mason of the Masonic Temple of Jasper, and a member of American Legion Post #78. He also sits on the Jasper-Newton Health District board of directors, and the deacon board at Dixie Missionary Baptist Church.

In addition, Horn received the Congress of Racial Equality Racial Harmony Award in Washington, D.C. He is also a recipient of the Highest Recognition Award from the U.S. Department of Justice.

He has been married to Mary Lue Horn for 45 years, and they have five children and grandchildren.

THE HONORABLE

MONICA M. HUDDLESTON

MAYOR OF
GREENDALE, MISSOURI

The Honorable Monica M. Huddleston was elected mayor of the City of Greendale, Missouri in St. Louis County on April 8, 2003. This is her first time holding public office. She is the first female and the first African-American mayor of Greendale.

Huddleston engineered several other 'firsts' for the city. She was successful in getting a capital improvement sales tax and bond issue passed in her first year as mayor. The revenue raised funded the replacement of the city's deteriorated sidewalks and driveway aprons that were neglected for many years. Also, more than $74,000 in grants received in 2004 and 2005 funded an increased recycling awareness campaign, the planting of many new trees, and construction of a new park pavilion. The City of Greendale has 722 people, 350 households, and seven businesses.

Huddleston received a bachelor of arts degree in economics from the George Washington University, Washington, D.C. in 1975, and a master of arts degree in telecommunications management from Webster University in St. Louis, Missouri in 1999. After more than 25 years of service to SBC, Inc., Huddleston retired as director of central office operations-Eastern Missouri in 2000.

Huddleston received the 2005 Woman of Excellence Award from Nerinx Hall High School in Webster Groves, Missouri, her alma mater, for fostering diversity. She also received the 1989 KPLR-TV St. Louis Community Leadership Award, 1991 United Negro College Fund Volunteer of the Year, 1993 *St. Louis Sentinel* newspaper Signal Award, and selection as a 1996 Olympic Torch runner.

Huddleston was president of the National Association of Black Telecommunications Professionals, Inc. (NABTP) from 1996 to 2000. Her past board memberships include Nerinx Hall High School, University City Residential Service, Equity Community Foundation, and St. Louis Federation of Block Units, an Urban League affiliate.

THE HONORABLE

FRANK D. JACKSON

MAYOR OF
PRAIRIE VIEW, TEXAS

The Honorable Frank D. Jackson was born and raised in Luling, Texas. He is the second of three sons born to Robbie Jackson, Sr. and Willie Louise Jackson.

Jackson graduated from Luling High School in 1969, and entered Prairie View A&M College during the fall semester of the same year. He majored in geography and earned a four-year scholarship as a naval science student. He graduated from Prairie View A&M in 1973 with a bachelor of arts degree, and was commissioned as an ensign in the United States Navy. In 1995, Mayor Jackson was promoted to the rank of captain in the U.S. Naval Reserves.

He served on City Council for the City of Prairie View for 12 years, and spent eight years as county commissioner of Precinct Three, Waller County, Texas. Jackson was elected mayor of the City of Prairie View on May 4, 2002, and was reelected to serve a second term on May 8, 2004.

In addition, Jackson is president and fire chief of the Prairie View Volunteer Fire Fighting Association, Inc., and a past master of Lone Star Lodge #85 in Hempstead, Texas. He currently serves as grand historian for the Most Worshipful Prince Hall Grand Lodge of Texas.

He is married to the former Marian Elaine Jones, and is the father of four children, Tracy, Ayanna, Cheikh, and Okofo. The Jacksons have one grandson, Chazrel.

As mayor, Jackson has been very instrumental in moving the City of Prairie View forward. He works closely with the faculty, staff, and students of Prairie View A&M University. As a historically African-American city, it is vital that everyone work together for the greater good to transcend both internal and external threats.

Jackson's motto is, "It will be a whole lot better if we just do it together."

THE *HONORABLE*

JOHN JACKSON

MAYOR OF
WHITE HALL, ALABAMA

The Honorable John Jackson, a native of Lowndes County, has served as mayor of White Hall for the past 22 years. He has worked tirelessly to help elect black city, county, and state government officials. In 1972, he ran unsuccessfully for tax assessor of Lowndes County. Thus began his political career. In 1978, he conceived the idea and initiated the incorporation of the City of White Hall. He became its second mayor in 1982. Over the last 22 years, he has constructed a community complex, a million-dollar water system, improved the streets, and added fire, police, and ambulance services. These accomplishments were made possible by collaboration with other cities, such as Washington, Atlanta, and Selma.

Jackson appointed the first black female judge and police chief in Lowndes County, and he completed major renovations to senior homes. He is a founder of Sellers Memorial Christian Church, Sellers Day Care Center, and the NBA Christian Services for Children in Alabama and Northwest Florida.

Jackson organized the Jonathan Daniels monument movement, and ran for governor of Alabama against George C. Wallace in 1986. In 1987, he was awarded an honorary doctoral degree from Selma University. Jackson was chosen as one of the Outstanding Young Men in America in 1981. He received the Trailblazer Award from Alpha Kappa Alpha Sorority, Inc., Zeta Eta Omega chapter in 2005. Additionally, he has been featured in numerous news articles and has traveled to China, Russia, and Puerto Rico.

Jackson studied at Tuskegee Institute, Alabama State University, and the University of Michigan. He is married to Dr. Katie Welch Jackson, and is the father of two children, Nina and Kevin. Jackson is the son of the late Matthew and Emma (nee Peterson) Jackson. He is "Papa" to three grandchildren.

THE HONORABLE

VELMA HILL JENKINS, PH.D.

MAYOR OF
SHUQUALAK, MISSISSIPPI

The Honorable Dr. Velma Hill Jenkins is the mayor of Shuqualak, Mississippi. A retired educator of more than 33 years, she is currently a contract consultant for the Mississippi State Department of Education Office of Assessment and Evaluation.

During her tenure in Shuqualak, Mayor Jenkins has sought federal and state grant funds to help improve the quality of life for the citizens, receiving a total sum of some four million dollars. This has funded projects including six new homes for families who lived in substandard housing, a sewer upgrade, new and resurfaced streets, a new fire station, and a youth program that has resulted in zero youth offenses and violence.

Jenkins has spent her adult life trying to make a positive difference in the lives of the boys and girls of Noxubee County. She taught senior English for 13 years, and later served as principal of B. F. Liddell Middle School, Earl Nash Elementary School, and Noxubee County High School.

A Prince Hall Affiliate Eastern Star, Jenkins is a member of Nu Epsilon Omega Chapter of Alpha Kappa Alpha Sorority, Inc., and the ladies auxiliary of the Veterans of Foreign Wars. She is a board member of Community Counseling, Inc., and United Management Systems, Inc.

Jenkins is an honor graduate of B. F. Liddell High School, a 1971 cum laude graduate of Jackson State College, and she holds a master's degree from Mississippi State University. She earned a doctorate of philosophy degree in educational leadership.

Mayor Jenkins is married to Hal Lee Jenkins. She is the biological mother to Hal Lavelle, Holli Lavette, and Lonnie Alonzo Jenkins, II, and a chosen mother to Franklin and Gregory Hill, and Trichia Hill Moore. She is the youngest of 16 children born to the late Alonzo Hill, Jr., and Pauline Slaughter Hill.

THE HONORABLE

REV. MALCOLM S. JOHNSON

MAYOR OF
DOVER, NORTH CAROLINA

The Honorable Malcolm S. Johnson is a native of Dover, North Carolina and the town's first African-American mayor. He is currently serving his third term as the mayor of Dover. Some of his major focuses are the youth and senior citizens programs that provide opportunities and assistance for the Dover residents. One of Mayor Johnson's major goals is to provide the town with its first sewage system. Work for the new system should become a realistic project this spring.

Johnson attended the Craven County School System and graduated from West Craven High School in 1972. He completed further study at Mt. Olive College and received a bachelor's degree in business management and a master's degree in biblical studies from Friends International Christian University.

Johnson has been in the ministry for 26 years, with 25 of those years as a pastor. He is a member of the Church of Christ's Goldsboro-Raleigh Assembly. The district elder of the Ghana, West Africa Assembly, he is an honorary African tribal chief.

Mayor Johnson is currently the pastor of St. Rose Church of Christ, DOC in Wilson, North Carolina.

THE *HONORABLE*

CAROLYN JONES

MAYOR OF
KENDLETON, TEXAS

The Honorable Carolyn Jones is currently serving her fourth term as mayor of the City of Kendleton. Her goal is to promote an open forum between the mayor's office, the city council, and the citizens. Prior to serving as mayor, Jones was a councilperson and mayor pro tempore for approximately 12 years. She was entered into state and national registries as the first African-American woman to be elected to a city council and as mayor pro tempore in the Texas Gulf Coast area.

Mayor Jones served many years with the Richmond State School for Mental Health and Mental Retardation. She assisted in organizing the Kendleton Senior Citizens Center, where she was site coordinator/nutritionist for several years. Also an entrepreneur, she established the Blue Jay Janitorial Service.

A graduate of the Fort Bend Chamber's Leadership Class of 2002-2003, Jones is a member of the National and State Conferences of Black Mayors, and a former member of the Houston-Galveston Area Council and the Fort Bend County 99 Year Flood Planning Committee.

Jones' involvement extends to the Kendleton Independent School District as a volunteer, substitute, and a member of the Powell Point PTO. Her other memberships include the Kendleton Floral Club, Worthy Counselor of the Silver Star Court of Calanthe #184, Deputy of the Regional III District Courts of Calantheans, and the AARP.

Jones was born in and remains a life-long resident of Kendleton and Fort Bend County, where she is the fifth generation of freed slaves. She is the proud mother of four children, Nellie, John, Larry, and Sheila, and ten grandchildren. She continues to serve the church as a lay leader, administrative board chairperson, usher board president, and a member of the United Methodist Women.

Her hobbies include traveling, crabbing, and sewing.

THE *HONORABLE*

CECIL JONES

MAYOR OF
TATUMS, OKLAHOMA

The Honorable Cecil Jones has served as mayor of Tatums, Oklahoma for 26 years. He served on the town council for 31 years, and was town clerk/treasurer for three years.

The eldest child of Clarence, Sr. and Delia Mae Worley Jones, Cecil was born on June 11, 1927 in Tatums, Oklahoma. He attended Tatums High School and went on to attend various other schools of higher education. He completed studies at Mechanical Arts Training School, Ardmore Higher Education, the University of Oklahoma, Tinker Field Air Force Base, the University of Atlanta, and the University of Florida.

Jones was president of the Tri-County NAACP and president of the local Tatums T-Okie Club for two years. A member of the Urban League, he is a past president of the Community Action Agency. He was a scoutmaster in Oklahoma City for four years and in Tatums for two. Jones is one of the five originators of the Oklahoma Conference of Black Mayors, where he served on the board for 12 years. He is also a charter member of the National Conference of Black Mayors, and he been a national board member of the organization for 12 years. Under Governor Henry Bellman, Jones was an Oklahoma fire safety improvement commissioner for the southeast quarter of the state.

Additionally, Jones served in the United States Army. He retired from the Phillips Oil Company after 20 years, and retired from Tinker Air Force Base after 21 years of service. He is the building/fund secretary/treasurer for Bethel Baptist Church.

Jones was married to Cecilia B. Tydings Jones (deceased) and Flora M. Houston (deceased). He has seven children, Cecil II, Clevonia, Ceon, Celano, Cleta, Cemitri, and Cedre; and 17 grandchildren. He is currently married to Lynetta Timmons-Jones, and he has one stepdaughter, Andrea R. Johnson, and four step-grandchildren.

THE HONORABLE

LINZEY D. JONES

VILLAGE PRESIDENT OF
OLYMPIA FIELDS, ILLINOIS

The Honorable Linzey D. Jones became the first African-American village president of Olympia Fields, Illinois in April of 1997. This election underscored the transition of Olympia Fields from a virtually all-white community into one of the most diverse, yet affluent communities in the United States.

Situated near Chicago, with a median annual household income in excess of $120,000, this predominantly African-American community has become home to many prominent African-American business owners, professionals, entertainers, and athletes. It also played host to the 1997 USGA Senior Open and the 2003 USGA U.S. Open at the Olympia Fields Country Club.

Jones has been active for many years in regional leadership activities as a past president of the South Suburban Mayors and Managers Association, and as a member of the executive committee of the Metropolitan Mayors Caucus, which includes 274 mayors who represent several million people.

Jones is a partner in the law firm of Pugh, Jones, Johnson & Quandt, P.C., one of the largest black-owned law firms in the country specializing in public finance, real estate, and litigation. After his graduation from the University of Illinois College of Law, magna cum laude, he spent his first 21 years as an attorney with the international law firm of Sidley Austin Brown & Wood, where he was a partner for 12 years.

THE *HONORABLE*

W. J. JONES

MAYOR OF
COAHOMA, MISSISSIPPI

The Honorable W. J. Jones became the first mayor of the Town of Coahoma, Mississippi in 1981, after working diligently with the community to facilitate the town being incorporated.

Mayor Jones offered the residents of Coahoma a vision for improving the quality of life and the enhancement of the over-all infrastructure of the town. Through his leadership, a series of firsts were implemented in Coahoma, including running water with an elevated water tower, an EPA-approved sewage system, paved streets, street lights, a town hall with a full-time clerk, and police protection for residents.

The elimination of substandard housing for most of the residents of Coahoma was a major priority for the mayor. As a guiding force, Jones and the residents worked collaborative-ly to eliminate substandard housing with Habitat for Humanity/World Vision, who constructed 40 homes; Rural Development and private funding, which constructed a 14-unit housing project; and CDBG, which facilitated the construction of seven single-dwelling homes.

As a retired school administrator, education is of utmost importance to Jones. He has worked with many volunteers and friends of Coahoma to establish Education for Coahoma, Inc., which includes a public library, a computer lab, and a tutorial program with workers to tutor children after school.

Jones has received numerous awards and appreciation. He was featured in *Home Magazine's* "Home's Heroes," and received national recognition as the 1996 recipient of the NEA's H. Councill Trenholm Memorial Award.

Mayor Jones earned a bachelor of arts degree from Rust College, and a master of arts degree from Tuskegee Institute. He has volunteered many years of time, energy, and resources to better the lives of his constituency.

THE HONORABLE

JOSEPH L. KELLEY

MAYOR OF
OPA-LOCKA, FLORIDA

The Honorable Joseph L. Kelley, mayor of Opa-Locka, Florida, is described as anointed, powerful, gifted, and compassionate. He has been the senior pastor and teacher of the Holy Temple Missionary Baptist Church of Opa-Locka since 1989.

Under Kelley's administration, the church has expanded the sanctuary, added a fellowship hall, and made other renovations. There are 13 active auxiliary ministries in the church, with three associate ministers and 22 evangelists. Kelley appears on Comcast Cable, and under his leadership Holy Temple Human Services, Inc. was established to reach out to the needs in the community.

A native of Opa-Locka, Kelley is the son of the late Eddie Kelley and Ollie B. Kelley. He and wife Tangela Reneé have one son, Joseph Isaiah. After receiving his call to ministry, Kelley served under Reverend Willis Jackson. In 2000, Kelley resigned from his job as a park supervisor, a position he had held for 17 years, and followed God's mandate to turn to full-time ministry.

Kelley attended Miami-Dade Community College and Florida International University. He is a volunteer for the local South Florida Food Recovery Program, and holds membership in the African-American Council of Christian Clergy, Miami-Dade League of Cities, NAACP, and the 5000 Role Models Project of Excellence.

Kelley was elected to a four-year term as a city commissioner in Opa-Locka in 2000, and served as vice mayor of the city for the first year of his term. On September 7, 2004, he was elected mayor of the City of Opa-Locka.

Mayor Kelley's determination to help others is rooted in the concept that God has not blessed people for them to sit down, but rather to be a blessing to someone else. He is working to move Holy Temple from "membership to effective ministry."

THE HONORABLE

JAMES A. KNOX

MAYOR OF
NORTHWEST, NORTH CAROLINA

The Honorable James A. Knox, mayor of the City of Northwest, North Carolina, was elected as mayor in 1995. He has been elected five times in a town of just less than 1,000 people. Mayor Knox played a vital role in getting city water and a town hall. He was also successful in getting a $6 million sewer grant.

Knox is currently involved in the NAACP, and is secretary of the Southern Black Mayors Association and the North Carolina Black Mayors Association. He is a tutor at Belville Elementary School in Brunswick County, North Carolina, pastor of Haw Branch AME Church in Richlands, North Carolina, and chairman of the Hood Creek Democratic Precinct.

Knox graduated from Shaw University in Raleigh, North Carolina with a bachelor of arts degree in religion and philosophy, and a bachelor of science degree in business administration.

Mayor Knox has been married to Debra Knox, a schoolteacher, for 20 years, and they have five children. His favorite quote is "The Lord will make a way somehow." He retired from E.I. Dupont after 32 years of service.

THE HONORABLE

JOE LANDRY

MAYOR OF
OLD RIVER-WINFREE, TEXAS

The Honorable Joe Landry is the first black mayor of Old River-Winfree, Texas, and continues to remain the favorite for mayor in a predominantly white city.

Mayor Landry has served the city as mayor for ten years. He began serving his country when he entered the Army and served as a sergeant in Vietnam for three years. He received the National Defense Medal, the Vietnam Service Medal, and a Bronze Star.

A member of the Masons, Landry serves as the worshipful master at the Gibraltar Lodge 406. He is also an ordained minister and serves as pastor for Little Rock Church of Old River-Winfree.

The position of mayor in a small town only brings success with much hard work and dedication, which is exactly what Landry exudes. He was instrumental in obtaining funds estimated at $10,000 to purchase equipment for a park within his community and at the City's park location. He saw the future need for Old River-Winfree's citizens to get in shape, and oversaw the installation of a walking track on the City's park grounds.

One of Landry's platforms has always been the safety of the citizens. This concern includes the many travelers who come through Old River-Winfree. Landry was able to have traffic signals installed at two major intersections. Another result of his safety concern over the years has been the installation of more than 45 streetlights within this very small community. This is notable in comparison to the neighboring cities that have more money and fewer or no streetlights.

THE *HONORABLE*

LORENZO T. LANGFORD

MAYOR OF
ATLANTIC CITY, NEW JERSEY

After 150 years, Atlantic City has never been better, thanks to the Honorable Mayor Lorenzo T. Langford, who has ushered in more than $2 billion in new projects in only three years. He secured a $15 million grant to help Atlantic City Medical Center, formulated a three-year tax stability plan endorsed by Wall Street, held employment summits, and created numerous youth and senior citizen initiatives.

Langford was born and raised in Atlantic City, the second of four children. He attended public school and graduated from Atlantic City High School in 1973. He then went on to graduate from Atlantic Community College and North Carolina Central University. He has a bachelor of science degree in business administration.

Langford was one of the first casino dealers at Caesars Boardwalk Regency. He moved to Playboy Casino Hotel in 1981 as a floor person, and eventually rose to the position of pit boss. He worked there until the demise of the then-Atlantis, and went on to work as a pit clerk for Trump Taj Mahal when it opened in April of 1990.

In 1992, Langford ran for the office of city councilman and defeated the incumbent council president. He has been reelected twice to represent Atlantic City's Fourth Ward. Langford ran for mayor in 1994 and 1998 unsuccessfully. On November 6, 2001, he was elected mayor and is currently seeking reelection.

Langford is a member of New Hope Baptist Church, the NAACP-Atlantic City branch, the Atlantic City Police Athletic League, 101 Women Plus, Omega Psi Phi Fraternity, Inc., and Prince Hall Lodge #27.

Langford's interests include singing, reading, and spending time with family and friends. He and his wife, Nynell, have two children, Elijah and Isaiah.

THE HONORABLE

WILLIE JAMES LARRY

MAYOR OF
MONTEZUMA, GEORGIA

The Honorable Willie James Larry was installed in December of 1999 as the first African-American mayor in the 150-year history of the City of Montezuma. He was reelected in November of 2003. During his first term in office, he successfully brought two industries with more than 400 jobs to Montezuma. Since he has been mayor, the city has received more than $3.5 million in economic department grants and $540,000 in airport upgrade grants.

A Montezuma native, Mayor Larry received his early education in the public schools of Marion County. After being drafted into the United States Army in 1956, he graduated from Anne Arundel County High School in Laurel, Maryland. Larry received post-secondary education at Northwestern State University in Natchitoches, Louisiana.

After retiring as a first sergeant from the U.S. Army, Larry worked in inventory management and retired from Robins Air Force Base in March of 1999. He served 11 years on the Montezuma City Council, four years as the first chairman of the Macon County Planning Commission, and three years on the board of directors at South Georgia Technical College.

Larry is a past master of Herman Lodge #51. While serving as worshipful master, he founded a scholarship fund that has awarded more than $20,500 to outstanding graduates of the Macon County Public School System. Larry is a member of the Chamber of Commerce and Union Baptist Church. He is a former member of the Macon County Development Authority board of directors.

In 1983, Larry organized the Community Youth Leadership Development League. This program sends 50 at-risk Macon County children to an annual summer camp at Camp John Hope.

Larry and his wife, Elizabeth Anne, have been married for 47 years. They have four sons, James, Geoffrey, Ronald, and George. They also have 12 grandchildren and two great-grandchildren.

THE *HONORABLE*

WILLIAM C. LAWRENCE

MAYOR OF
HIGHLAND VILLAGE, TEXAS

The Honorable William C. Lawrence is serving his third term as the 16th mayor of the City of Highland Village, Texas. He was first elected in May of 2000, and is the city's first African-American mayor. Bill is also the owner of Dakiman Company, a dispute resolution firm.

With a population of 14,300, Highland Village has been named one of the top five places to live in the Dallas-Fort Worth Metroplex by *D Magazine* several times during Bill's administration. In each of the last three years, Highland Village was named the safest city in North Texas by the FBI.

Bill's professional background includes service as a tax attorney with the United States Internal Revenue Service, and corporate management positions with Verizon Corporation and Cummins Engine Company. He is a retired colonel in the Air Force Reserves. Bill holds a bachelor of science degree from Tuskegee University, a master of science degree from St. Mary's University, and a law degree from Indiana University School of Law.

Bill's public service career includes serving on the Highland Village Planning and Zoning Commission, a term on City Council, and sitting on the Denton County Advisory Board for Wells Fargo Bank. He is also on the board of directors for the Lewisville Education Foundation, a Rotarian, a member of the Tuskegee Airmen, and a member of the Denton County Republican Men's Club. Bill is also on the Texas Board of Professional Engineers, a gubernatorial appointed position.

The son of a career soldier, Bill was born at Tuskegee Army Air Field in Tuskegee, Alabama. He is a Baptist and a member of Alpha Phi Alpha Fraternity, Inc. Bill and his wife, Grace, have three adult children, Kimberly, David, and Antoinette, and a beloved dog, Murphy.

THE HONORABLE

WARDELL LEACH

MAYOR OF
YAZOO CITY, MISSISSIPPI

The Honorable Wardell Leach is currently serving his second term as mayor of Yazoo City, Mississippi. He was elected in April of 1998. He is a member of the board of directors for the Mississippi Municipal League, and serves on the liability board of the Mississippi Service Company. He served two years as an alderman, and was mayor pro tempore in the absence of Mayor Hugh McGraw.

Wardell served in the United States Army from June of 1962 until his honorable discharge on June 13, 1965. He spent 24 months in Germany as director of the American Youth Association, which provided recreational activities for American children in Germany.

Wardell was named Citizen of the Year in 2000 by the Xi Kappa Kappa chapter of Omega Psi Phi Fraternity, Inc. He received Mayor of the Year honors from the committee that organized the Martin Luther King Day parade in Jackson, and this year, he was elected president of the Mississippi Black Mayors Conference.

He holds a bachelor of science degree, a master's degree in health and physical education, and a master's degree in administration from Jackson State University, where he was a three-year letterman in football and a four-year letterman in baseball.

A school principal from 1990 to 1994, Wardell has coached high school baseball and football in Yazoo City and Yazoo County schools for 29 years, and has received Coach of the Year honors in both sports. He has been inducted into the Mississippi Baseball Coaches Hall of Fame, the Jackson State University Sports Hall of Fame, and the Mississippi High School Baseball Hall of Fame.

Wardell and his wife, the former Mattie J. Thomas, have two children, Sheila and Gary, and three grandchildren, Jonjala, Jesten, and Kelsey. He and his family are members of St. Stephens United Methodist Church.

THE HONORABLE

MAURICE LUCAS, SR.

MAYOR OF
RENOVA, MISSISSIPPI

The Honorable Maurice Lucas, Sr., mayor of Renova, Mississippi, is proud of his achievements. His philosophy is, "Someone must take the time to do it. Why not me?"

Born in Mound Bayou, Mississippi on October 10, 1944, Mayor Lucas was the third of eight children born to Julius and Gladys Lucas. His hard work and diligence were instilled in him by his parents on the family farm. Lucas' wife, Carolyn, and their son, Maurice, Jr., have offered additional incentive for him to use his unique gifts.

Lucas received his elementary education in Renova and attended junior and senior high school at East Side High School in Cleveland, Mississippi. He received an associate of arts degree from Coahoma Junior College in 1969 and a bachelor of business administration degree from Delta State University in 1971. He earned his degrees while working full time at Baxter Laboratories, where he continued to work for 25 years as a cost analysis and accounting supervisor. All the while, he has been self-employed as a bookkeeper and tax accountant.

Lucas has been mayor of Renova for 26 years, and has served 17 years on the Cleveland School District's board of trustees. He also serves as a Bolivar County Hospital Medical Foundation trustee, a United Way board member and treasurer, and a Community Action Agency (Headstart) board member in Bolivar County. A member of the Bolivar County Chamber of Commerce, he was the first African American to serve as president of that agency. He sits on the Industrial Development Foundation board of directors, the Mississippi Public Service Commission advisory board, and is a member of the Mississippi Manufacturing Association and the National Conference of Black Mayors.

Mayor Lucas is the grand master of M.W. Stringer Grand Lodge-Prince Hall Affiliated. He has numerous other Masonic memberships and affiliations.

THE HONORABLE

DEBRA A. MABRY

MAYOR OF
GOODMAN, MISSISSIPPI

The Honorable Debra A. Mabry became the first African-American mayor of Goodman, Mississippi in July of 2001, a municipality that was founded in 1865. This is the first time she has held a political office.

Mayor Mabry brought to Goodman a vision of change that she felt was needed to move the community forward. This vision included better homes, cleaner communities, and relationships forged where there had been none previously. Mabry wanted to awaken in the citizens a burning desire to improve their quality of life. She brought a new grocery store to the community, which had been without one since 1994.

During her term in office, Mabry received Woman of the Year honors from the Holmes County Chamber of Commerce in 2002, the Municipal Excellence Award for downtown improvement, and the Governor's Home Program Reconstruction Award in 2002. She was the runner up for that award in 2003.

Mabry received her early education in the schools of Holmes County, and she studied further at Mississippi Valley State University.

Mabry's vision is for Goodman to be a beacon off I-55 and U.S. Highway 51 that causes people to want to stop, shop, and live. She feels that the community is living up to the motto, "The Lil' Town That's Making a Difference!"

Mayor Mabry has one son, Eric.

THE HONORABLE

SONYA A. MALLORY

MAYOR OF
JEFFERSONVILLE, GEORGIA

The Honorable Sonya A. Mallory, one of seven children, was born to Emmitt and Daisy Carswell in the real middle of Georgia, the City of Jeffersonville. She attended Jeffersonville Elementary School for her first nine years of education, where she received the firm old school background she needed to survive in this world.

A 1972 graduate of Twiggs County High School, Mayor Mallory continued her education at Macon Technical Collage and became a licensed practical nurse. Realizing how hard it was to be a parent, and wanting more for her children, she joined the United States Army, where she was a 91C medic. Her Army tour was for five years, and she also served eight years in the National Guard.

After her tour, Mallory accepted a position at the V.A. Medical Center in Dublin, Georgia, where she was employed for ten years. During that time, she was vice president of the local union.

Still searching for something more for her family, Mallory attended Macon Tech School of Barbering and soon discovered that men were harder to please than women. She then attended Nirobi School of Cosmetology under the direction of Mrs. Cornelious Tucker, one of the greatest role models she has ever known. After she received her cosmetology license, Mallory continued school for another two years to receive her license to teach cosmetology.

Mallory began to notice that Jeffersonville was in decline. She ran for the office of mayor three times and won. Having faced several obstacles, she continues to fight for what she believes in.

Mayor Mallory is the owner of RosSams Beauty Salon, and hopes to build a school of cosmetology one day. She is married to Joseph R. Mallory and has two children, Shawn and Sherale, and three grandchildren, Sonjala, Jazma, and LaShawndra.

THE HONORABLE

HERMAN MALVEAUX

MAYOR OF
CHATAIGNIER, LOUISIANA

The Honorable Herman Malveaux began his service in the village of Chataignier, Louisiana as a councilman by appointment in 1974. He served in that capacity until 1989. That year, he decided to run for mayor of the village, and was elected with 70 percent of the vote.

Mayor Malveaux became the first African-American mayor to be elected in Chataignier. At present, he remains the only elected African-American mayor in the parish of Evangeline.

Malveaux offered citizens a better hope for improved government and a passion for making Chataignier a safer, cleaner village. His intent was to improve quality of life for families, seniors, and children and to provide a more open, responsive, and effective village government.

During the course of his outstanding career, Malveaux has received many science awards and served on numerous parish and state committees. He earned a bachelor of science degree from Grambling State University, and a master's degree from Southern University.

Mayor Malveaux has tackled the tough challenges in village government and lived up to his campaign promise, "If you elect me mayor, I'll make you proud." His continuing slogan is, "Don't Watch Us Grow, Come Grow With Us."

THE HONORABLE

ARTHUR MARBLE

MAYOR OF
INDIANOLA, MISSISSIPPI

The Honorable Arthur Marble became the first elected African-American mayor of Indianola, Mississippi, the birthplace of the White Citizen's Council, in January of 2002. Mayor Marble provides a new vision and outlook for a once-divided city.

Since becoming mayor, Marble has worked to support schools, improve and secure housing, and improve the overall quality of life in Indianola. He intends to continue economic development, including the promotion of blues music, and development of a B.B. King Blues Museum and Learning Center.

Marble served his country in the U.S. Air Force. He completed Combined Intelligence School in 1977. Serving as a special intelligence officer, he worked with U-2 and SR-71 Blackbirds, reporting directly to national intelligence authorities and the White House. He received numerous commendations for services rendered.

Marble is affiliated with Omega Psi Phi Fraternity, Inc. and Overton Lodge #62, F&A M, Prince Hall Affiliate. He is a lifelong member of Little Rock Missionary Baptist Church of Gulfport, Mississippi.

Most of Marble's early education was at Thirty-Third Avenue High School in Gulfport, with the last two years completed at South Park High School in Buffalo, New York. His first two years of college were at Grambling State University with completion occurring at the University of Southern Mississippi in Hattiesburg.

Mayor Marble's special interest includes a love of water sports and a special affection his family. His family includes his wife of 33 years, Pamela Byas Marble, and Vivian Nicholas (Dedia and Naomi) of Normandy, France, Arthur III (Tara, Kennedy and Olivia) of Mississippi State University, and Vanessa Marble of Atlanta, Geogia.

His motto is, "I am the captain of my ship, I am the master of my soul."

THE *HONORABLE*

TITUS W. MCCLARY

MAYOR OF
HIGHLAND PARK, MICHIGAN

The Honorable Titus W. McClary was elected mayor of Highland Park, Michigan in November of 2003. He began serving the City of Highland Park when he was appointed to the Highland Park Police Department as a patrolman in January of 1965. While serving as the police community relations officer, he was approached by a community group who asked him to run for the Highland Park Board of Education.

Mayor McClary served for more than 16 years as a member of the board of education and the Highland Park Community College board of trustees. He was elected for five consecutive terms. In 1993, he was appointed to the Highland Park City Council, after the death of a councilman.

In 1994, McClary was elected to serve the remaining period of the unexpired term. He ran for reelection in 1995 and was elected president pro-tempore. In 1999, he was elected president of the Highland Park City Council.

McClary is the longest continuously serving black elected official in the history of Highland Park. He has served his community in many different capacities. He has been honored as "Man of the Year," in 2003 by his church, Ebenezer AME; served as district governor of the International Lions Club; and honored by the city, county, and state for outstanding services to the community.

A graduate of Highland Park High School, McClary also graduated from Highland Park Community College, Mercy College of Detroit, the Metropolitan Police Academy of Michigan, and the National Crime Prevention Institute.

Mayor McClary is married and has three adult children and six grandchildren. He has been a member of Ebenezer AME Church for 52 years.

He is a man who feels that it is his duty to serve mankind.

THE HONORABLE

AL MCCOWAN

MAYOR OF
UNIVERSITY PARK, ILLINOIS

The Honorable Al McCowan was elected mayor of University Park, Illinois in April of 2003. He served on the village board for seven years and held numerous appointments, including planning commission and finance chairman. He is senior vice-president of The Habitat Company, one of the nation's premier residential development and management companies. McCowan is a member of the Silver Cross Hospital board of directors and the Chicago Area Transportation Study executive committee.

Often referred to as a visionary and strong leader by his peers, Mayor McCowan has devoted considerable effort to positioning University Park to have meaningful influence in the growth and development of this region. His vision is for University Park and the Southland area is to enjoy lower real estate taxes, jobs closer to home, and high quality educational opportunities.

Under McCowan's leadership, the quality of residential development has shown significant improvement. He has led efforts to reduce the cost of public services, including water and sewer services. Creative methods of realizing economic benefits from industrial park development have been realized with the more than five million square feet of new industrial space created over the past two years.

Along with U.S. Congressman Jesse Jackson, Jr., McCowan led efforts to establish University Park as one of two founding members of the Abraham Lincoln National Airport Commission. McCowan serves as chairman of this Commission, and University Park will be one of the bond-issuing authorities.

University Park plays a meaningful role in the greatest economic development opportunity in the Southland for many decades, which represents thousands of jobs, lower taxes, and more funding for schools. Additionally, McCowan's vision and creativity led to critical land acquisitions important to the future growth of University Park including the procurement and annexation of the University Golf Club and Conference Center.

THE HONORABLE

MONIQUE MCDUFFIE-DAVIS

MAYOR OF
CLEVELAND, TEXAS

The Honorable Monique McDuffie-Davis became the 24th mayor of Cleveland, Texas in May of 2003, at the age of 37. She made history by being elected as the first African-American and first woman to serve as mayor in the city and in Liberty County.

Mayor McDuffie-Davis offers the citizens of Cleveland the desire to grow and expand. Cleveland has experienced stunted growth, due to people with large capital wealth who dominated the economic sector. The town has had many examples of short-sighted planning, including a new hotel without a swimming pool, restaurants operating out of inadequate facilities, and a one-screen theater. Now, the economic development is advancing as Cleveland is building an 18-hole PGA golf course, upscale housing, a civic center, a new city hall, and many other improvements.

Monique wants to be a role model to the young adults. She believes that it is important to be a part of the local community, and that people can make a world of difference by being as concerned for others as they are for themselves. Monique has a desire to become the first African-American and first woman judge in the county in order to help the community on a deep level.

Monique is secretary of the Texas Conference of Black Mayors. She attends C.C. Driver Revival Center, where she is an altar worker, church nurse, and in the choir.

She graduated from Cleveland High School in 1983, and then attended the Liberty County Sheriff Academy, Lamar University, and Kingwood College, where she studied nursing.

Monique is married to John W. Davis, III, a deputy sheriff in the Liberty County Sheriff's Department. They have two children, Gabrielle, 18, and Jonathan, 15.

THE HONORABLE

ESSIE L. MCINTOSH

MAYOR OF
TAFT, OKLAHOMA

The Honorable Essie L. McIntosh was born and raised in Taft, Oklahoma. "I know the people of Taft very well. In fact, I know them just about as well as I know myself," says Mayor McIntosh.

The oldest of six children, McIntosh grew up in the community that she now serves. A 1967 graduate, she received her education at Moton High School and through the wisdom that her elders passed on to her. She has always worked in the field of education, as both a teacher's aid and as a teacher, and has amassed 30 years of teaching living skills to blind children.

McIntosh is a volunteer who thrives on helping others. In addition to her service on the board of the Muskogee Community Action organization, she is a volunteer at a local nursing home, a member of the Taft Volunteer Fire Department, and the treasurer of New Life Ministries Women's Committee.

McIntosh was elected mayor of Taft after having first served as vice mayor. She has worked to improve the community and is responsible for several grants that have been beneficial to her people. Under her administration, the city received grants that brought about the Taft Senior Center, an expansion of sewer lines, repairs to roads, and renovations to the town hall.

Mayor McIntosh says, "I have seen changes come to our town, but now, I have the power to bring about change and to assist in the economic development of our community. I want Taft to be a town that everyone wants to visit and live in. I believe that great things will come but we must have unity among our people. One person cannot stand alone, it will take the entire community to make a difference."

THE HONORABLE

JONATHAN MOORE

MAYOR OF
PICKENS, MISSISSIPPI

The Honorable Jonathan Moore was elected as the first African-American mayor of the town of Pickens, Mississippi in 1993. Before being elected mayor, he was one of the first African Americans elected to the Board of Aldermen in 1977.

During Mayor Moore's tenure, the town has made improvements in the areas of housing, water and sewer services, parks and recreation, business development, and the overall aesthetics of the town.

Moore earned his degree in biological science from Mississippi Valley State University. He then taught junior high school science for 32 years before retiring in 1995. During his years in education, he also served as an assistant principal and boys basketball coach. Moore was an active member of the teachers association, where he served as association president and vice president. While president, he served as a delegate for the state of Mississippi to the National Education Association (NEA) conventions in Los Angeles and New Orleans.

Moore maintains membership in various organizations and committees such as the Chamber of Commerce, where he served as the first black president. He is also a member of the State Municipal League, the NAACP, the FDP, Habitat for Humanity, and the Baptist church; he is a life member of the NEA. Moore serves his church as a deacon, clerk, Sunday school teacher, and in the male chorus.

Mayor Moore is married to Laura Johnson Moore, and they have four daughters and one son. His hobbies include collecting antiques, making videos, and practicing photography.

His favorite quote is from Matthew 5:9, "Blessed are the peacemakers, for they shall be called the sons of God."

THE HONORABLE

STANLEY MORRIS, ESQ.

MAYOR OF
MENIFEE, ARKANSAS

The Honorable Stanley Morris, Esq., is the mayor of Menifee, Arkansas and a licensed practicing attorney with Sears Roebuck and Co. as in-house counsel. He has been the mayor of Menifee for more than six years. He is also licensed to practice law in Texas, Georgia, and Illinois, and with federal bars.

Mayor Morris has extensive experience in all litigation phases in state and federal courts, and has conducted depositions and managed trials in public liability, product liability, workers' compensation, and commercial cases for several years. He is a skilled litigation manager who has reduced time spent by others on litigation projects through work supervision, as well as avoided unnecessary litigation through concise, well-written contracts.

He has successfully negotiated real estate contracts, operating agreements, and estoppels documents; planned, negotiated, and litigated construction contract issues; and developed standard contracts.

Morris achieved a $1.8 million settlement in a breach of contract matter and achieved defense verdicts in complex trade practices cases through meticulous fact development. He also obtained a defense summary judgment in a wrongful death case that was affirmed by the United States Supreme Court.

Morris is a graduate of Texas Southern School of Law and Philander Smith College.

THE HONORABLE

SYLVESTER MUCKELROY

MAYOR OF
NEW ROADS, LOUISIANA

The Honorable Sylvester Muckelroy, mayor of New Roads, Louisiana, was born to Joseph and Marie Parker Muckelroy. A native of Kilgore, Texas, he has two brothers and two sisters. He is married to Leona Veronica Duhe Muckelroy, and they are the parents of five children, Leslie, Dennis, Karen Collette, Mary Lynette, and Paul Drexel.

Mayor Muckelroy retired in 1989, after 40 years as a classroom teacher in elementary and high school. He served as assistant principal at Rosenwald High School and supervisor of elementary education with the Pointe Coupee Paris Public School System.

On April 1, 1989, Muckelroy was elected mayor of New Roads, and he assumed office on July 1, 1989. He believes in the importance of youth receiving a high school education. He began an initiative to provide job training for young people to prepare them for the job market, to ensure that they can take part in an ever-changing society.

Muckelroy believes that education should be the number one priority for both national and state governments, and he strongly supports public education. He believes that all children should have a right to a well-rounded education, and that there is nothing greater than the betterment of oneself with knowledge, for education is the key to prosperity.

Muckelroy graduated from Kilgore High School, then earned a bachelor of science degree and a master of education degree in administration and supervision from Southern University.

Mayor Muckelroy is past president of the Knights of Peter Claver Council #41, New Roads False River Rotary, and the St. Augustine Parish Council. He is past president and current board member of the Louisiana Energy & Power Authority. A board member of Guaranty Bank & Trust Company, he is a current member of the National Conference of Black Mayors (NCBM) and the Louisiana Chapter of NCBM.

THE HONORABLE

MARILYN MURRELL

MAYOR OF
ARCADIA, OKLAHOMA

The Honorable Marilyn Murrell was born and raised in Arcadia, Oklahoma. After leading a successful four-year legal battle to reestablish the identity of Arcadia as an official town, Murrell was elected Arcadia's first mayor in May of 1988. She has been reelected to the post four times.

Mayor Murrell was instrumental in creating town ordinances where none existed before, fully functional police and fire departments, a municipal court system, and other required governmental entities for town management.

Murrell has been a member of the Oklahoma Conference of Black Mayors and the National Conference of Black Mayors (NCBM) since 1988. She has served in numerous positions with both organizations. She served as president of the NCBM during the 2002-2003 year, the second woman to hold the position of president.

Murrell has served on many local and state boards and commissions representing her community. Those organizations include the Oklahoma Municipal League, the Oklahoma Conference of Mayors, the Central Oklahoma Regional Economic Development Task Force, and the ACOG 911 board of directors. She is an executive committee member of the Oklahoma Rural Development Council.

She serves as chairman of the Small Town Alliance, an organization with a mission of assisting small and rural communities throughout the country to improve growth and development through technology, education, and advocacy.

Murrell's professional career spans more than 30 years as an advocate for small business and as a business consultant providing management and technical assistance to small and minority businesses.

Murrell's civic duties continue as she participates with the Women's Foundation of Oklahoma board of advisors, the Youth Services for Oklahoma County board of directors, the NAACP, and the National Association of Colored Women's Clubs.

Mayor Murrell has three adult children and one grandson.

THE HONORABLE

ROBERT L. NASH

**MAYOR OF
HIGHLAND HILLS, OHIO**

The Honorable Robert L. (Bob) Nash has been mayor of the village of Highland Hills, Ohio since its inception as a municipality in 1990. Before the incorporation of Highland Hills, Bob served on the board of trustees for the village's forerunner, Warrensville Township.

Since Highland Hills' formation 15 years ago, Bob's leadership and drive have transformed the Cleveland suburb from a quiet hamlet to a premiere municipality. It is home to some of America's most prestigious corporations and institutions, all while maintaining the quaintness of the village.

When Highland Hills was first formed, it had a little more than $8,000 in the bank. Thanks to Bob's prudent fiscal management and "can-do" spirit, the village now boasts cash reserves in the seven-figure range.

Village residents and corporate citizens alike enjoy first-class municipal services in addition to quality of life initiatives that are the envy of cities throughout Cuyahoga County (Ohio), due in large part to Bob's energetic management style and dedication to constituents.

He is truly "a mayor's mayor."

THE HONORABLE

SHARON NICHOLSON

MAYOR OF
YELLOW BLUFF, ALABAMA

The Honorable Sharon Nicholson became the fourth mayor of Yellow Bluff, Alabama in September of 2000. She is the third African-American woman to serve as mayor of Yellow Bluff.

During Sharon's first term as mayor, the town was awarded a housing rehabilitation and street improvement grant. She is working hard to improve Yellow Bluff Community Park to have a safe play area for the town's children.

A graduate of Pine Hill High School in Pine Hill, Alabama, Sharon received an associate degree in computer clerical and graduated with honors from Riley College.

Sharon is a member of St. Lewis Primitive Baptist Church in Yellow Bluff. She is the director of the youth ministry and serves on other auxiliaries. Sharon enjoys working with children and caring for elderly people.

Happily married to Jesse Nicholson, Sharon is the mother of one son, two daughters, one stepdaughter, and four grandchildren.

Sharon has faced tough challenges in city government and still lived up to her campaign slogan, "If you don't stand up for something, you will fall for anything!"

THE HONORABLE

JOYCE AYERS NIXON

MAYOR OF
CAPITOL HEIGHTS, MARYLAND

The Honorable Joyce Ayers Nixon was elected the tenth mayor of the Town of Capitol Heights, Maryland in May of 2002, the second African-American woman to serve the township in that capacity.

Mayor Nixon campaigned on two major promises. She said she would generate economic development by attracting businesses to the town, and that she would be a champion for the cause of restructuring the town to achieve efficient management and services for constituents. She continues to make great strides in both areas.

Throughout her career in nursing and in federal and state government, Nixon has received countless awards, including the distinguished service award from the Maryland House of Delegates and the Blacks in Government honor award for exceptional community services.

Nixon was recently elected president of the PG Black Mayors Association. She has been featured in several major publications, including the *Washington Post*, the *Maryland Gazette*, the *Washington Informer*, and the *Christian Recorder*. She recently received local television coverage for the implementation of a major initiative to help eradicate crime and drug traffic between Washington, D.C. and Capitol Heights.

Nixon earned an associate degree and a bachelor of arts degree from the University of the District of Columbia. She earned a master of arts degree in teaching from Trinity College in D.C. She is an active member of Ward Memorial AME Church in Washington, and a member of Alpha Phi Chi Sorority, Inc.

A woman of many interests and pursuits, Nixon relishes life and finds strength and commitment in the words of Mark Yost, "History, although sometimes made up of a few acts of the great, is more often shaped by the many acts of the small."

Mayor Nixon is married to Vernon Raye Nixon, and they have two sons. She enjoys singing, word games, dancing, and reading.

THE HONORABLE

CARL EDWARD OFFICER

MAYOR OF
EAST ST. LOUIS, ILLINOIS

In May of 2003, the Honorable Carl Edward Officer raised his hand to serve a fourth term as mayor of the great city of East St. Louis, Illinois. In 1979, at the age of 26, Officer made American history by becoming the nation's youngest mayor when he was elected.

While mayor, Officer attended the prestigious Harvard University's John F. Kennedy School of Government for State and Local Officials. He also attended seminary classes in the United States, Israel, and Egypt.

At the age of 23, Officer became director of Driver Services for the Illinois Secretary of State's Office, and he instituted the State of Illinois' First Photo Driving License Program.

Despite enduring one of the most devastating financial periods in the city's history and glaring media attention, Officer strived and succeeded in securing economic development for the city. His biggest coup was securing a lifetime gaming license, which made East St. Louis the only city in Illinois with a gaming license.

Officer graduated from Marmion Military Academy in Aurora, Illinois. Following graduation, he explored his passion of politics by attending Western College of Miami University in Oxford, Ohio, where he received a bachelor's degree in political science and history. He fulfilled his family's legacy by obtaining an associate degree in mortuary science from Southern Illinois University in Carbondale, Illinois.

He is a member of Kappa Alpha Psi Fraternity, Inc., a lifetime member of the NAACP, a second lieutenant in the Illinois National Guard, a 33° Mason, and a member of the National and State Funeral Directors' Associations.

Officer is an ordained elder in the African Methodist Episcopal (AME) Church. He is married and is the proud father of one daughter.

THE HONORABLE

JOHN F. OVERTON, SR.

MAYOR OF
MARINGOUIN, LOUISIANA

The Honorable John F. Overton, Sr. became the second African-American to serve as mayor in the town of Maringouin, Louisiana.

Mayor Overton has worked aggressively to promote economic growth and development in this diverse area. He has worked to upgrade the condition of the neighborhood through a better utility system. Likewise, he has achieved a better working relationship with law enforcement and fire departments to improve the safety of the community.

Overton is a former police juror for District 12 in Iberville Parish, where he served for three years, and a retired minority farmer with 15 years of experience. The Iberville Parish Council currently employs him as the supervisor of the drainage department.

A member of the Farm Bureau and the Maringouin Volunteer Fire Department, Overton has served on the USDA advisory board.

He is a board advisor to the Iberville Parish Social Service Department and the Iberville Chamber of Commerce. He is also serving as a commissioner of the Capital Region Planning Commission.

Overton is a member of Shiloh United Methodist Church. He attended the University of Southwestern Louisiana (currently the University of Louisiana at Lafayette) for two-and-a-half years majoring in agricultural business.

Overton is married to the former Cynthia Gilbert. They are the proud parents of Desiree Nicole, Dexter Fitzgerald, and John Fitzgerald, Jr. Overton's hobbies include weight lifting, fishing, and watching sports and the stock market.

Mayor John F. Overton always says a hero doesn't live long, but a legend lives forever.

THE HONORABLE

ROBERT PATTON

MAYOR OF
SHELBY, MISSISSIPPI

The Honorable Robert Patton became the fourth African-American mayor of the City of Shelby, Mississippi on June 8, 2004. Patton came into office on a campaign theme of New Leadership.

Patton has proven for a short time that hard work, persistence, flexibility, and a high degree of intelligent common sense can change a city for the better. A clean, attractive city, decent housing, more and better jobs, and better streets and drains help to improve the infrastructure of the city.

During his outstanding career, Patton has served as alderman, vice mayor, and now, mayor.

Patton has tackled many tough challenges in city government and lives up to the campaign slogan, "If you make me mayor, I will give you New Leadership."

THE HONORABLE

SALLIE SIMS PEAKE

MAYOR OF
WELLFORD, SOUTH CAROLINA

The Honorable Sallie Sims Peake was elected mayor of Wellford, South Carolina in 1995. She was the first elected black woman in the state of South Carolina since the Reconstruction. Previously, Sallie was elected to Wellford City Council and was president of the Wellford Precinct.

Sallie's record of community and organizational involvement is extensive, including service in a variety of capacities with more than 35 different organizations. She was appointed by Governor Riley to serve on the advisory board to the governor, and received gubernatorial appointment to serve on the Commission for the Future of South Carolina.

Currently, she serves on the boards of directors for the Council on Aging, Inc., the Middle Tyger Area Chamber of Commerce, Urban League of the Upstate, and the Community Advisory Panel. She is a member of Women in Government of South Carolina; the National Association of Counties; the Black, Spartanburg County, and South Carolina Municipal Associations; the National Council of Negro Women, Inc. of Spartanburg; the Spartanburg County Union of Churches; the Spartanburg County Enhancement Committee; and the Spartanburg County Policy Committee.

Some of Sallie's awards and honors include completion of the Leadership Institute for Mayors in 1995; the Spartanburg County Council Service Award; the University of South Carolina Appalachian Council of Government Award; the National Association of Black County Officials Lifetime Distinguished Service Award; and the South Carolina House of Representatives Contribution Award.

Sallie graduated from Florence Chapel School and attended Spartanburg Technical College, where she minored in business administration.

She is a mother of four, three boys and one girl, and resides in Wellford. Sallie is very involved with her church, Mayfield Chapel Baptist Church, where she is a member of the Usher Board, the Missionary Circle, the Sympathy Club, and Order of the Eastern Star Chapter 150.

THE HONORABLE

JAMES PERKINS, JR.

MAYOR OF
SELMA, ALABAMA

The Honorable James Perkins, Jr. has a rich and proven community service record in Selma and across the state. Presently, he serves as mayor of the City of Selma and a member of the Selma Public School System Drug Advisory Council.

In 1975, Mayor Perkins accepted a job with Caterpillar Tractor Company, and later joined Martin Marietta Corporation. In 1980, he returned to Selma to start his own business, Business Ventures, Inc. (BVI). Perkins also taught mathematics and computer science courses at Selma University.

Perkins is co-founder and organizer of the Selma to Montgomery National Historic Trail Friends Association. He is a life member of Kappa Alpha Psi Fraternity, Inc., and a member of the Leadership Birmingham class of 1992, Alabama Democratic Conference, and New South Coalition. Perkins was the chairman of the Black Leadership Council Samson Crum, Sr. Scholarship Fund and a board of directors member for the Selma/Dallas Community Action Agency.

He served as a Birmingham United Way Visiting Allocation Team member, Selma-Dallas County NAACP president, and Minority Business Council president. He is a recipient of the Project Head Start Award.

Perkins is a product of the Selma Public System. He was a member of the first graduating class of Selma High, May 1971. He holds a bachelor of science degree in mathematics from Alabama A&M University and master of business administration courses at Auburn University at Montgomery.

The son of Etta Smith Perkins and James Perkins, Sr., Perkins is married to Cynthia Paige Perkins and is the father of four children, Reginald Antwan, Tiffini Monique, Justin Rashad, and Jarius Renard. He has two sisters, Remigia Perkins, and Synethia Pettaway.

Mayor Perkins is a member of Ebenezer Baptist Church, where he serves as deacon, Sunday school young adult teacher, and male chorus member.

THE HONORABLE

RALPH PETERSON, SR.

MAYOR OF
PLEASANTVILLE, NEW JERSEY

The Honorable Ralph Peterson, Sr. was elected mayor of Pleasantville, New Jersey on November 2, 1992 by an overwhelming mandate of the total community. The first African-American mayor of Pleasantville, Ralph is currently serving his fourth term.

Ralph has played a powerful role in leading the City of Pleasantville into the 21st century. He established Pleasantville as an Urban Enterprise Zone (UEZ). The city has developed the Yacht Basin, the Marina District, a new transportation center that serves New Jersey Transit, the Central Business District Façade, and the Streetscape Program. Ralph continues to move the city forward with the revitalization plans for the Waterfront District. The Waterfront District has received state designation as a Neighborhood Preservation District, along with the city's existing UEZ, UCC, Transit Village, and Abbot District designations. These designations have made the City of Pleasantville one of the few municipalities with all five designations.

Ralph has been very instrumental in the construction of the new middle and high schools, and the creation of the Industrial Park and Veteran's Memorial park.

As mayor, Ralph has received numerous awards, commendations, and recognition for his service, including the Governor's Volunteerism Award, the City News Publishing Company's award for the 100 Most Influential, and the Department of Transportation's Public Service Award.

In addition, he continues to partner with Pleasantville Public Schools to assist in providing quality education and better job opportunities for the city's youth. His goal is to continue making the City of Pleasantville "A City on the Move."

Ralph earned an associate degree in law enforcement from Atlantic Cape Community College, and a bachelor's degree in criminal justice from Stockton State College. He has completed graduate studies in municipal management at Rowan College and Rider College.

Ralph and his wife, Shirley, have four children, six grandchildren, and three great-grandchildren.

THE HONORABLE

MARY STRAWDER PONDS

MAYOR OF
GRANITE QUARRY, NORTH CAROLINA

The Honorable Mary Strawder Ponds became the mayor of Granite Quarry in November of 1999, and is currently serving a term from her reelection in 2002. Mary made history when she was elected the town's first woman mayor, and the first African-American woman to serve Granite Quarry.

Mary offers her small town compassion and a vision of learning as she strives to keep the town clean and safe, and emphasizes family, teaching, economic growth, and environmental awareness.

During the course of her career, Mary has received numerous awards including Teacher of the Year, the Martin Luther King Humanitarian Award, and the Outstanding Professional Accomplishment and Community Service Award.

She has served on the boards of Community Care of Rowan County, the Rufty Holmes Senior Center, the Rowan Regional Medical Center, The Partnership for Children, Rowan Homes, Black Achievers, the Nazareth Children's Home, Information and Referral of Rowan County, the Rowan County Health Department, ARC, and the Grateful Heart Youth Center.

Mary earned a bachelor's degree in biology from Livingstone College in 1966. She is a choir member, a former trustee, and a former steward of White Rock AME Zion Church. Mary is also a proud member of Delta Sigma Theta Sorority, Inc.

Mary has risen to the challenge of difficult decisions that arise in leading the Town of Granite Quarry. Some of the comments one might hear from a citizen of Granite Quarry are, "She is the best thing that ever happened to our town," or "I cannot imagine what we would be like without her leadership."

THE HONORABLE

CARL ANTHONY REDUS, JR.

MAYOR OF
PINE BLUFF, ARKANSAS

The Honorable Carl Anthony Redus, Jr., a native of Pine Bluff, was educated in the public schools and received a bachelor of science degree in mathematics from A M & N College (University of Arkansas-Pine Bluff) in 1971. His education led him to Atlanta, Georgia to pursue a curriculum in business at Clark Atlanta University School of Business, where he received a master of business administration degree with a concentration in finance during May of 1973. Further studies have been completed at the New York Institute of Finance and the Wharton School of Banking Operations.

Mayor Redus has an extensive, multi-faceted career in corporate sales and management with technology firms, focusing on the financial services industry. He was consistently recognized and rewarded for superior sales leadership and the ability to develop technology solutions that supported the client's business' strategies.

While residing in Atlanta, Redus spent approximately 30 years cultivating and developing relations with senior-level executives throughout the southern states and the New York banking markets. Although his skills were nurtured in the corporate environment, his desire to fulfill potential entrepreneurial goals led to the field of real estate. He has had an opportunity to impact his community through investing, developing and restoring housing.

Community involvement runs parallel to Redus' sales and management career. He has a history of distinguished work in civil rights and community organizations such as the Southern Christian Leadership Conference, BusinessLinc Chapter, NAACP, Junior Achievement of America, and the University of Arkansas-Pine Bluff Foundation Board. He has also served as a YMCA board member.

Mayor Redus is married to the former Trudy C. Bruster, and they are the proud parents of an infant son. He also has an adult daughter living in Atlanta, Georgia.

THE HONORABLE

LEONARD REED

MAYOR OF
WILLIS, TEXAS

The Honorable Leonard Reed became the 12th mayor of Willis, Texas on May 5, 2003. Reed is only the second African American to serve as mayor of Willis since its incorporation in 1937.

Reed offered Willis an opportunity to elect someone who was capable of bringing everyone to the table for the benefit of all its residents.

Since being elected mayor, Reed has implemented a master park plan, and overseen the construction of the first neighborhood parks in the city. He submitted a proposition to adopt a Home Rule Charter, and has worked with the county government to build a multi-purpose convention and community center. The city has taken on a new life through the active pursuit of grants, loans, donations, and volunteers to assist in the cleaning and rebuilding process.

Reed recently received an award from the Texas Municipal League for receiving a Municipal League Continuing Education Certificate for five consecutive years.

Reed serves on the board of directors for the International Brotherhood of Electrical Workers Local 2286, the Texas Conference of Black Mayors, and the Willis Community Development Corporation. He is also first vice president of the Texas Association of Black City Council Members.

Reed is a member of the Thergood Memorial Church of God in Christ. He is married to Mary, and has four sons, Shannon, Brionne, Cody, and Erick. A veteran of the U.S. Army, Reed was employed as a reliability technician with Entergy Corporation for 25 years.

THE *HONORABLE*

KEVIN G. SANDERS

MAYOR OF
ASBURY PARK, NEW JERSEY

On May 8, 2001, Kevin G. Sanders was elected to serve as mayor of the City of Asbury Park in Monmouth County, New Jersey. He is the fourth African-American mayor, and the youngest ever elected. Sanders is currently a member of the National Conference of Black Mayors, and he serves as chairman of the arts and recreation committee. In addition, he is a member of the New Jersey League of Municipalities and State Senator Ron Rice's statewide urban housing committee. He is also a member of the planning and recreation boards for the City of Asbury Park.

Sanders graduated from the Community College of the Air Force in Japan, with a bachelor's degree in business management. While serving his country in the United States Air Force, Sanders reached the rank of E-4. He held an honored, top secret, highest security clearance position in command and control for the base commander.

Born and raised in Asbury Park, Sanders' goal as mayor is to help the city return to greatness. He is actively leading the revitalization and redevelopment efforts, along with local developers, architects, and public polity and urban renewal specialists.

Sanders put into motion actions that resulted in the most progressive and comprehensive summer arts and entertainment program in Asbury Park history. The mayor's initiative provided top-of-the-line entertainment in jazz, gospel, pop, big band music, and Broadway productions. Additionally, the children of the city's school district were provided with a summer-long program that offered the opportunity to participate in theatre, music, fine arts, and dance.

Sanders has more than a passing appreciation for the fine arts; he is an accomplished musician. A contemporary Renaissance man, Sanders plays all percussion and keyboard instruments, and writes and performs. He has played locally, nationally, and internationally for more than 20 years.

THE HONORABLE

SILAS SEABROOKS, JR.

MAYOR OF
SANTEE, SOUTH CAROLINA

The Honorable Silas Seabrooks, Jr. is the mayor of Santee, South Carolina. He was the first black mayor of the town, and previously served in the same capacity from 1972 to 1983.

Mayor Seabrooks was born on November 11, 1931. He is the son of the late Silas and Clara Gadson Seabrooks of Santee.

Seabrooks attended the Mount Holly School, and then enlisted in the U.S. Army. He served for two years in the Army, 16 months of which was during the Korean conflict. In addition, he is a graduate of South Carolina Area Trade School, where he completed his studies in plumbing and brick masonry.

A deacon at Chapel Hill Baptist Church in Santee, Seabrooks served as a county councilman for Orangeburg County District Two. He presently serves as a member of Briner Lodge # 365 of Holly Hill, South Carolina; the Elloree-Santee Branch NAACP; the Robert Shaw Consistory of Orangeburg, South Carolina; and District #66 Concerned Citizens. Seabrooks is also a notary public in South Carolina.

Mayor Seabrooks is married to Ms. Annie Mae Adgerson. He is the father of three children, Melvin, Vanester, and the late Darnell Seabrooks. He has five grandchildren.

THE HONORABLE

JAMES SHIPMAN

MAYOR OF
MIDWAY, GEORGIA

The Honorable James "JC" Shipman was elected mayor of Midway, Georgia in November of 2001. He hit the ground running in January of 2002, even though he had not held public office before.

JC has annexed his old high school, which was to be abandoned, moved the city hall to the site, and established the first civic center in the county. He launched a massive cleanup and beautification campaign and expanded the city limits and infrastructure.

A member of the Georgia Conference of Black Mayors, JC is the Region 12 director of the Georgia Municipal Association (GMA) and first vice president of the GMA. He serves the Small Cities Council, the National Black Caucus of Local Elected Officials, and the Leadership Training Council of the National League of Cities. He is also president of the Liberty County Branch of the NAACP and a member of the National Council of Black Mayors.

The National League of Cities certified JC with its highest rank, leadership statesman. He is one of only 24 elected officials in the nation certified as such. He also received a Certificate of Excellence from the Georgia Municipal Association.

JC earned a bachelor of science degree from the University of the District of Columbia and a certificate from Bryant Theological Seminary. He is an ordained Baptist minister and the pastor of historic Bolton Street Baptist Church in Savannah, Georgia.

JC is married to Dr. Kermetta Clark Shipman, a local educator. They have three children and five grandchildren.

THE HONORABLE

LINDA W. SHORT

MAYOR OF
MAYERSVILLE, MISSISSIPPI

The Honorable Linda W. Short is mayor of Mayersville, a rural community located in the Mississippi Delta. She became the third and youngest mayor of Mayersville in June of 2001. Born and raised in the Mayersville community, Linda graduated from Rolling Fork High School in 1984. Her greatest asset is her professionalism and added personal touch.

Through such programs as the Yard of the Month program, Linda has cleaned the community of unsightly debris and gained residential appreciation for a cleaner town. She established the town's annual homecoming event, which is very similar to a family reunion. The homecoming is an all day event for the entire community and for guests from around the country to enjoy. Linda was instrumental in the improvement of the water tower and water system infrastructure, and she extended the sewerage system for citizens outside of the city limits. She also implemented tobacco awareness (anti-smoking) programs for the youth in the community.

Additionally, Linda is promoting a healthier community. Previously, residents had to travel great distances for medical resources. Now, through a collaborative effort between the mayor, the University Medical Center, and the Sisters of Mercy, Mayersville residents enjoy free medical screening for diseases such as diabetes, cholesterol, and high-blood pressure.

Linda is married to Larry D. Short, and is the mother of three lovely children, James, Jercelle, and Jasona. She is an active member of the Rose Hill Missionary Baptist Church, where she serves as the primary Sunday school teacher and senior choir director.

THE HONORABLE

ANNA C. SIMMONS

MAYOR OF
OPELOUSAS, LOUISIANA

The Honorable Anna C. Simmons became the 16th mayor of Opelousas, Louisiana in October of 2002 and redefined history by being the first woman elected to serve as mayor of the city. She is also the first African-American woman to serve as mayor of Opelousas.

Anna gave the citizens of Opelousas a vision of rising together as the city soars to new heights. She has attended many seminars and conferences, gathering abundant knowledge to make the city move forward and flourish. She has been conducive in getting the citizens to work with the city government in moving Opelousas forward.

Anna earned a master's degree in social work from Florida State University. She attended law school at Southern University, was a member of the law review, and received her juris doctorate degree in 1984. She graduated magna cum laude from both institutions.

Anna has been responsible for many new businesses coming to Opelousas and the great economic development impact that is constantly growing in the city. She will continue to tackle the tough challenges in city government to make sure that the city continues "Rising Together as Opelousas Soars to New Heights."

THE HONORABLE

LORRAINE DANDRIDGE SMITH

MAYOR OF
WRIGHTSVILLE, ARKANSAS

The Honorable Lorraine D. Smith became the second mayor of Wrightsville in November of 1987. She is currently serving her fourth consecutive term in this city of 1,400 citizens.

Under Smith's leadership, Wrightsville developed and implemented its first sewer and waste system, and constructed a new city hall and community center complex. Wrightsville is proud of its Fire Volunteer Commission, and the construction of the city's first apartment complex for low-income citizens.

Smith has partnered with surrounding local entities and private donors to build infrastructure in the city. The Senior Net program for seniors and the basketball league for youth are just two examples. She serves on various boards and commissions that serve the Greater Little Rock and Pulaski County area.

Smith earned a bachelor of arts degree from Philander Smith College in Little Rock, Arkansas, and a master of arts degree from the University of Central Arkansas in Conway, Arkansas. She has completed further graduate studies at the University of Mississippi in Oxford and at the University of Arkansas in Fayetteville.

Smith grew up in Wrightsville. Her dream for the city is for it to be a place that the young and old will be proud to say, "Wrightsville is my home."

THE *HONORABLE*

NOBLE T. SMITH

MAYOR OF
ROCKY MOUND, TEXAS

The Honorable Noble T. Smith is the first and only mayor in the history of Rocky Mound, Texas. He has served as mayor for 28 years.

Smith was the second black city police officer of Pittsburg, Texas, population 4,500. He was the first black constable and the first black deputy sheriff of Camp County, Texas in the community of Rocky Mound. Rocky Mound had a population of 300, but that number is now down to approximately 125 due to people moving out or dying.

One day while on patrol, Smith stopped in Rocky Mound to visit his mother, and a neighbor who was burning garbage in her yard lost control of the flames. After putting in a call to the Pittsburg Fire Department, located four-and-a-half miles away, Smith decided it was time for Rocky Mound to have its own fire department. A group of citizens met and decided to incorporate and establish the fire department. In the process, it became apparent that someone needed to make applications for the city offices, and Smith eventually took the position as mayor of Rocky Mound. He has been reelected in each subsequent election.

Smith is the senior member of the Rocky Mound Church of God in Christ, and has engineered its remodeling and the building of its new fellowship hall. He is also the fire chief of Rocky Mound's volunteer fire department. Because all of the city positions Smith holds are on a volunteer basis, he has been employed in the transportation department of Pittsburg Independent School District for 21 years.

Born and raised in Camp County, Texas, Smith graduated from Douglas High School in the early 1950s. He has been married for almost 50 years, and has three children, two sons and one daughter. He also has seven grandchildren and three great-grandchildren.

THE HONORABLE

ROBERT TAYLOR

MAYOR OF
MARIANNA, ARKANSAS

The Honorable Robert Taylor became the first black mayor of Marianna, Arkansas in November of 1995, and he set a precedent for future hopefuls in the Delta region of Arkansas. Since his election, three first-time black mayors have been elected in municipalities just north and south of Marianna.

During his career, Mayor Taylor has worked very hard to bring industry to the area and maintain collaborative efforts among all the citizens. Presently, he is working on rebuilding the fire and police department facilities. One of his major accomplishments was the widening of a state highway that intersects within the town.

Taylor attended the University of Arkansas at Little Rock and later earned a psychiatric nursing license. He worked for several years within the mental health field before entering politics. He is also an ordained minister and has been a pastor for more than 20 years. He has been a volunteer for several years with the Omega Little Brothers organization.

Taylor received the Arkansas Impact Award, the Delta Leadership Award, and several other awards presented by local organizations, fraternities, and sororities.

Taylor's hobbies include reading, fishing, and watching college basketball. He also enjoys spending time with family and friends. His favorite book is the Bible, favorite color is blue, favorite food is traditional southern sweet potato pie, and his motto is, "do what you can while you can."

THE HONORABLE

RAYMOND TERRELL

MAYOR OF
WOODLAWN, OHIO

The Honorable Raymond Terrell became mayor of the Village of Woodlawn, Ohio in January of 2004. During his campaign, Mayor Terrell offered the residents new leadership, new vision, and new direction. The focus has been to expand retail and industrial development, to develop additional moderate and upscale housing, and to complete the Woodlawn Project, a combined village recreation center and national guard armory.

Ray earned a bachelor's degree in English and a master's degree in educational administration from Xavier University in Cincinnati, Ohio. He then earned a doctorate in educational administration from Wayne State University in Detroit, Michigan.

Ray has been a public school English teacher, elementary principal, assistant superintendent, and a college professor. He also served for five years as dean of the School of Education at California State University in Los Angeles. He has co-authored a book and written numerous articles on diversity and cultural issues.

After retiring from the California State system and returning home to Woodlawn, Ray stood first for village council and then successfully acquired the seat as mayor. He also currently serves as special assistant to the dean of the School of Education and Allied Professions at Miami University in Oxford, where he is working on various diversity initiatives.

Ray is married to Eloise Terrell, and they have two adult offspring, Dina and William.

It is Mayor Terrell's vision to move beautiful Woodlawn to a world class status as a small, predominantly African-American community.

THE *HONORABLE*

JOHNNY B. THOMAS

MAYOR OF
GLENDORA, MISSISSIPPI

The Honorable Johnny B. Thomas became the second African-American mayor of Glendora, Mississippi in March of 1982, and he continues to serve in that post.

Mayor Thomas brought hope of a brighter future to this impoverished rural community. Throughout his distinguished service, he has worked tirelessly to create a healthier, wealthier, and better-educated community for the citizens of Glendora.

Thomas brought vision and a sense of commitment to empower the people. He has undertaken the creation of jobs, construction of homes for low-wealth persons, and brought the first fire protection to the 105-year-old community. He also established a new town hall and provided childcare services. In addition, he is reclaiming the youth through a Boys to Men Program.

Thomas graduated from West Tallahatchie High School and attended the Mississippi Valley State University.

Mayor Thomas was featured in the 1985 edition of *Who's Who Among African Americans*.

THE HONORABLE

BOBBY R. WASHINGTON

MAYOR OF
CULLEN, LOUISIANA

The Honorable Bobby R. Washington became the fourth mayor of Cullen, Louisiana in 1988. He made history as the first African-American mayor elected in Cullen and in Webster Parish. Washington served the constituents of Cullen with dignity, tenacity, and passion for three terms before stepping down. Before leaving Cullen, the town was known as a safer, aggressive, and positive community. After sitting out of office for four years, the citizens asked Washington to come back and serve as mayor, and they reelected him with 76 percent of the vote.

During the course of his career, Washington has received numerous awards and recognition. He is a recipient of the Reese Van Hooser Memorial Award for Outstanding Elected Official; the Springhill/North Webster Chamber of Commerce's Ambassador of the Year; the School of Religious Study in North Little Rock, Arkansas' 2002 Outstanding Community Leader Award; and Alpha Kappa Alpha Sorority, Inc.'s 2003 Outstanding Public Service Award.

Washington received a bachelor of arts degree from Grambling State University in 1974. He was also a member of the Grambling State University Marching Band.

Washington did not buckle under the pressures of municipal government in a small town. Being its first African-American mayor, he let everyone know that he was not the mayor of black folks or white folks, he was the mayor of the Town of Cullen.

Washington is the pastor of the Holy Temple First Church of God in Christ in Cullen. He enjoys playing golf, and his favorite word from the Lord is, "We walk by faith and not by sight." He has been married to Frances Lucille Smith Washington for 33 years, and they have three children, André (Teresa), Priscilla (Chris), and Samuel. They have two granddaughters, D'Andrea and Dreunna.

THE HONORABLE

TERRY R. WELLS

VILLAGE PRESIDENT OF PHOENIX, ILLINOIS

The Honorable Terry R. Wells is a lifelong resident of the Village of Phoenix, Illinois. He was elected village president in 1993. He is currently serving his third term and is presently running for reelection.

Before being elected village president, Wells served for ten years as a village trustee and president of the Phoenix Library Board.

Wells has worked as an educator at Coolidge Middle School, located in Phoenix. He now teaches history at nearby Thornton High School. He is a member of the board of directors of South Suburban College.

Wells holds a bachelor's degree from Illinois State University and a master's degree from National Louis University.

Wells and his wife, Loretta, have two children, Terry, Jr. and Brianna.

THE HONORABLE

MARLIN WEST

MAYOR OF
URBANCREST, OHIO

The Honorable Marlin West became the tenth black mayor of Urbancrest, Ohio in November of 2000. He is Urbancrest's second mayor to be elected for two back-to-back terms since the late 1950s. He also served on council for eight years before becoming mayor.

Mayor West has offered the residents a cleaner, safer village to live in, provided help for seniors, and kept the center open for children. He has also helped to provide a more responsible and effective government.

West received recognition from Florida Memorial College for the Leadership Institute for Mayors, and the National Conference of Black Mayors three times. He has served on the Franklin County Board of Health, the board of the Central Ohio Municipal Council, and the board of CMACAO.

West attended high school in Grove City, Ohio, and thereafter served his country in the Marine Corps. He has been married for 30 years and has two children, Sabrina and Sheldon, and four grandchildren.

Mayor West's philosophy is, "There is a day in sight where everyone will come together and there is love from one brother to another. Everyone with and without need will come together and help, no matter who you are."

THE HONORABLE

JOHN WHITE

MAYOR OF
AMES, TEXAS

The Honorable John White became mayor of Ames, Texas, in 1993. The City of Ames has seen major improvements during the 11 years Mayor White has served the city.

During the course of his outstanding leadership, he has completed projects involving rehabilitation and improved housing for the low income and elderly; initiated infrastructure enhancements and development; and improved safety conditions in the community. Enhancements made under his tenure have greatly improved quality of life for the citizens of Ames.

Mayor White became the president and chairman of the Texas Conference of Black Mayors (TCBM) in 1999 and currently continues to hold that position. His goal for the TCBM is to see that all 40 black mayors in Texas have access to the opportunities to make the needed improvements in their communities.

Under Mayor White's leadership, TCBM provides a forum in which corporate managers and the TCBM members can have direct interaction and explore innovative and cooperative solutions to important challenges for both urban and rural Texas. He was elected to the board of directors of the National Conference of Black Mayors in 2002.

THE *HONORABLE*

RILLASTINE R. WILKINS

MAYOR OF
MUSKEGON HEIGHTS, MICHIGAN

The Honorable Rillastine R. Wilkins has served as a trailblazer in the City of Muskegon Heights, Michigan for the last 30 years. She is the city's 21st mayor and the first of the 21st century.

Wilkins is a graduate of Muskegon Community College, Muskegon Business College, and the University of Wisconsin-Eau Claire.

She has successfully negotiated an array of political affiliations to become a credible leader. Wilkins is a founding member of both the National Caucus of Women in Government (1974), and Michigan Women in Government (1977). Wilkins has served as president of the National Black Caucus of Local Elected Officials. Since taking office as mayor in 1999, she has received the Love in Action Award, the Muskegon Community College Women of Accomplishment Award, and the Woman of Distinction/Courage Award from the Michigan Women's Foundation.

An avid women's rights activist, Wilkins has been listed in *Who's Who of American Women* (13th edition, 1983-1984) as well as the *Who's Who of Black America* (1985). She was the first mayor pro tem to serve three consecutive terms in this position.

Now mayor of Muskegon Heights, Wilkins finds great fulfillment in her role as a civil leader. This recognition of her commitment to the people has sustained her constituents' trust in her ability to listen and get results.

When asked to speak about the long list of Wilkins' accomplishments in her thirty years of service to the community, the local elders replied, "A bird does not sing because it has an answer, it sings because it has a song." It was during those years that her song has become the soundtrack to the service of Muskegon Heights.

THE *HONORABLE*

ERMA JEAN WILLIAMS

MAYOR OF
GUNNISON, MISSISSIPPI

The Honorable Erma Jean Williams, mayor of Gunnison, Mississippi, was born and raised in Gunnison. At the age of 16, she and her youngest sister, Earnestine, along with other friends, became close associates of notable civil rights workers such as Fannie Lou Hamer, Amzie Moore, Doris Dozier Crenshaw, and Unita Blackwell.

Erma and Earnestine went door to door and urged blacks to register so that they would be able to vote.

Erma is past president of the Gunnison Section National Council of Negro Women, Inc. She was elected to the board of aldermen in June of 2001. She is the third African-American mayor elected in this diversely populated town.

Erma attended Bob Woods Elementary School in Gunnison, West Bolivar High School in Rosedale, and Coahoma Community College in Clarksdale, Mississippi. She received a certificate of achievement in entrepreneur training from the Delta State University Small Business Center.

Erma is married to Louis. She is the mother of one son, Stedman.

THE *HONORABLE*

LEONARD M. WILLIAMS

MAYOR OF
GIBSONVILLE, NORTH CAROLINA

The Honorable Leonard M. Williams was elected as the first black mayor of the Town of Gibsonville in November of 2001. He was elected by defeating Sandi Moulton, a white female college administrator who was appointed by the majority vote of the board of aldermen in March of 2000. Gibsonville is 80 percent white, 17 percent black, and three percent other minorities. Mayor Williams was elected in 2001 with 53 percent of the vote. He was reelected in 2003 when he defeated a hometown white male with 71 percent of the vote. He is the only black mayor in a predominantly white town in the Piedmont area.

The Town of Gibsonville was established in 1871. The first black alderman was elected in 1987. Mayor Williams was elected as the second black alderman in 1993.

Mayor Williams is a retired IRS manager, where he worked for more than 35 years. A veteran of the U.S. Army, he formerly served as a member of the board of aldermen in Gibsonville for eight years, and as a member of the town planning board for five years.

In addition to many other affiliations, Mayor Williams is chairman of the Burlington-Graham Transportation Advisory Committee. He is a member of the Piedmont Regional Transportation Board, the United Way of Alamance County, and the North Carolina Black Mayors Association.

Mayor Williams holds a bachelor of science degree in business administration from A&T State University and a master of arts degree in management and supervision from Central Michigan University.

Mayor Williams was elected with this slogan: "Let us make Gibsonville a better place for all of us to live."

He is married to Connie Williams and has three grandchildren, Kalvin Sierra, Antoine Sierra, and Anthony Woodard, Jr., and one great grandchild, Kaylen Sierra.

THE HONORABLE

MAE ROSIE WILLIAMS-JOHNSON

MAYOR OF
PACE, MISSISSIPPI

The Honorable Mae Rosie Williams-Johnson became a little-known black history fact on June 5, 2001 by becoming the first African-American woman mayor of the Town of Pace, Mississippi.

As her first term began, Mayor Williams challenged her citizens and constituents to "Rise up for progress! For pride! For Pace!" Under her leadership, the board of aldermen and the community are meeting this challenge through numerous and continuous revitalization projects for Pace. Through the receipt of community grants, the acquisitions of land, maintenance equipment, and vehicles and the improvement of recreational facilities, Williams has offered the citizens of Pace a safer, cleaner, and healthier community.

Williams was born on August 23, 1961. She graduated second in her class from Rosedale High School in Rosedale, Mississippi in 1979. She received a bachelor of business administration degree in office administration from Delta State University in Cleveland, Mississippi in 1998.

The motto for the Town of Pace is "A small time with a big future." During her tenure, the town adopted its theme, "Working together to improve our conditions and to empower our citizens." As mayor of Pace, Williams promised her citizens and constituents that with the help of the Lord, she would do her very best to improve the conditions of the town. To this day, she has kept that promise.

Williams is married to Sam Johnson and they have three wonderful children, Laderious, Lajustin, and LaSandreá, and one precious granddaughter, Aujané.

THE HONORABLE

EULIS A. WILLIS

MAYOR OF
NAVASSA, NORTH CAROLINA

The Honorable Eulis "Scrap" Willis was elected as the second mayor of the Town of Navassa, located in southeastern North Carolina, on November 4, 1999. Navassa was incorporated in 1977 and Willis has served on the town council since the incorporation. His predecessor, Mayor Louis "Bobby" Brown, had served in the office of mayor for 22 years, and is considered a pioneer for black mayors throughout the state of North Carolina.

Mayor Willis quickly put his stamp on Navassa when he and his town council annexed some adjacent communities to their town, which tripled the population, quadrupled the annual budget, and increased the corporate boundaries of Navassa fivefold. Navassa was granted a charter amendment, which changed the mayor's term from two years to four years. Willis ran unopposed and was elected to a four-year term in 2001.

Navassa has completed some major infrastructure improvements during Willis' term. These include $4 million in water and sewer services improvements, more than $5 million in highway and street improvements, and a $3 million major bridge replacement. The town also attracted a boat manufacturing facility, which currently employs 400 workers and has a goal of hiring 600 workers by mid-2006. This facility represents a $30 million investment.

On November 29, 2005, the State of North Carolina's Department of Transportation honored Willis by dedicating the new bridge and naming a section of the main road into Navassa after him.

Mayor Willis, a 1971 graduate of North Carolina A&T, emphasizes that the education he received there, both academic and worldly, is a reflection of his personal motto and the theme of the town, "People Working For People."

THE HONORABLE

H. ABRAM WILSON

MAYOR OF
SAN RAMON, CALIFORNIA

The City of San Ramon, the dynamic jewel of Northern California, made history in 2003 by selecting the Honorable H. Abram Wilson as the first elected mayor in the city's 22-year history. He is also the first mayor of African-American heritage to head this city.

During his short political career, Mayor Wilson has served on numerous city and county boards and commissions. His public service includes ten years on the San Ramon Arts Council, serving as president for three years, and ten years of service on the Parks and Community Services Commission, serving as chairman for three terms. Wilson is the 2005 recipient of the California Association for Music Education's Legislative Leadership Award in recognition of his support of music education in schools. He is a member of the Kappa Alpha Psi Fraternity, Inc.

Wilson is a former vice president of Wells Fargo Bank Investment Division, San Francisco, and a former principle of Bank of America Securities, LLC, San Francisco.

Mayor Wilson is married to Dr. Karen B. Wilson. They have two children, Natausha A. Wilson, Esq. and P. Nathan Wilson. His motto, "Together we can. Together we will," continues to make San Ramon one of the best cities in the United States to raise a family, educate children, and build a successful large or small business.

THE HONORABLE

MARY MCCASKILL YOUNG

MAYOR OF
KILMICHAEL, MISSISSIPPI

The seventh child of Mr. and Mrs. Sammie Edwards McCaskill, the Honorable Mary Young became the first African-American female mayor of the town of Kilmichael, Mississippi on February 18, 2003. It was, coincidently, on her father's birthday.

Mary's hope for her town is to establish a structure where citizens will be the most important element in the town's daily efforts by becoming partners for a better Kilmichael. She plans to achieve this goal by allowing citizens a voice and opportunity to participate in helping form and improve their surroundings. Moreover, her goal is to create an open form of government for the citizens of Kilmichael.

Mary plans to work with county schools by setting up a program called "A Day with the Mayor," and plans to institute town policies and other guidelines for better efficiency. One achievement has been starting a project with the Mississippi Development Authority to obtain a grant for dealing with raw sewage within the town city limits. In 2004, Mary applied for the Home Program but missed success. The town still hopes to obtain funding for the needed cause. Mary has received a $400,000 grant, earmarked for the town streets, through Congressman Bennie Thompson.

In 1998, Mary received a bachelor of science degree from Mississippi Valley State University in public administration, with hopes to obtain a master of science degree.

Mary is a thankful mother of four children, who are pursuing their college careers. She has been married for 31 years to Rochester Young, who is the president of the Concerned Citizens of Kilmichael. She is a member of the Mount Olive Missionary Baptist Church, where she is an active member.

Mayor Young enjoys serving her family, studying different materials and music, meeting people, and gardening.

Her favorite quote is, "God knows!"

THE HONORABLE

WILBERT A. YOUNG

MAYOR OF
WILKINSBURG, PENNSYLVANIA

The Honorable Wilbert A. Young is the mayor of the Borough of Wilkinsburg, Pennsylvania. Previously, he worked in the area of planning and community development. He was chosen to participate in the National Internship in Community Economic Development at the Development Training Institute for his commitment to the redevelopment and revitalization of inner city communities.

Mayor Young has always believed in the value of public service and has held a number of positions in the public sector. It is his tenure as a legislative staff member on Capitol Hill in the U.S. House of Representatives that was the turning point in his political career. After much success in this capacity, Young began to receive positive attention from the legislative community. He was staff for the LA Legislative Black Caucus and went on to hold a number of positions on the local, state, and federal levels.

Young was chosen as senior executive fellow at Harvard University and John F. Kennedy School of Government, both of which he maintains frequent association with through membership in their Alumni Associations. Later, chosen as a Ralph Bunche fellow while at Dillard University, he was recognized as an Outstanding Young Man in America. He was also chosen as a graduate fellow at the Graduate Center for Planning and Environment of the Pratt Institute, School of Architecture.

Young has been a board member of Federal Home Loan Bank of Pittsburgh, and served with the Landmark Development Corporation Board and the Neighborhood Housing Service. He is an active participant in the mentoring programs at the Wilkinsburg, Pennsylvania Boy's and Girl's Club.

Mayor Young is the survivor of the recently deceased Meredith Watson, nationally known Pittsburgh artist and teacher. The father of five children, Young is a dedicated, full-time father, in addition to his many civic affiliations.

Black *Mayors* In America

At the time of publication, there were no photos available for the following mayors.

THE HONORABLE

IRMA L. ANDERSON

MAYOR OF RICHMOND, CALIFORNIA

The Honorable Irma L. Anderson is the mayor of the City of Richmond, California.

Upon retiring as director of public health nursing in 1992, Mayor Anderson ran for Richmond City Council. She was successful and became the first black female city councilperson on the Richmond City Council. She also enjoyed the honor of receiving the highest number of votes ever in the history of council elections. In 1997, Anderson was reelected to the Richmond City Council, again receiving the highest number of votes. In 2001, Anderson ran for the office of mayor and was successful, becoming the first black female elected mayor of a major California city.

During her brief tenure as mayor, Anderson has been instrumental in developing a historic partnership with the West Contra Costa Unified School District, dubbed Kids! First, to cultivate and expand after-school programs throughout Richmond. This past January, the Kids! First partnership secured over $1.8 million to begin five pilot after-school programs in the city. Currently, the partnership is outlining a long-term sustainability and expansion plan for after-school programs at every school site in Richmond. Additionally, Anderson has been successfully lobbying to secure Richmond a fair share of transportation dollars, which include $12 million from the State of California for a Richmond ferry service in 2010.

Mayor Anderson earned a bachelor of science degree from Cornell University and a master's degree in public health from University of California, Berkeley.

THE HONORABLE

CLARENCE E. ANTHONY

MAYOR OF SOUTH BAY, FLORIDA

The Honorable Clarence E. Anthony has served his community since his election to the city commission in March of 1984. He was elected mayor of South Bay in 1985. A creative and thoughtful leader, Anthony has brought a wealth of experience and personal energy into his work.

Over the last 17 years, Anthony has been on the forefront of politics in Florida and the nation having very productive presidencies with the Florida League of Cities (FLC) and the National League of Cities (NLC), respectively. As NLC president, Anthony was chief spokesperson of the oldest and largest organization of municipal officials in the United States. He has served on the NLC board of directors and several NLC committees. Anthony was president of the FLC in 1995. Now vice chair of FLC's Federal Action Strike Team, he has served on the executive board since 1992.

He is a member of the National Black Caucus of Local Elected Officials, the Federal Judicial Nomination Commission, the Florida Environmental Land Management Study Commission, and the Federal Government Everglades Ecosystem Task Force. Also a trustee of the nature conservancy, he serves on the boards of directors for Bealls, Inc., and the National Conference of Black Mayors.

A lifelong resident of the South Bay area bordering Lake Okeechobee, Anthony completed his undergraduate studies and earned a master's degree in public administration at Florida Atlantic University.

Anthony is president of Emerge Consulting Corporation and remains active in many professional and service organizations in South Bay and Palm Beach County. His community service has earned him many honors, including the Florida Jaycees Mayor of the Year Award (1989-1990); Distinguished Alumnus Awards from Florida Atlantic University and Palm Beach Community College; *Ebony's* Future Leader Award; the Outstanding Young Men in America Award; and the Outstanding Community Leaders in America Award.

THE HONORABLE

RUBYE BYRD, Ph.D.

MAYOR OF GREENVILLE, GEORGIA

The Honorable Rubye Byrd, Ph.D., completed a doctor of philosophy program in counseling and psychological services. She is certified in special education and has attended law school. Currently, she is director of federal programs at Morehouse College for the U.S. Department of Education. Byrd is a national trainer for the department and travels the nation as well as its trust territories. She has secured several million dollars for colleges and universities. She has received many awards across the country, and she serves on several national, regional, and state boards and committees.

Byrd was reared by her grandparents, Henry and Rosa Stinson, in the quaint town of Stovall. Her late father was a railroad man and she traveled the country extensively as a child. She attributes all of her success to the nurturing community of Stovall and her many mentors.

As a national speaker, Byrd always reminds her audiences that she is a southern girl reared in a small, warm village in Meriwether County. A proud member of Delta Sigma Theta Sorority, Inc., Byrd is glad to serve in the top capacity for the City of Greenville.

THE HONORABLE

ALEX DAVIS

MAYOR OF NEWELLTON, LOUISIANA

Alex Davis is the first black mayor in the town of Newellton, Louisiana. Davis' election was historic as he defeated an incumbent who had held the office for more than 30 years.

A man of humble beginnings, Davis worked a series of odd jobs ranging from working in the fields to working in sawmills and grain elevators, before entering the field of education. A graduate of Southern University, he received his degree in 1966. Davis is a retired teacher who taught social studies and accounting in the Tallulah public school system until the year 2000.

Davis has served as a deacon at Newellton Chapel Baptist Church for more than 30 years. He has two children by his first wife, the late Carrie Pollard, and one child by his second wife, Helen Marie Hunter. Davis considers his family and friends to be his wealth.

DONALD G. DAVIS

MAYOR OF SNOW HILL, NORTH CAROLINA

The Honorable Donald G. Davis is the mayor of Snow Hill, North Carolina. At age 30, he was elected as the first African-American and youngest mayor in the town's 173-year history. He is also the youngest serving mayor in the state. Don has brought progressive leadership to Snow Hill.

Under Don's leadership, residents of Snow Hill have experienced enormous growth in quality affordable housing, street resurfacing, recreational and community activity enhancement, and community revitalization. Likewise, the town has experienced growth in housing rehabilitation, downtown revitalization, historic preservation, beautification, resident participation, and strategic planning.

Don was selected as one of the "50 Young Leaders of Tomorrow" by *Ebony* magazine. He has been labeled by many as an "up and rising star."

Currently, Don serves on the North Carolina League of Municipalities Committee for Economic Development and is a member of the North Carolina Conference of Black Mayors. He was chairman of the First Congressional District Democratic Party for one year and resigned to run for the United States Congress. After withdrawing from the congressional race, he was unanimously reelected chairman of the First Congressional District Democratic Party. A 2003 graduate of the Congressional Black Caucus Political Bootcamp, Don was elected in June 2004 as an at-large delegate to the Democratic Party National Convention.

Don is a 1994 graduate of the United States Air Force Academy with a bachelor of science degree in social sciences. He graduated from Central Michigan University with a master of science degree in administration and from East Carolina University with a master of arts degree in sociology. He is completing a doctorate in educational leadership with a concentration in higher education.

Don is a person who is ahead of his time and whose leadership is best characterized as energetic and innovative.

HENRY ESPY

MAYOR OF CLARKSDALE, MISSISSIPPI

It has often been said that leadership should be born out of understanding the needs of those who would be affected by it. Born in Yazoo City, Mississippi, the Honorable Henry Espy was destined not only to lead, but to understand those who would follow him.

A homegrown community servant, Mayor Espy earned his bachelor of science degree in business education at Southern University.

Before his career as a public servant, Espy was a long-time employee of the Century Funeral Home. He held the positions of associate manager and vice president before becoming the corporation's president in 1980.

Espy was elected to the office of mayor of the city of Clarksdale after having spent considerable time in the community serving its people. Even more impressive was his election as city commissioner of Clarksdale.

With this win, Espy became the first black elected to any office in the city. He held the office for 14 years.

Espy is a long-time member of Bell Grove Missionary Baptist Church. He is a 33° Mason, a member of the Coahoma County Chamber of Commerce, and a former Basileus of Omega Psi Phi Fraternity. In addition to his civic memberships, he maintains both personal and business relationships with those he met at the Century Funeral Home. He continues as a member of the Mississippi Funeral Directors and Morticians Association and the National Funeral Directors and Morticians Association.

A member of the executive board of the National Conference of Black Mayors, after having served for two terms as president, Mayor Espy proves that he can not only lead, but he can follow. Presently serving in his third term as mayor of the City of Clarksdale, his constituents have made their position clear. They would much rather him lead.

DIANA M. FENNELL

MAYOR OF COLMAR MANOR, MARYLAND

The Honorable Diana M. Fennell has served as mayor of Colmar Manor, Maryland since May of 2000. Her goal is to serve the constituents of the community through her volunteer and elected positions. Prior to her election as mayor, Fennell served as a town councilmember representing Ward Three.

In addition to her current duties, Fennell has served in the capacity of office manager/information management with the Prince George's County Fire Department since May of 1999. She is also a member of the Recreational Council of Colmar Manor, the Neighborhood Watch Committee, the Prince George's County Municipal Association, the Ladies Auxiliary of the VFW, and the National Arbor Day Foundation. Fennell is also the current secretary of the Maryland Black Mayor's Association.

From October of 2001 to October of 2002, Fennell was vice president of the Prince George's County Elected Women. From January of 2002 to July of 2003, Fennell served as secretary of the Maryland Mayor's Association; she is currently serving as vice president of the association. She also served on the Maryland State Affordable Housing Board in 2003.

Fennell graduated from Greensville County High School in 1986. She then attended one year at Catholic University studying business administration. In 2002, she became a state certified fires science instructor. Since 2003, Fennell has continued to pursue her education at DeVry University.

VIOLA M. FOSTER

MAYOR OF PLANTERSVILLE, MISSISSIPPI

The Honorable Viola M. Foster is the mayor of Plantersville, Mississippi. She has held that office since April of 1998. A retired teacher, Foster's resume reflects a life dedicated to public and community service.

Foster is a member of the National Conference of Black Mayors, the Mississippi Municipal Association, Women In Municipalities, and the Lee County Executive Committee of the Democratic Party. She received designation as a Certified Municipal Official by the Mississippi Municipal League.

Foster is a member of New Zion Missionary Baptist Church where she is a Sunday school teacher, teacher of the new members class, and president of the Senior Women's Missionary Union, a position she has held for the last ten years. Foster is currently president of the General Progressive Baptist State Convention of Mississippi, Inc.; secretary for the trustee board at the Ministerial Institute and College; instructor for the National Baptist Convention of America, Inc. Congress of Christian Workers; and a field missionary for the Mississippi area of the National Baptist Convention of America, Inc.

Foster's fraternal affiliations include Delta Sigma Theta Sorority, Inc., the Order of the Eastern Star #515, and Queen Elizabeth Court #124. She also holds memberships with the National Council of Negro Women, Inc., the Black Business Association in Tupelo, and the NAACP, where she is a lifetime member.

Foster received a bachelor of science degree from Mississippi Industrial College in Holly Springs, and a master of science degree and a master of education degree from the University of Mississippi. She also received a bachelor of religious education degree from the Mississippi Baptist Seminary in Jackson, and an honorary doctorate degree from the Ministerial Institute and College in West Point, Mississippi.

Foster is married to Leatrich Foster, Sr., a deacon, and is the mother of four adult children.

CARRIE F. FULGHUM

MAYOR OF GAINESVILLE, ALABAMA

The Honorable Carrie F. Fulghum made history when she was elected as Gainesville, Alabama's first woman and first African American to serve as mayor.

Mayor Fulghum shares the passion of the residents of Gainesville to preserve the town's history and make it a better place for families, children, and visitors.

An accomplished corporate strategist, Fulghum's vision and expertise in business performance have driven notable growth in Gainesville. Her work as general manager of Panola Land Buyers Housing Development Corporation reflects her strategic approach to building a business.

Fulghum is a founder and board member of First Steps Child Care Center, a board member of The Federation of Southern Cooperatives Land Assistance Fund, and a chapter coordinator of the Mandela Chapter of 21st Century Youth Leadership Movement. Her passion and commitment for social justice is highlighted by her accomplishments as president of Gainesville's Commission of Southern Rural Black Women Initiative.

Fulghum has embarked on countless tough challenges as mayor. In spite of this, she managed to increase the population, develop new businesses, create new jobs, improve the physical appearance of the town, and make her dream a reality by creating Gainesville's Senior Citizens Program. She has received several awards during her exceptional career and is know to many people as the "Village Mother."

Fulghum received a bachelor of science degree from the University of West Alabama. Her enthusiasm, dedication, and devotion are reflected in her children, Douglas and Valarie.

CLARENCE W. HAWKINS

MAYOR OF BASTROP, LOUISIANA

The Honorable Clarence W. Hawkins is the mayor of Bastrop, Louisiana and has held the office since 1989. Prior to his election as mayor, Hawkins was a representative of Horace Mann Companies from 1985 to 1989. He had 20 years of experience in education before moving into the government sector.

From 1965 to 1985, Hawkins worked with the Morehouse Parish Public School System as a teacher, assistant principle, curriculum supervisor, co-director of personnel, and supervisor of textbooks and adult education.

Hawkins' call to lead and passion for service is undeniable. An active and committed public servant, he currently serves on the boards of directors of numerous civic and professional associations and organizations, including the Foundation for the Mid South, the Louisiana Asset Management Pool, and the University Foundation (ULM).

Hawkins serves in leadership positions on several other boards including secretary of the board of the National Conference of Black Mayors, and vice chairman of the board for the Firefighter's Retirement System. He is also a member of the Louisiana Workforce Commission and the Democratic State Central Committee of Louisiana.

Hawkins was the first black president of the Louisiana Municipal Association Executive Board. He is a past president of the boards of a host of organizations including the Ouachita-Morehouse Workforce Alliance; the Morehouse School Employees Federal Credit Union; the Macon Ridge Economic Development Region, Inc.; Club 21 Men's Club of Bastrop; the Louisiana chapter of the National Conference of Black Mayors; the Morehouse Library Board; the Northeast Supervisors Association; and the Bastrop High School Band Association.

A man of faith, Hawkins is member of St. Mary's Christian Methodist Episcopal Church, where he serves as assistant superintendent of the Sunday school, director of the adult choir, member of the finance committee, and is a past president of the steward board.

WALTER S. HILL

MAYOR OF MOSSES, ALABAMA

The Honorable Walter S. Hill is at the helm of Mosses, Alabama, a 2,000-plus, largely African-American town. At 31 years of age, Hill is far more experienced than his three decades of living would allow.

He is a member of the Alabama State Conference of Mayors and the 21st Century Leadership Movement. He is vice chair for the Door II Community Center, the Economic Development Committee, and the Alabama Municipal League. Hill is also chairman of the Lowndes County Mayors Coalition, the Lowndes County Head Start Program, and the Lowndes County Juvenile Justice Board. In addition, he is a Miles College National/State Alumni and Central High School State Alumni.

Currently, Hill is the technology supervisor for the Lowndes County Head Start program, and he owns Bell's Funeral Home.

Hill decided to run for office because of a desire to uplift his community through public service. When the opportunity came for him to run for office, Hill pledged that he would provide effective and responsive leadership that would contribute to the progress of his community.

Hill completed high school in the Town of Mosses. He then went on to Miles College in Birmingham and earned a bachelor's degree. In high school and college, he dabbled in writing, public speaking, and acting. However, he remained committed to his home and he came back to become a public official.

Hill realized he wanted to be a politician after hearing a speech by John F. Kennedy. These words challenged Hill: "Some men see things as they are and ask why, I see things that never were and ask why not?"

Hill is the single father of three-year-old Dremequa Lasha Hill.

EARLENE JOHNSON

MAYOR OF COLONY, ALABAMA

The Honorable Earlene Johnson retired from her 30-year service career with the Alabama pubic education system only to answer another calling, to serve her community as mayor of Colony, Alabama. Recently elected to her second term as mayor, Johnson is dedicated to the community of Colony, which has a population of more than 400. Johnson never had political aspirations, but there was just a job that needed to be done.

She is a former elementary school teacher and library supervisor for the Cullman County public school system, where she first formed her philosophy of giving back to her fellow man. Johnson's life philosophy is that of John Wesley, founder of Methodism: "Do all the good you can, in all the ways you can, in all the places you can, at all the times you can, to all the people you can, as long as ever you can."

Johnson completed her elementary and high school education at Colony High School She went on to complete her teacher's certification from what was formerly known as Alabama State Teacher's College in Montgomery, now Alabama State University, where she earned a bachelor's degree. Her post-graduate work was completed at Alabama A&M University in Huntsville.

Johnson is active in many civic and social organizations including the Lion's Club, Delta Kappa Gamma Society International, the Retired Teachers of Alabama, the Alabama Democratic Women, the Retired Teachers of Cullman County (NEA and AEA), and the United Methodist Women.

Johnson admires the politics of Shirley Chisholm and continues to work part-time at Wallace State Community College. She believes that "success is working toward a needed goal, and achieving that goal."

KENNEDY V. JOHNSON

MAYOR OF MOUND BAYOU, MISSISSIPPI

The combination of both need and desire to do something for my community," is the eager reply from Mayor Kennedy V. Johnson when asked for the motivation behind his commitment to public service, established more than eight years ago. This dedication has been displayed since his election to office in July 2001, after a lifetime involved in politics.

Mayor Johnson was raised in Mississippi. The son of the late Eddie Johnson, Sr. and Olevia M. Johnson, Mound Bayou's mayor proudly boasts "fore-parents" who were co-founders of the community in 1887.

A 1980 graduate of the Mound Bayou School District, Johnson attended I.T. Montgomery Elementary School and Mound Bayou High School. He later went on to earn a political science degree from Mississippi Delta Junior College.

Johnson's transition to a large political arena did not come as a surprise to those who had witnessed his maturing business acumen. He made clear his commitment to both serve and protect as a Mississippi Department of Corrections officer and as a Mound Bayou Police Department patrolman. He then campaigned successfully for the office of alderman, serving from 1997 to 2001. He was elected to the office of mayor in July 2001.

Despite his busy schedule, the Mississippi native finds time to devote attention to several local and national organizations, stressing a desire to remain a visible and approachable servant of the people.

Mayor Johnson's dedication to service extends beyond the veil worn by the average politician. He has managed to maintain the same relationship with his community as he does with his family. Moreover, he has managed to make his community his family as well.

Married and the father of two children who attend school in Mound Bayou, he guards his responsibility to the younger members of his constituency.

KEVIN L. JOHNSON

MAYOR OF MANNING, SOUTH CAROLINA

The Honorable Kevin L. Johnson is mayor of Manning, South Carolina. He currently serves as the second vice president of the South Carolina Conference of Black Mayors, and is one of only four mayors appointed by SLED and the Municipal Association of South Carolina to serve on a Regional Counter Terrorism Task Force. Kevin served on the Manning City Council for six years before being elected mayor in April of 2000.

Kevin is first vice chairman of the board of directors of Santee Lynches Regional Council of Governments, and is a member of the boards of directors for the South Carolina Association of Regional Councils, and Wateree Community Actions, Inc. He is also a member and chairman of the trustee board of Ebenezer Missionary Baptist Church in Manning.

He received a bachelor of science degree in business administration from the University of South Carolina in 1982. Upon graduating in 1982, Kevin began a career with the South Carolina Department of Revenue, where he held several positions and currently serves as manager of the collection services division. He is also a 1995 graduate of Leadership South Carolina.

Previously, Kevin served as a member of the boards of Harvin Clarendon County Library, the Clarendon County Chamber of Commerce, Black River Healthcare, Inc., the South Carolina School Board Association's Workers' Compensation Board, and Clarendon County School District Two.

Johnson was born to Sallie M. Johnson and the late Willie L. Johnson on September 27, 1960. He is married to the former Gloria Richardson, and they are the proud parents of three children, Kimberly, Kenneth, and Kyndra. Kimberly and Kenneth, both U.S. Army veterans, are currently students at the University of South Carolina. Kyndra is a seventh grader at Manning Junior High School.

THE HONORABLE

ERIC KELLOGG

MAYOR OF HARVEY, ILLINOIS

The Honorable Eric Kellogg is the mayor of Harvey, Illinois. Having served in the field of education for more than 20 years, Kellogg's resume reflects a life dedicated to public service, community support, and fostering education.

In addition to his charge to move the City of Harvey into the future, Kellogg is the assistant superintendent for School District 152. He has worked in the past as a teacher, coach, dean of students, and director of administrative services.

Kellogg's commitment to the City of Harvey and its young people has led him to serve on numerous boards and foundations. He has served as executive director and contributed to the financial wellbeing and support of such organizations as Harvey Little League, the Harvey Twisters Wrestling Program, the Harvey Colts Football Team, the United Negro College Fund, and area churches.

Kellogg holds a bachelor's degree in physical education from Illinois State University; a master's degree in curriculum from National-Louis University in Evanston; and an administrative certificate from Lewis University in Romeoville. In 2002, he graduated from Lewis University's Graduate School with a superintendent's endorsement. He is currently working on a doctor of philosophy degree.

Kellogg is a dedicated public servant.

THE HONORABLE

ANNIE M. MICKENS

MAYOR OF PETERSBURG, VIRGINIA

The Honorable Annie M. Mickens is mayor of Petersburg, Virginia. She is a councilwoman of Ward Five, and has served on City Council from 1986 to the present.

Mickens' goal is to serve the citizens of Petersburg by helping enable the city's staff, employees, and council to provide the most effective and efficient city services, facilities, programs, and positive growth possible for the City of Petersburg. Her major areas of focus are education, neighborhood revitalization, and youth services.

Currently, Petersburg is in the process of continuing economic recovery and stabilization. The city's continual progress is improving the area's need to provide an excellent quality of life for all its citizens.

Mickens graduated from Virginia State University with a bachelor of science degree in mathematics and a master's degree in mathematics education. Her full-time occupation is serving as a teacher and department chairperson in the mathematics department of Petersburg High School (1972 to present).

Mickens' organizational membership includes serving on the National, Virginia, and Petersburg Education Associations; the Petersburg Democratic Committee; the Petersburg Police Athletic League Board; the Citizens' Review Board Oversight Committee; the city audit committee; and Virginia Municipal League's human development and education policy committee.

A native of Nelson County, Virginia, Mickens is married and has two children. She is a member of Good Shepherd Baptist Church in Petersburg. Her hobbies and interests include reading, church activities, high school sports, sewing, music, and watching *Star Trek*.

CHARLES E. STOKES

MAYOR OF UTICA, MISSISSIPPI

The Honorable Charles E. Stokes became the 17th mayor of Utica, Mississippi in June of 1997 and made history as the first African American to serve in that position in Utica.

Mayor Stokes offered the residents of Utica a vision and passion for making a safer, cleaner city; a better city for families, seniors, and children; and is providing a more open, responsive, and effective city government.

Stokes is a graduate of Utica High School and Hinds Community College, formerly Utica Junior College.

Stokes is a man who believes in family values and personal integrity. He is a positive role model and is actively involved in the educational process of the students at Utica Elementary School and Hinds A.H.S., where he serves on the advisory committee. In addition, he is a former member of the Hinds County Community Development Task Force, and a former commissioner of the Utica Police Department. He currently serves as a deputy with the Hinds County Sheriff's Department.

Mayor Stokes has tackled the tough challenges in Utica's government, and lived up to his campaign slogan, "It's Time For A Change."

LOYDLEETTA JOHNSON WABBINGTON

MAYOR OF UNION, ALABAMA

The Honorable Loydleetta Johnson Wabbington became the third mayor of the Town of Union in October of 2004. She is the first woman mayor in Union's 25-year history.

Through positive and responsive leadership, Loydleetta endeavors to serve the town with diligence, wisdom, and a sincere passion to lift, enlighten, and encourage. Some of the growth and positive changes her administration is offering the citizens of Union include a safer, cleaner environment, resurfaced roads, parks and recreational facilities, and a multi-complex center.

Formerly, Loydleetta served on the Town Council for 16 years, and she taught health and physical education for 30 years, now retired. Currently, Loydleetta is a Primerica Financial Service Representative and president of the Greene County Education Retirees Association. Additionally, she is a health/physical education school area contact for state workshops.

Her awards and honors include certificates from the local chapter of the SCLC, and the Alabama Education Retirees Association. Loydleetta is a parliamentarian, charter member, and former president of the Greene County Alumnae chapter of Delta Sigma Theta Sorority, Inc. She is also a member of First Baptist Union Church, where she is a youth advisor, assistant secretary, and serves on several committees.

Loydleetta received a bachelor of arts degree from Stillman College in Tuscaloosa, Alabama, and bachelor of science and master of arts degrees from Livingston University, now the University of West Alabama. She completed further studies at the University of Alabama.

Loydleetta is married to Ross William Wabbington, III and is the mother of one son, Ross IV, and three adopted sons, Daryll F. Hunt, Nehemiah Kenyatta Johnson, and Wilfred Michael Thomas.

Mayor Wabbington loves traveling and enjoys anything sweet. Her life slogan reflects this attitude: "Lord, I put my trust in you. Send me, I'll go!"

THE HONORABLE

ROSCOE WARREN

MAYOR OF HOMESTEAD, FLORIDA

The Honorable Roscoe Warren, mayor of Homestead, Florida, was born in Georgetown, South Carolina. His family moved to Homestead when he was three years old. He is the fifth of 13 children raised by his mother.

Mayor Warren attended the University of Miami as an Upward Bound student and graduated from Florida Presbyterian College in St. Petersburg, Florida. He then pursued and earned his master of business administration degree from Georgetown University. In 1978, he attended Harvard University's JFK School of Government for one year to enhance his skills and education.

Warren returned to Homestead and was elected president of the NAACP for the Homestead/ Florida City community. In 1981, he ran for the City Council of Homestead and won a four-year term. He has won reelection for seven consecutive terms, and was elected vice mayor of Homestead on three occasions. On February 15, 2001 he was appointed mayor. He was reelected in November 2001 and again in 2003. Warren was the first African American elected as mayor of Homestead.

For more than 22 years, Warren has been employed at Florida Memorial College, the only historically black college in South Florida and one of the oldest colleges in the state. He serves as the college's vice president of enrollment management.

Warren's professional work experience consisted of administrative positions with the U.S. Department of Education, the Mathematical Policy Research Institute in Princeton, New Jersey, Florida International University, and Metropolitan Dade County. He has also owned and operated his own consulting business, Warren & Associates, Inc.

Mayor Warren, with partner, Dr. Willie C. Robinson, helped make state history by opening Florida's first black-owned Denny's restaurant. More importantly, the ownership represented the first in the entire southeastern portion of the U.S.

Warren is a member of numerous social and civic organizations.

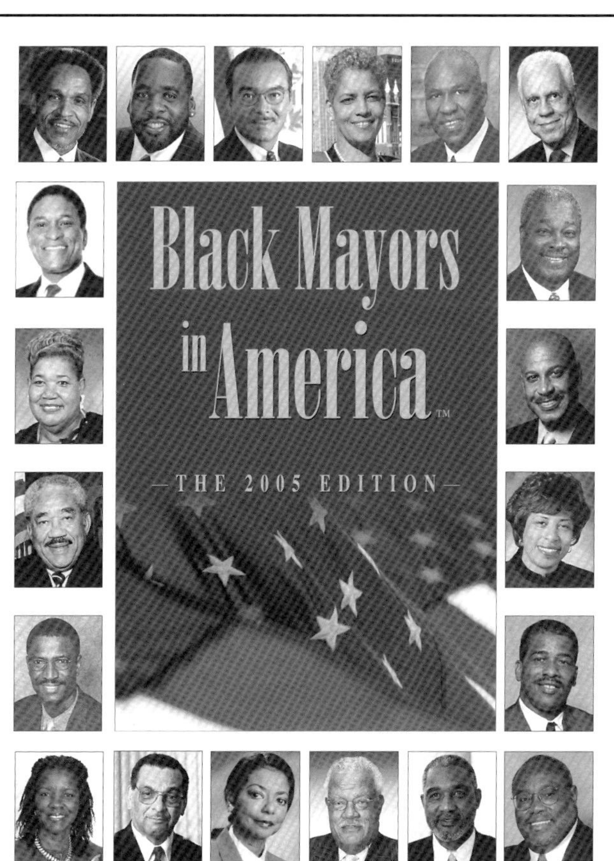

AFRICAN-AMERICAN MAYORS BY STATE

ALABAMA

Helenor Bell	Hayneville, AL
Geneva Bledsoe	Five Points, AL
Cleon Bolden	Mt. Vernon, AL
Rufus Carson	Tuskegee, AL
Charles B. Cole	New Brockton, AL
Eddie Cooper	Brighton, AL
Edward Daniel	Marion, AL
Ron Davis	Prichard, AL
Danny Evans	Camp Hill, AL
Cynthia Evans	Vrendenburgh, AL
Robert Finley	LaFayette, AL
Johnny Ford	Tuskegee, AL
Fletcher Fountain, Sr.	Fort Deposit, AL
Marvalene Freeman	Madison, AL
Carrie Fulgham	Gainesville, AL
Carolyn Gosa	York, AL
John Jackson	White Hall, AL
Thomas Jackson	Lisman, AL
Fred James	North Courtland, AL
Earlene Johnson	Colony, AL
Bernard Kincaid	Birmingham, AL
Essie R. Madison	McMullen, AL
Albert Mason	Lipscomb, AL
Edward E. May	Bessemer, AL
Henry Miles	Akron, AL
Vicki Moore	Slocomb, AL
Sharon Nicholson	Yellow Bluff, AL
Herbert H. Payne, Sr.	Geiger, AL
James Perkins, Jr.	Selma, AL
Willie Mae Powell	Shorter, AL
Robert Ricks	Leighton, AL
William Scott	Mosses, AL
Ozell Smith	Gordon, AL
Sadie Stanford	Faunsdale, AL
Raymond Steele	Eutaw, AL
Walter Taylor	Boligee, AL
Bessie D. Twine	Attala, AL
Loydleetta Wabbington	Union, AL
Johnnie B. Washington	Greensboro, AL
Phillip White	Uniontown, AL
Roy Willingham	Emelle, AL
Eddie Woods	Forkland, AL
Ralph Woods	Hobson City, AL
Larry Yates, Sr.	Epes, AL
Billy Young	Hillsboro, AL

ARKANSAS

Helen Adams	Jericho, AR
James Lee Brooks	Madison, AR
Christine Brownlee	Gilmore, AR
Larry S. Bryant	Forrest City, AR
Willie C. Carringan	Ozan, AR
Kervin Dolphin	Allport, AR
Richard Ealy	Twin Groves, AR
Floyd E. Gray	Dermott, AR
Patricia Henderson	Edmondson, AR
Martha Hendrix	Tollette, AR
Curly Jackson	Wilmar, AR
Eddie Johnson	Cotton Plant, AR
Robert Johnson	Birdsong, AR
Shirley Johnson	Alexander, AR
Plex Frank Lucas	Jennette, AR
Kirby Massey	Sunset, AR
Chester McGee	Turrell, AR
Robert Miller	Helena, AR
Stanley Morris	Menifee, AR
James Murry, Sr.	Wabbaseka, AR
Spencer Nixon	Wilton, AR
Bobbie Norman	Dumas, AR
Leon A. Phillips, Jr.	Lakeview, AR
Leo Rasberry	Altheimer, AR
Carl Redus, Jr.	Pine Bluff, AR
Lorraine Smith	Wrightsville, AR
Sherman Smith	Earle, AR
Tommie Smith	Reed, AR
Yvonne Smith-Dockery	Garland City, AR
Robert P. Taylor	Marianna, AR
Willie Toney, Jr.	Carthage, AR
Lula Tyler	Holly Grove, AR
Charlie Tyson	Buckner, AR
Henry Warren	McNeil, AR
Johnny Weaver	West Helena, AR
Ethel Westbrook	Lexa, AR
Eddye Wilson	Gould, AR
Leroy C. Wright	Anthonyville, AR

CALIFORNIA

Irma Anderson	Richmond, CA
Louis Byrd	Lynwood, CA
Roosevelt F. Dorn	Inglewood, CA
Jim Lawrence	Foster City, CA
Eric Perrodin	Compton, CA
H. Abram Wilson	San Ramon, CA
David Woods	East Palo Alto, CA

DELAWARE

James M. Baker	Wilmington, DE

DISTRICT OF COLUMBIA

Anthony A. Williams	Washington, D.C.

FLORIDA

Clarence Anthony	South Bay, FL
Earnest O. Barkley	Gretna, FL
Michael D. Brown	Riviera Beach, FL
Samuel S. Brown	Lauderdale Lakes, FL
Josaphat "Joe" Celestin	North Miami, FL
Audrey M. Edmonson	El Portal, FL
Karl Nathaniel Flagg	Palatka, FL
Shirley Gibson	Miami Gardens, FL
Anthony Grant	Eatonville, FL
Riley Henderson	Cottondale, FL
Joseph L. Kelly	Opa-Locka, FL
Delores Madison	Midway, FL
John Marks	Tallahassee, FL
Otis T. Wallace	Florida City, FL
Roscoe Warren	Homestead, FL

GEORGIA

Willie Adams, Jr.	Albany, GA
Robert Albritten	Dawson, GA
Herman Baker	Wadley, GA
Dewaine T. Bell	Barnesville, GA
Edna Brown	Irwinton, GA
Justine Thomas Brown	Oliver, GA
Ralph Brown, Jr.	Buena Vista, GA
Willie Burns	Washington, GA
Rubye Byrd	Greenville, GA
James Carter	Woodland, GA
Willie J. Davis	Vienna, GA
Tholen Edwards	Baconton, GA
C. Jack Ellis	Macon, GA
William Evans, Jr.	Sparta, GA
Olan Faulk	Richland, GA
John N. Fluker	Waycross, GA
Shirley Franklin	Atlanta, GA
Henry Frasier, Sr.	Walthourville, GA
Phaedra Graham	Riverdale, GA
Emma Gresham	Keysville, GA
Floyd L. Griffin Jr.	Milledgeville, GA
Ruben Hawkins	Bronwood, GA
Patsy Jo Hilliard	East Point, GA
Darold Honoré, Jr.	Lithonia, GA
Otis S. Johnson	Savannah, GA
Willie J. Larry	Montezuma, GA
Sonja A. Mallory	Jeffersonville, GA
Willie R. Martin	Cuthbert, GA

AFRICAN-AMERICAN MAYORS BY STATE

Ralph Moore	Union City, GA	Bobby Braxton	Clarence, LA
Jerry Myrick	Smithville, GA	Edward L. Brown	St. Joseph, LA
Harvey Norris	Flovilla, GA	Maurice Brown	White Castle, LA
Fred Oliver	Morgan, GA	Frank D. Broxton	Fenton, LA
Tony Paulk	Douglas, GA	Marshall Brumfield	Folsom, LA
John Reid	Eatonton, GA	Jean Coco	Grand Coteau, LA
Gregory Richardson	Riceboro, GA	Mariah J. Cooper	Waterproof, LA
James C. Shipman	Midway, GA	Margie Davenport	Powhatan, LA
Kenneth E. Smith, Sr.	Kingsland, GA	Alex Davis	Newellton, LA
Roger Smith	Toomsboro, GA	Donald R. Davis	Campti, LA
Roxie L. Wilkins	Stillmore, GA	Leroy Davis	Baker, LA
Glenn Wright	Greensboro, GA	Willie Davis	Farmerville, LA

Eugene W. Grant — Seat Pleasant, MD
Carol Johnson — District Heights, MD
Joseph C. Lomax, Jr. — Aquasco, MD
Lillie T. Martin — Fairmount Hts, MD
Joyce Ayers Nixon — Capitol Heights, MD
Paula R. Noble — Forest Heights, MD
Irving L. Robinson — Morningside, MD
Lee P. Walker — Landover Hills, MD

IOWA

Lametta K. Wynn — Clinton, IA

IDAHO

Joe B. McNeal — Mountain Home, ID

ILLINOIS

Saul L. Beck	Ford Heights, IL
Irene H. Brodie, Ph.D.	Robbins, IL
William A. Browne	Hazelcrest, IL
Shirley Byrd	Sun River Terrace, IL
Ralph W. Conner	Maywood, IL
Jon E. Dyson	Hopkins Park, IL
Tyrone Echols	Venice, IL
Linzey D. Jones	Olympia Fields, IL
Eric Kellogg	Harvey, IL
Martha Loggins	Dixmoor, IL
Alvin R. McCowan	University Park, IL
Dennis Miller	Brooklyn, IL
Lorraine Morton	Evanston, IL
Carl E. Officer	East St. Louis, IL
Frankie J. Seaberry	Centreville, IL
William Shaw	Dolton, IL
Sherman Sorrell	Washington Park, IL
Bette Thomas	North Chicago, IL
David Webb, Jr.	Markham, IL
Terry R. Wells	Phoenix, IL
Carolyn Williams	Alorton, IL

LOUISIANA

Ramon Harris, Jr.	Franklin, LA
Gloria Anderson	Sicily Island, LA
Martha Andrus	Grambling, LA
Lloyd Benjamin, Sr.	Natchez, LA
Bobby Joe Boston	Lucky, LA
Dennis Boston	Bienville, LA

Clarence Fields	Pineville, LA
Clarence J. Fultz	Tangipahoa, LA
George L. Grace, Sr.	St. Gabriel, LA
Edward L. Harris	Richwood, LA
Clarence W. Hawkins	Bastrop, LA
Willie Haynes	Melville, LA
Melvin "Kip" Holden	E. Baton Rouge, LA
Bennie C. Jones, Jr.	Wilson, LA
Rosa S. Jones	LeCompte, LA
Darrell C. Jupiter, Sr.	Napoleonville, LA
Odell Odis Key	Gibsland, LA
Ernest Lampkins	Greenwood, LA
Harry "Kayo" Lewis	Rayville, LA
Theodore Lindsey	Tallulah, LA
Herman Malveaux	Chataigner, LA
Jamie Mayo	Monroe, LA
Curtis McCoy	Mansfield, LA
Harry Mims	East Hodges, LA
Sylvester Muckelroy	New Roads, LA
C. Ray Nagin	New Orleans, LA
John Overton, Jr.	Maringouin, LA
Julius Patrick, Jr.	Boyce, LA
Dessie Lee Patterson	S. Mansfield, LA
Joseph A. Pitre	Washington, LA
David Riggins	Vinton, LA
Joyce A. Roberson	Campti, LA
Anna C. Simmons	Opelousas, LA
Harold J. Smith	Kentwood, LA
Leroy Sullivan, Sr.	Donaldsonville, LA
Betty Thomas	Pleasant Hill, LA
Bobby Washington	Cullen, LA
Wilbert Washington	Clayton, LA

MARYLAND

Lillian K. Beverly	North Brentwood, MD
Elaine Carter	Glenarden, MD
Diana Fennell	Colmar Manor, MD

MICHIGAN

Julia Bell	Cassopolis, MI
Donel Brown	Yates, MI
Wilce Cooke	Benton Harbor, MI
Hilliard L. Hampton, Jr.	Inkster, MI
Robert Jones	Kalamazoo, MI
Wilmer Jones-Ham	Saginaw, MI
Kwame Kilpatrick	Detroit, MI
Brenda L. Lawrence	Southfield, MI
Titus W. McClary	Highland Park, MI
Dwayne A. Parker	Buena Vista Twp, MI
Willie W. Payne	Pontiac, MI
Rillastine Wilkins	Muskegon Heights, MI
Beverly Young	Vandalia, MI

MISSOURI

Joseph Adams	University City, MO
James Anderson	North Lilbourn, MO
Johnny Avance	Haywood City, MO
Mary Louise Carter	Pagedale, MO
Keith Conway	Kinloch, MO
Jim Farr	Howardville, MO
Felton L. Flagg	Country Club Hills, MO
Nichole Ghant	Wilson City, MO
Reginald Grant	Wardell, MO
Alex Green	Hayti Heights, MO
James A. Harvey	Wellston, MO
Robert Hensley	Velda City, MO
Monica Huddleston	Greendale, MO
Clarence King	Beverly Hills, MO
Earlene Luster	Velda Village Hills, MO
Roger Mason	Hanley Hills, MO
Carmen McClendon	Upland Park, MO
George H. Murphy	Moline Acres, MO
Everett R. Thomas	Northwoods, MO
Randolph E. Toles	Cool Valley, MO
Kyra Watson	Berkeley, MO
Adrian Wright	Pine Lawn, MO

AFRICAN-AMERICAN MAYORS BY STATE

MISSISSIPPI

Mary L. Ajoku	Cruger, MS
Shirley S. Allen	Metcalfe, MS
Amelda Arnold	Port Gibson, MS
Dwight A. Barfield	Marks, MS
Juan Barnett	Heidelberg, MS
James Bateaste	Crosby, MS
Torrey Bell	Doddsville, MS
Cecil Belle	Aberdeen, MS
Mary Bolton	McLain, MS
Clyde Brown	Shubuta, MS
Yvonne Brown	Tchula, MS
Lawrence Butler	Bolton, MS
Patrick Campbell	Jonestown, MS
Sherman Carouthers	Okolona, MS
John E. Carpenter	Moorhead, MS
Charles Carter	Summit, MS
Roger D. Carter	Shaw, MS
Jimmie Collins	Potts Camp, MS
Gregory Cooley	Lumberton, MS
Joey Cooley	Duck Hill, MS
Emma Cooper-Harris	Anguilla, MS
Lucinda Dailey	Beaumont, MS
Andre DeBerry	Holly Springs, MS
Earnestine Dixon	Webb, MS
Johnny L. DuPree	Hattiesburg, MS
Shirley Edwards	Ruleville, MS
Fred Esco, Jr.	Canton, MS
Henry Espy	Clarksdale, MS
Viola Foster	Plantersville, MS
Betty Fowler	Sunflower, MS
Diana Freelon-Foster	Grenada, MS
Robert Grayson	Tutwiler, MS
Reginald G. Griffin	Lambert, MS
Clifton Harris	Arcola, MS
Linda F. Harris	Wesson, MS
Charles Harvey	Duncan, MS
Alvin Hodo	Falcon, MS
Heather Hudson	Greenville, MS
Velma Jenkins	Shuqualak, MS
Harvey Johnson, Jr.	Jackson, MS
Kennedy Johnson	Mound Bayou, MS
W.J. Jones	Coahoma, MS
Rogers King	Fayette, MS
Wardell Leach	Yazoo City, MS
Azria Lewers	Como, MS
Eddie Logan	Durant, MS
Maurice Lucas	Renova, MS
Debra A. Mabry	Goodman, MS
Arthur MacLittleton	Bude, MS
Arthur Marble	Indianola, MS
Mary McCaskill-Young	Kilmichael, MS
Robert McNair	Mt. Oliver, MS
Jonathan Moore	Pickens, MS
Helen O'Neal	Crawford, MS
Robert Patton	Shelby, MS
Darron Pritchard	Edwards, MS
Jimmy L. Sanders	Atesia, MS
Linda Williams Short	Mayersville, MS
William W. Smith	Brooksville, MS
Charles E. Stokes	Utica, MS
James R. Swearengen	Oakland, MS
Willie Tanner	Isola, MS
Herbert Thomas	Friars Point, MS
Johnny B. Thomas	Glendora, MS
Roseber Thomas	Coldwater, MS
Luscius Tucker	Beulah, MS
Milton Tutwiler	Winstonville, MS
Butch Walker	Rolling Fork, MS
Phillip C. West	Natchez, MS
Erma Williams	Gunnison, MS
Mae Rosie Williams-Johnson	Pace, MS
Lorenzo Windless	Sledge, MS

NORTH CAROLINA

Ulysses Barrett, Jr.	Taylortown, NC
Tom A. Bayliss	New Bern, NC
Roy Bell	Garysburg, NC
William V. Bell	Durham, NC
Doug Boyd	Knightdale, NC
Melvin Broadnax	Seaboard, NC
Theodore Carr	Morven, NC
Ethel Clark	Spring Lake, NC
Lula H. Council	Parmele, NC
Donald Davis	Snow Hill, NC
Alfred Dixon	Greenevers, NC
Perry Dixon	Sandyfield, NC
Willie Dixon	East Arcadia, NC
J.B. Evans	Fair Bluff, NC
Priscilla Everette-Oates	Princeville, NC
Milton Farmer	Wagram, NC
Nedward Graddy	Fairmont, NC
John Gyalog	Bayboro, NC
James Harper	Maysville, NC
James Harrington	Lilesville, NC
Wilbert Harrison	Speed, NC
Aekins Huell	Wade, NC
Erma Jefferies	East Spencer, NC
Malcolm Johnson	Dover, NC
Edward W. Jones	Enfield, NC
Alfonzo King	Goldsboro, NC
James S. Knox	Northwest, NC
Harris McCall	Rowland, NC
John McKellar	Jackson, NC
Lillie McKoy	Maxton, NC
Emmett McRae	Rennert, NC
Shirley Mitchell	Fountain, NC
Johnnie Mosley	Kinston, NC
Darryl Moss	Creedmoor, NC
John Pellan	Rich Square, NC
Marshall B. Pitts, Jr.	Fayetteville, NC
Mary Ponds	Granite Quarry, NC
Hermea Pugh, Sr.	Cofield, NC
Jeanne Rudd	Fountain, NC
Bunny Sanders	Roper, NC
Grady N. Smith	Elm City, NC
Algene Tarpley	Green Level, NC
Jo-Ann Thomas	Hoffman, NC
William M. Ward, Sr.	Dobbins Heights, NC
Leonard Williams	Gibonsville, NC
Sheila Williams	Sharpsburg, NC
Sylvia Willie	Trenton, NC
Eulis A. Willis	Navassa, NC
Frank A. Wilson	Bolton, NC
Clarence Withrow	Kingstown, NC
Richard Worrells	Eureka, NC
Fredrick L. Yates	Winfall, NC

NEW JERSEY

Robert L. Bowser	East Orange, NJ
Mark Bryant	Lawnside, NJ
Eddie Campbell, Jr.	Willingboro, NJ
Gwendolyn A. Faison	Camden, NJ
Mims Hackett	Orange, NJ
Sharpe James	Newark, NJ
Deborah Johnson	S. Brunswick Twp, NJ
Lorenzo Langford	Atlantic City, NJ
Albert I. McWilliams	Plainfield, NJ
Karen McCoy Oliver	Hillside, NJ
Douglas Palmer	Trenton, NJ
Ralph Peterson, Sr.	Pleasantville, NJ
Arland W. Poindexter	Chesilhurst, NJ
Kevin G. Sanders	Asbury Park, NJ
L. Harvey Smith	Jersey City, NJ
Wayne Smith	Irvington, NJ

AFRICAN-AMERICAN MAYORS BY STATE

NEW YORK

Edward L. Arrington	Owego, NY
George Darden	Spring Valley, NY
Ernest D. Davis	Mt. Vernon, NY
James A. Garner	Hempstead, NY
William A. Johnson	Rochester, NY

OHIO

Yolanda Broadie	Woodmere Village, OH
Michael B. Coleman	Columbus, OH
Dennis D. Davis	Delaware, OH
Stephanie S. Dumas	Forest Park, OH
Jack Ford	Toledo, OH
Marcia L. Fudge	Warrensville Hts., OH
Saratha A. Goggins	East Cleveland, OH
Rhine McLin	Dayton, OH
James Mills	Lebanon, OH
LaVerne Mitchell	Lincoln Hts., OH
Robert Nash	Highland Hills, OH
Shelton Richardson	N. Randall, OH
Raymond Terrell	Woodlawn, OH
Marlin West	Urbancrest, OH

OKLAHOMA

Clarence Ashley	Okay, OK
Anna B. Brooks	Meridian, OK
Mildred Burkhalter	Rentiesville, OK
DeNay Burris	Ft. Coffee, OK
Helen JoAnn Fox	Grayson, OK
Benice Joy Gaines	Tullahassee, OK
Tammie Hill	Lima, OK
Marsha Jefferson	Spencer, OK
Cecil Jones	Tatums, OK
Tom Lucas	Clearview, OK
Mary Joan Matthews	Boley, OK
Essie McIntosh	Taft, OK
Marilyn Murrell	Arcadia, OK
Lee Oliver	Brooksville, OK
Eugene Osborn	Redbird, OK
Clyde Shaver	Okema, OK
Greg Smith	Summit, OK
Jake Spencer	Langston, OK

PENNSYLVANIA

John F. Street	Philadelphia, PA
Wilbert A. Young	Wilkinsburg, PA

SOUTH CAROLINA

Tyrone Aiken	Lincolnville, SC
Carl LaRue Alford	Lake City, SC
William H. Alston	Awendaw, SC
Irene Armstrong	Atlantic Beach, SC
Christopher K. Campbell	Eastover, SC
John R. Carter	Gray Court, SC
Moses L. Cohen, Jr.	Fairfax, SC
Curtis Dorsey	Andrews, SC
German Glasscho	Greeleyville, SC
Bobby Gordon	Livingston, SC
Janie G. Goree	Carlisle, SC
Wilmot Hayes	Williams, SC
Harvey Henderson	Waterloo, SC
Jackie T. Holman	Blackville, SC
Willie Jefferson	Mayesville, SC
Kevin Johnson	Manning, SC
Levorn Von Mack	McBee, SC
Samuel E. Murray	Port Royal, SC
Floyd Nicholson	Greenwood, SC
Thomas Owens	Estill, SC
Sallie Peake	Wellford, SC
Zelda Pelzer	Bowman, SC
Henry B. Peoples	Timmonsville, SC
James Risher, Sr.	Gifford, SC
Silas Seabrooks	Santee, SC
Sylvia G. Shinger	Vance, SC
Wanda Stringfellow	Chester, SC
Johnnie Waller	Calhoun Falls, SC
Leroy Woods	Clio, SC
Levenia Wright	Sellers, SC
Terry Wright	Brunson, SC

TENNESSEE

Roland Dykes, Jr.	Newport, TN
Willie W. Herenton	Memphis, TN
Mary Ann Jarrett	Henning, TN

TEXAS

James Adkins	Kyle, TX
Frances Anderson	Terrell, TX
Joe Barron	Caney City, TX
Essie Bellfield	Orange, TX
Oscar Birdow	Cuney, TX
Willie Boddie	Van Alstyne, TX
Travis Bronner	Detroit, TX
Bobby Byars	San Felipe, TX
Marvin Campbell	Domino, TX
Robert Campbell	Crawford, TX
Calvin Cooper	Seven Oaks, TX
Albert L. Davis	Rosser, TX
Monique McDuffie Davis	Cleveland, TX
Ennis Degrate, Jr.	Golinda, TX
Arthur Earl	LaRue, TX
Charles Eaton	Leander, TX
Herman Edwards	China, TX
George English	Annona, TX
Bill Goodson	Whitewright, TX
James Gosey	Forest Hill, TX
Donald Hill	Taylor, TX
Clarence Holliman	Mineral Wells, TX
R.C. Horn	Jasper, TX
Jesus Humphrey	Glenn Heights, TX
Frank Jackson	Italy, TX
Frank D. Jackson	Prairie View, TX
Artis Johnson	Hutchins, TX
Carolyn Jones	Kendleton, TX
Joe Landry	Old River-Winfree, TX
Bill Lawrence	Highland Village, TX
Robert C. Lewis, Jr.	Wolfe City, TX
John Linton	Manchaca, TX
Freddie Newsome, Jr.	Thompsons, TX
Viola Randle	Fulshear, TX
Leonard Reed	Willis, TX
Bruce Robinson	Sour Lake, TX
Willis Sammons	Easton, TX
Charlie S. Scott	Buffalo, TX
Bernetta Shannon	The Colony, TX
Noble Smith	Pittsburg, TX
Carl Swanson, III	Bellmead, TX
Michael Warren	Coffee City, TX
Willie H. Washington	Goodlow, TX
John White	Ames, TX
David Williams	Leroy, TX
Fred Williams	Kountze, TX
Gary Williams	Thorndale, TX
Robert L. Willrich, Sr.	Lexington, TX
Kathy Wilson	Greenville, TX
Michael Wolfe	Hempstead, TX
Keith Woods	Brookshire, TX

UTAH

George Garwood, Jr.	South Odgen, UT

VIRGINIA

William D. Euille	Alexandria, VA
James Holley, III	Portsmouth, VA
Annie M. Mickens	Petersburg, VA
William E. Ward	Chesapeake, VA
L. Douglas Wilder	Richmond, VA

BIOGRAPHICAL INDEX

ADVERTISERS' INDEX

Who's Who Publishing Co., LLC

would like to express its sincere appreciation

for all sponsors and advertisers and those featured in

the 2005 Edition of *Black Mayors In America.*

Your individual and collective contributions

help us to highlight the forward

progress of the communities you serve.

Commemorate your appearance in Black Mayors In America with a beautiful, handcrafted plaque.

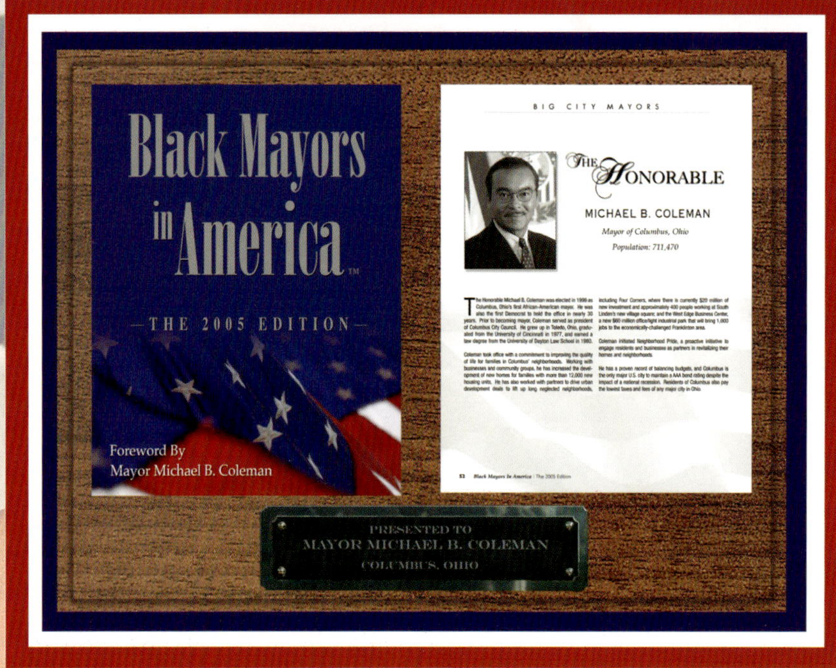

Your picture and biographical data will be mounted on a 16" x 20" rich, hand staine 3/4" birchwood plaque and sealed with a non-glare finish.

Perfect for your office or lobby!

Only $169.95 + S&H

Order Your Commemorative Plaque Today!

Order online or call (614) 481-7300

www.whoswhopublishing.com